A History of
Bridgwater

The centrally located parish church dedicated to St Mary the Virgin is Bridgwater's oldest building. The 117-foot-high spire added in 1367 has provided a major landmark ever since.

A History of
Bridgwater

J.F. Lawrence

revised and completed by
J.C Lawrence

Phillimore

2005

Published by
PHILLIMORE & CO. LTD
Shopwyke Manor Barn, Chichester, West Sussex, England
www.phillimore.co.uk

© J.C. Lawrence, 2005

ISBN 1 86077 363 X

Printed and bound in Great Britain by
THE CROMWELL PRESS
Trowbridge, Wiltshire

Contents

	List of Illustrations	vii
	Preface and Acknowledgements	ix
1	An Introduction and the Town's Origins	1
2	The Lordship of Bridgwater	10
3	The Castle	17
4	The Borough	23
5	The Medieval Street Plan	29
6	The Hospital of St John, The Friary and the Leper Hospital	39
7	The Parish Church	48
8	The Medieval Port of Bridgwater	57
9	The End of the Middle Ages	61
10	The Burgess Hall and the High Cross	67
11	Bridgwater under Edward VI, Mary and Elizabeth	71
12	An Unusual Municipal Enterprise	80
13	The Problem of Poverty	85
14	Town Life under the Early Stuarts	90
15	The Siege of Bridgwater	97
16	The Commonwealth	104
17	Town Life under Charles II	109
18	The Monmouth Rebellion, 1685	113
19	Town Life, 1685-1774	119
20	The Age of Improvement	134
21	Victorian Times	150
22	Bridgwater in the Twentieth Century	166
	Appendix	183
	Bibliography	191
	Index	193

List of Illustrations

Frontispiece: St Mary's church, Bridgwater

1	Map showing Bridgwater in relation to Somerset places	1
2	Location of places close to Bridgwater	2
3	Pleasure barges on the Bridgwater-Taunton canal	4
4	Bridgwater milestone	5
5	Lady Maud Mortimer's Seal	11
6	Seal of the Reeves	12
7	Portion of castle wall	17
8	The Watergate	18
9	Base of a corner tower	18
10	The castle gatehouse	19
11	The castle gatehouse	20
12	Choir screen in Plymtree parish church	22
13	Seal of the Commonality	25
14	Drawing of Mary Tudor on a charter	27
15	Map of medieval Bridgwater	29
16	The North gate	31
17	Medieval stonework in High Street	34
18	Location of archaeological remains in Bridgwater	35
19	The High Cross	37
20	A Friary tile showing the Royal Arms	46
21	A Friary tile showing the arms of Richard of Cornwall	46
22	A Friary tile showing the arms of Warenne or St Barbe	47
23	Seal of the Chantry of the Blessed Virgin Mary	50
24	The Parish Church, 1834	51
25	The Old Vicarage	53
26	The medieval town bridge	58
27	The arms of Trivet	59
28	Map of medieval coastal trade of Bridgwater	60
29	Map of medieval foreign trade of Bridgwater	60
30	The *Mansion House* inn in High Street	62
31	Salmon Butts in the River Parrett	71
32	A salmon trap	72
33	A note of pew rents, 1549	73
34	'The Turret' – originally a horse mill	81
35	Remains of a 16th-century doorway	90
36	The Blake Museum in Blake street	98
37	Siege of Bridgwater – a cartoon	102
38	The Marycourt, pre-alterations	116
39	The Marycourt, post-alterations	116
40	Front page of an Act to repair the bridge	120
41	Preamble to an Act to repair the bridge	120
42	Terraced houses in Taunton Road	121
43	The Glass Cone	125

44	The Glass Cone remains	126
45	Castle Street	126
46	The Gibbs doorway in Castle Street	127
47	'The Lions'	128
48	An 18th-century cottage in King Square	128
49	The Cornhill in about 1780	135
50	'The island' in the High Street	136
51	The arch above Langport Quay	137
52	Langport Quay after removing the arch	138
53	Chimneys in Fore Street	139
54	St Mary's church from Mansion House Lane	140
55	The *Royal Clarence Hotel*	141
56	An 1850 building in King Square	143
57	Taunton Road tollhouse	144
58	Monmouth Street tollhouse	144
59	The Cornhill in 2002	151
60	The County Court	152
61	Castle House	152
62	A Bath brick	153
63	Soldiers and police in the Town Hall, 1896	154
64	Union workhouse hospital	155
65	Brunel's dredger *Bertha*	156
66	The former customs house	157
67	The tug *Petrel*	157
68	The floating harbour	158
69	The telescopic bridge	159
70	Ice on the river in 1867	159
71	Fragments of the old wooden wharf	160
72	Somerset and Dorset railway	160
73	Bridgwater Hospital in Salmon Parade	161
74	The *Golden Ball* in High Street	162
75	A Bath brick soil-retaining wall	170
76	A Bridgwater brick	171
77	Brickyard locations	171
78	Barham Brothers catalogue	173
79	Shipping seen from the Town Bridge in 1907	173
80	Boat containing slate from Portugal	174
81	West Street Canal Bridge	174
82	The *Crowpill* - a collier	175
83	The *Tiny* - a cargo vessel	175
84	The *Sandholm* - a suction dredger	176
85	The Priory	176
86	Venetian window in the Priory	177
87	The George Williams Memorial Hall	178
88	Market Street	178
89	Shell porch, 15 Friarn Street	179
90	Mansard roofs in Friarn Street	179
91	Regency houses with iron-work veranda	180
92	Old dockside features	180
93	Angel Place shopping centre	181
94	St Mary's altar picture	183
95	Unitarian chapel	186
96	Baptist chapel	187
97	St Matthew's Fair	188

Preface and Acknowledgements

My father, Jack Lawrence, developed an interest in local history when he came to Bridgwater in 1931 to join the staff of Dr Morgan's School, then still in Mount Street, as their history and physical training master. One of his first contributions was co-authoring with the then headmaster, Mr Cyril Trenchard, a school production of the Siege of Bridgwater. In the years following the 1939-45 war Jack Lawrence regularly contributed a concise history of Bridgwater for the town guide. About 1970 he devised a 'Bridgwater Walkabout' for the local Civic Society and then started actively to research material for his own version of the town's history. His invitation to revise *Squibbs' History of Bridgwater*, published in 1982, somewhat delayed his own project.

Simultaneously Jack Lawrence's health started to deteriorate, resulting in an ever increasing loss of mobility together with other problems leading to a poor quality of life and his book was never finished. However, some eighteen months before his death early in 1996 he asked me to 'see if I could do anything with it' – this invitation was on the basis of an article I had written about the history of the hospital where I worked. Sadly, I was unable to pursue his suggestion until after my own retirement; thus there was no opportunity to revise the text jointly.

Revising and completing the text was not easy as although some chapters were complete others were not. The greatest difficulty was deciding what to omit as the original was much too long for publication; the errors of omission are attributable to me. Moreover, Bridgwater has changed somewhat since Jack Lawrence wrote his text. For example, he says: 'it will be interesting to see how the entrance to the proposed shopping precinct off High Street will be handled' – The Queen performed the opening ceremony in 1987.

The book traces the progress of Bridgwater from an insignificant Saxon settlement to the town that it is now via the astuteness of a feudal lord in obtaining a charter, the Incorporation which created a mayor and corporation, an elected council and finally the modern Sedgemoor District Council. I have endeavoured to update changes in names or uses of buildings. There may well be errors and omissions which I can partly attribute to the fact that for over fifty years my visits to Bridgwater have been relatively infrequent.

Jack Lawrence made the following acknowledgements: I owe much to Bruce Dilks who generously shared his knowledge and understanding of the archives with me as he prepared the first four volumes of the Bridgwater Archives for publication. Many years later I had the good fortune to meet Dr Dunning who was able to get the fifth volume into print. I have always valued his sound and shrewd advice.

Mr Shorrocks, the County Archivist who retired in 1988, has solved many a tangled problem for me, placing his knowledge at my disposal. All the members of his staff at the County Record Office have been equally helpful.

Many members of the staff of Sedgemoor District Council have assisted me. Mr Desmond Hunt produced a collection of Public Health Reports. Mr Kenneth Preston enabled me to examine deeds of old property that revealed facts which were not available from any other source (e.g. Angel Crescent, previously thought to be 18th-century, was built in 1816 by a man from Shurton as an investment). Mr Philip Meade showed me the special survey of Durleigh Brook which he had made for the former borough authority. Mr Dennis Heal enabled me to photograph documents that now belong to the Charter Trustees. Detailed information concerning the excavations at West Quay and at Friarn Street carried out by the Western Archaeological Trust were provided by Mr Peter Ellis.

Mr David Bromwich at the Local History Library in Taunton has identified or supplied numerous references with great efficiency. The staff of the County Library in Bridgwater, especially Mr Philip Stoyle in the Reference Department, have given much practical help with printed sources.

Some maps are the work of Mr Chris. Sidaway who also made drawings from seals attached to medieval manuscripts. Some photographs come from my collection, others were taken by my son, Dr Chris. Lawrence. I have to thank the Somerset Archaeological and Natural History Society for permission to use the two watercolours of St Mary's Church and Wessex Water for providing photographs (taken by Douglas Allen) of existing salmon butts. The photographs of the Glass House were generously provided by Mr Brian Murless who also photographed the watercolours of St Mary's Church.

J.C. LAWRENCE

October 2005

N.B. Some illustrations duplicate those in the local photograph collection in Blake Museum as Jack Lawrence's collection predates the museum's. Moreover, other persons may well possess prints from the original negatives. The Museum was originally loaned the Chubb pictures; recently they purchased the collection which is well worth seeing.

1

AN INTRODUCTION AND THE TOWN'S ORIGINS

Superficially the Somersetshire market town of Bridgwater is a small, ordinary country town. However, it has an interesting history and features worthy of more than a passing glance. Bridgwater lies between Bristol and Exeter, each 35-40 miles away. The busy A38 trunk road, a main route to the West Country

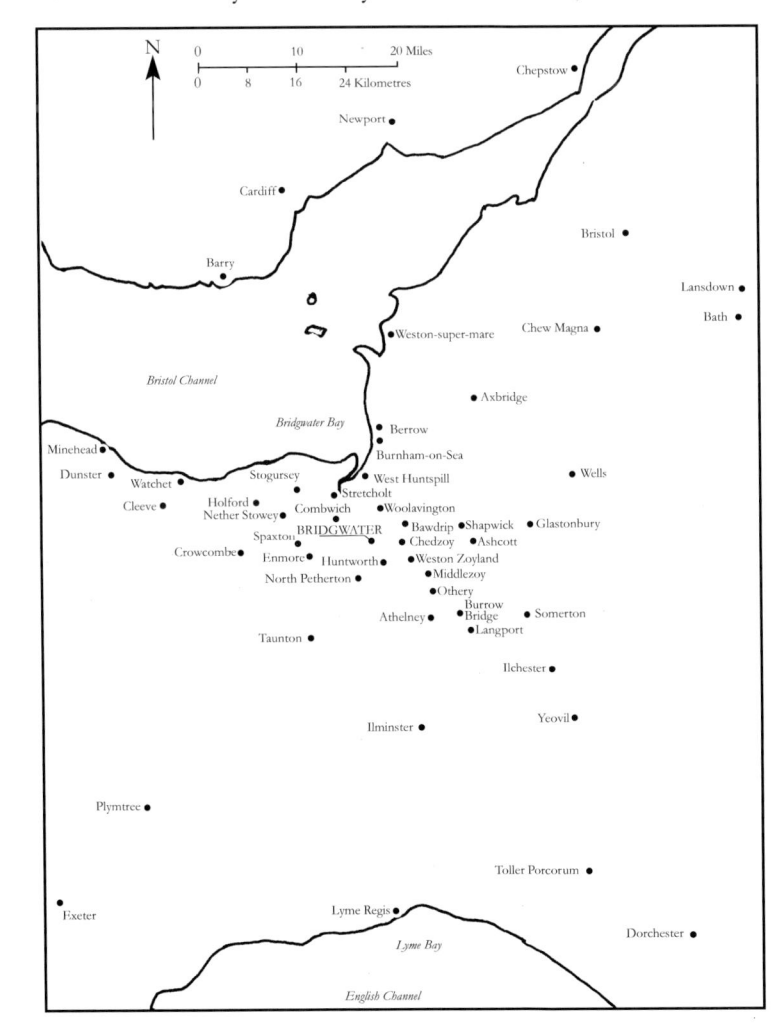

1 Map showing Bridgwater in relation to many of the places in Somerset and adjacent areas that are mentioned in the text.

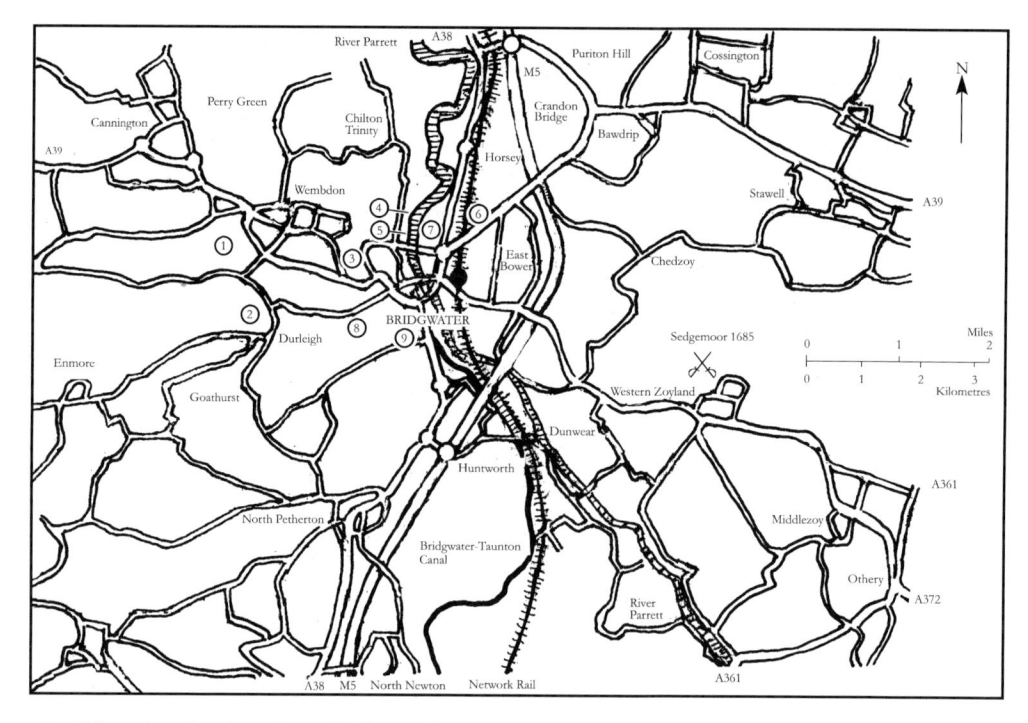

2   Map showing location of places close to Bridgwater:
   1. Sandford Manor (Private property)
   2. West Bower Manor (Private property)
   3. The Parks
   4. Site of a recently completed bridge which is on the boundary of the districts of Chilton (downstream) and Saltlands (upstream)
   5. Crowpill district
   6. Sydenham Manor (Private property)
   7. Castle Field
   8. Site of Haygrove Manor (Private property)
   9. Hamp district

from the Midlands and the North, runs through the town but nowadays most south-west-bound traffic uses the M5 motorway. The A39 connecting Bath and Minehead also passes through the town; going to Bath the road follows the Polden Hills towards Glastonbury and Wells; in the opposite direction it traverses the Quantock Hills to Minehead. Another main road (A372) leads to Langport. Minor roads serve the neighbouring villages of Chilton Trinity, Wembdon and Durleigh. (See also Fig 2.)

Bridgwater lies on the river Parrett, Somerset's major river, which flows into the Bristol Channel six miles away as the crow flies; it is 10½ miles by road. The river was navigable up to the Town Bridge and ships still dock at Dunball wharf some two miles downstream. The Parrett is tidal and the shape of its mouth creates a tidal bore which can be impressive, typically a three- to four-foot wave is seen which can reach nine feet in height in a westerly gale. The bore travels at a fast walking pace. Tide and bore times are displayed on East Quay by the town bridge.

The Parrett rises in the Dorset heights in South Perrott, two miles over the south Somerset border, and is joined by the Yeo and Isle before reaching Langport to enter the flat central area of the county, the Somerset Levels, to be joined by the rivers Tone and Cary. It is about 35 miles long from source to its estuary at Burnham-on-Sea. From Bridgwater the distance to the sea by river is 14 miles.

The Parrett divides Bridgwater. The east side of the town is flat with no ground over 25 feet above ordnance datum level. The western side is also low-lying though the land rises a little above 25 feet towards the north and west. Much of the town, especially the north and east, in common with the Somerset Levels, lies on alluvial deposits 20 to 30 feet in depth but occasionally over 85 feet.

Since 1901 the population has increased from 15,000 to 36,000. The boundary has been extended at times to encompass districts that were formerly separate entities. The ancient settlement of Hamp is now a housing estate on the west of Taunton road (A38) just before the Rhode Lane junction. Sydenham manor, east of the river (next to the A39 Bath road just before the town limits) is also a housing estate plus some industry. The 16th-century manor house is within Courtaulds factory boundary and not open to the public. Castle Field, a large area on the east river bank just beyond the telescopic bridge, has become a large industrial estate. Saltlands, a little further downstream on the west bank, is mainly covered with new houses.

The Parks, originally belonging to the castle, occupies an area opposite the west end of St Matthew's Field; local people call it the Fairfield. It starts where West Street joins the Durleigh road, an unclassified road leading to Durleigh, West Bower, Spaxton, Goathurst and Enmore. The Parks is mainly housing whose roads reflect old names, e.g. Park Road, but has little of interest. Continuing along Durleigh road the Manor of Haygrove was at the top of the short hill. Nothing remains today. (See also Fig 2.)

Neighbouring Villages

About a mile further is a junction. The left turn leads to Durleigh whose village church is on the left at the bottom of another short hill; there is a reservoir to the right. Bridgwater's boundary is about 200 yards before the junction. Continuing straight ahead instead of visiting Durleigh, the entrance to West Bower Manor is within a few yards, now a farm on private property. The medieval wing is visible across the reservoir. The road leads to Spaxton and over the Quantocks and in the 17th century was an important route from Bridgwater to the west, ending in Devon at Barnstaple.

Taunton is almost 12 miles away via the A38. Bridgwater's boundary now passes through part of Huntworth, but most of this settlement is off the main

3 Pleasure barge on the Bridgwater-Taunton Canal seen from the Newtown lock at the west end of the floating harbour. The canal, built in 1827, originally terminated at Huntworth, just outside the town, but was extended to link with the newly opened docks in 1841. From 1900 the canal was largely disused but it has been restored in recent years and was completely reopened in 1994.

road. The Bridgwater to Taunton canal starts at the docks; it has been restored and is used by pleasure boats. The towpath can be walked (Fig. 3).

The A38 Bristol Road goes through Dunball. The ancient settlement of Downend is a short lane off the spur road from Dunball leading to the M5. Downend has few houses and little to be seen though Pevsner mentions earthworks suggestive of a motte and bailey fortification.

Travelling west on the Quantock Road (A39), Sandford Manor (private property) is visible to the right about a mile past the town boundary. The main road now by-passes Cannington, another ancient settlement with interesting and attractive buildings, especially the church. Nether Stowey, where Coleridge lived, is four miles further. The Wordsworths briefly lived in the next village, Holford. Between Nether Stowey and Holford a lane on the left leads to Dead Woman's Ditch and Walford's Gibbet, site of an 18th-century murder and execution.

A road from Cannington leads to Combwich, a Romano-British settlement on the Parrett where the Romans possibly had a jetty. There was a small harbour until recently. The Parrett could be forded at low tide and at one time there was also a ferry-man, but both ford and ferry fell into disuse over a century ago. Stogursey is three miles further and, in medieval days, had some type of borough status. There are castle remains and a fine church.

Horsey lies along a lane off the A39 Bath Road just beyond Sydenham Manor and the town boundary but only comprises a few houses. East Bower is reached via a lane to the right further along. A little further on again is a lane to Chedzoy. The main road then crosses Kings Sedgemoor Drain at Crandon Bridge—originally on a meander of the Parrett and the location of a Roman port. The main road bears right to follow the line of the Roman road along the ridge of the Polden Hills as far as Ashcott where the Roman road turned towards Ilchester in the south of the county. The main road continues to Glastonbury, Wells, and Bath.

Travellers from North Somerset found crossing the low-lying ground south of the Poldens difficult after heavy rainfall as flooding was inevitable

4 The milestone at the foot of Wembdon Hill, a relic of the Bridgwater to Watchet Turnpike. Most of the original milestones placed on these routes have vanished. The Bridgwater Turnpike Trust was dissolved in 1869.

The route had been a road for centuries and attempts made to raise its height to create 'the great causeway'. The Bishops of Bath and Wells offered an Indulgence to all the faithful who would deposit loads of stone along this road (according to a document formerly in Cossington parish chest).

Chilton Trinity and Wembdon are close to Bridgwater. Chilton Trinity is a small, isolated farming community near the river and relatively unspoiled by modern developments though once it had a brickyard. The small church has some Saxon stonework. The village is reached by way of Chilton Street which starts at Bridgwater docks.

Wembdon is now reached via Quantock Road, built 80 years ago to avoid Wembdon and Sandford hills. At the foot of Wembdon Hill is a milestone stating 'Bridgwater 1 mile' (Fig. 4), a relic of the Bridgwater-Watchet turnpike. The toll cottage stands near the town boundary. Wembdon's parish includes Sandford Manor, Perry Green and Bridgwater's late Victorian and early 20th-century development called New Town.

The Bridgwater-Langport road starts from St John's Street and then crosses the railway to pass through an area of modern housing. Dunwear is just beyond the town boundary off a lane to the right but is now little more than worked-out clay pits. The first village is Weston Zoyland and the battle of Sedgemoor site is about a mile north across marshy fields. The 'zoy' portion of Weston Zoyland, Middlezoy and Chedzoy reflects the fact that they were originally islands which is readily appreciated whilst travelling towards Langport across the flat wetlands of the Somerset Levels. For centuries this area was the focus of the willow industry; early last century over 9,000 acres grew withies (the name given to the harvested willow cane) but now only 300 acres.

Bridgwater's Origins

Apart from a Bronze-Age urn discovered in a clay pit at Colley Lane and a Neolithic polished stone axe found at Hamp during the 19th century, there is little sign of early settlement in Bridgwater. There is no evidence of Roman occupation and the few Roman coins found between 1946 and 1951 near Crowpill were on an ancient travel route. However, there were Romano-British farms in Wembdon, Cannington, Spaxton and Bawdrip, and an urbanised settlement near Crandon Bridge.

The Parrett valley, made fertile by alluvial deposits, is bounded on the west by the Quantock Hills, and on the east by the Polden Hills. The Quantocks are composed of Devonian slates and grits. Their lower slopes contain Keuper Marl which is red sandstone. Near Bridgwater these deposits are covered with valley gravels providing well-drained sites suitable for settlement.

A factor affecting choice of settlement was the Parrett's tendency to change course and flood the low-lying ground between Bridgwater and the Poldens. Langport is 15 miles in a straight line from the river's mouth but the level only drops one foot per mile. Much of the surrounding land, the Somerset Levels, is scarcely above sea level and thus prone to flooding. The silting of the

Parrett valley with alluvium and sand was lengthy, starting thousands of years ago and far from complete when the Saxons reached the river in A.D. 658. A meander of the Parrett may explain why the original eastern parish boundary of Wembdon lay across its present course between Horsey and Bridgwater to encompass Sydenham Manor. The boundary was redrawn west of the river in the 19th century. The river changed course over the centuries because the Bristol Channel has the second greatest tidal movement in the world, such that a 30-ft. spring tide is not unusual. This, plus the enormous volume of water pouring down the river valley after storms, could readily cause changes of course on occasion. There was no major added drainage before the 18th century when King's Sedgemoor Drain was excavated.

Bridgwater's Boundary

Bridgwater has no Saxon remains but three Saxon charters relate to Hamp. Hamp belonged to Athelney Abbey and was entirely separate from Bridgwater; thus these documents contain no information about Bridgwater. The earliest charter, A.D. 794, defines Hamp's bounds but uses names no longer identifiable and the boundary has never been described since. It began with Swan Lake, presumably to the south and now covered with houses. As these perambulations were made clockwise they must have followed Bridgwater's northern boundary. The area was called 'The marsh of the river Pedride' suggesting that Hamp was isolated from Bridgwater by water flowing down the Durleigh valley. The third charter, A.D. 1007, uses the dative form of the place-name, 'Hamme', meaning 'at the water meadow'. It also stipulates that the land granted is to be free of all secular services but with exceptions, one being 'a general levy to construct a bridge', but there is no evidence to show that this was ever done. The place is named 'Ham' in the first and second A.D. 958 charter; the letter 'p' was added for ease of pronunciation, as in 'Southampton'.

Durleigh valley contains two streams arising in the Quantocks which originally met near Haygrove before flowing into the Parrett. At an unknown date each was diverted; Durleigh Brook 1¼ miles from the river to flow along a contour higher than its natural course; a similar alteration was made to Hamp Brook starting 1½ miles from the river. Currently a sluice at Durleigh Brook's diversion point sends excess water towards the original course. Water collecting in this area is drained by several rhines including one called 'Middle Stream Rhine' into the river.

'Middle Stream' is a significant name and it is, perhaps, surprising that it was not adopted for the whole series, but it was not and different sections of the system have different names. Another rhine, 'Witches Walk' on the Ordnance Survey, is not a whimsical modern name but a corruption of 'Weech's Wall'. In the 18th century the Weech family owned land there and added a boundary wall. At that time their family name was frequently spelt 'Witch'.

The trench cut to divert Durleigh Brook was over a mile long and created an efficient leat for the town mill. The town mill was usually called 'Lytell Mill', suggesting that there was at least one other mill. The diversion cut along the southern valley rim presumably provided power for another mill and at least one document mentions 'South Mill', thus confirming its existence. The mill site on Hamp Brook has never been identified but it existed and was still working in 1594 when the miller, Young Lockyer, bought a new millstone in Bridgwater. The town accounts state: 'Solde the Younge Lockar of Hame £1-15-4.'

The borough's original boundary followed the present course of Durleigh Brook and not that of Middlestream, indicating that the diversion was made at an early date. This huge task could only be done by a powerful authority, wealthy enough to provide the considerable capital investment. Undoubtedly this authority was the lord of Bridgwater, who must also have financed the Hamp Brook scheme which was always under the borough court's jurisdiction. On occasion the court condemned the Abbot of Athelney for failing to scour out the brook. (The land lying between the two streams belonged to Athelney Abbey.)

The borough boundary followed Durleigh Brook to the South Gate and then turned south-east, encompassing a large triangular piece of territory which included a stretch of the river bank long enough to include the outlet of the Middlestream Rhine.

The Early Community

The first document referring directly to a community in Bridgwater is Domesday Book. The settlement described is consistent with a late 11th-century development and in translation reads:

'Walscin holds Bridgwater. Merleswain held it before 1066. it paid tax for 5 hides. Land for 10 ploughs. In lordship 3 ploughs; 5 slaves; 2 hides.

13 villagers, 9 smallholders and 5 cottagers with 8 ploughs. A mill which pays 5s., meadow, 10 acres; underwood, 100 acres; pasture, 30 acres. 13 cattle; 7 pigs; 61 sheep.

Value when he acquired it, 100 s; now £7'

Walscin, otherwise known as Walter of Douai, owned the fee of Bridgwater (Ekwall) and was the Norman lord who replaced the Saxon thane Merleswain who, under King Harold, was Sheriff of Lincolnshire. Merleswain's lands had stretched across the Midlands and also included a long stretch of the river Parrett with the estates of Wembdon and Bawdrip.

'Ten ploughlands' gives an assessment of arable land. The number of ploughs is the number of plough teams available for preparing the soil. A full plough team had eight oxen. 'In demesne' means on the land reserved to the lord. The villeins were the ordinary farmers, holding their land of the lord. The smallholders held a lesser amount, and the slaves were simple ploughmen who held no land and were kept by the steward or bailiff. The cottagers, too, had very little land. Such men, trained as smiths or in other occupations, comprised the manorial work force. Cautious extrapolation of the population recorded in Domesday Book suggests a total of about 150 people.

An Introduction and the Town's Origins

The Domesday Survey enabled the king to have a rapid and easily accessible valuation of the land he had conquered. By reducing the information to its bare essentials it is possible to obtain a sound basis for comparing different settlements. Bridgwater was not large but it was more important than its neighbours and potentially head of a group:

	Hamp	Horsey	Wembdon	Bridgwater
1. Tax Assessment (in Hides)	1	2	2	5
2. Number of Ploughlands	4	7	8	10
3. Number of Ploughteams	2	7	6	8
4. Population recorded	12	19	12	32
5a. Value (in 1085)	£1½	£4	£4	£7
5b. Change since 1066		+£1	+£1	+£2

There was no sign of urban development – no mint and no market. There were no 'burgesses' although Ilchester had 107, Taunton 64 and Langport 34. There was no fortified burh as there was at Lyng, Axbridge and Watchet, but a rural manor with 13 farmers and 19 other peasants. Women and priests were not normally recorded although the Survey records a priest at Horsey. It is thus likely that Horsey had a chapel then; its site has been excavated. Hamp and Horsey were in the medieval parish of Bridgwater but this arrangement may be later than the Conquest.

Quantock villages such as Crowcombe, valued at £8 with a population of 47, and Stogursey, population also 47 and valued at £20, were more important than Bridgwater in 1085 but Bridgwater's site had the advantage of potential for economic growth.

The Saxon's called Bridgwater 'Brycg'. When the Domesday Commissioners wrote 'Brugie' as its name, they heard the West Saxon dialect and presumably should have written 'Bruge', the local rendering of the word 'brycg' meaning 'bridge'. Dr Dunning offers two alternatives: either the Old English word 'brycg' means a gang-plank between ship and shore, or the original word was from the Old Norse 'bryggja' meaning a quay or jetty. A letter in 1989 from Professor Cameron, Honorary Director of the English Place-name Society, emphasises that 'bridge' is the correct translation of 'brycg'. No evidence exists to show that there was a bridge at such an early date.

The town takes its name from the Norman lord and, at first, was called Brugie-Walter. Successively a series of alternative spellings was used, ultimately leading to the current name which has been used for a very long time. Professor Cameron pointed out that 'water' is the Middle English colloquial pronunciation of 'Walter'.

2

The Lordship of Bridgwater

Feudal lordship followed the Norman Conquest. The manor was a small part of Walter of Douai's great military fief but soon such estates were military in name only. The holder not only had to pay rents and perform services for the king but also remain subject to 'feudal incidents', the most dangerous being the rights of wardship and marriage which the overlord could enforce during a minority. The lord could occupy the land himself or intrude a guardian. If he wished he could sell off stock, timber, buildings, crops, etc. to leave the estate in ruins. He could also force the heir or heiress to marry any person he chose which often meant that the Crown put up the heir or heiress for sale. The families ruling Bridgwater were fortunate for over 150 years but after 1230 there were problems.

Walter was succeeded by his son, Robert of Bampton, who was something of a ruffian. When he died the manor passed by marriage to the Paynel family. William Paynel's son Fulk got into serious difficulties and solved them by seeking support from one of the most powerful men in England, William Brewer. The price he paid was the manor of Bridgwater.

William Brewer (or de Bruere) created medieval Bridgwater because he obtained the borough charter, built the castle, founded the Hospital of Canons Regular and probably built the first stone bridge. He died in 1226 and was succeeded by his son, also called William. William Brewer II died in 1231 having, according to tradition, seen the first Franciscans arrive in the town. He died childless, and the following years saw the succession in some confusion, with the intervention of the king as overlord.

Bridgwater was considered a safe place because in 1234 the collectors of a tax called 'a fortieth' in Cornwall were ordered to meet the Sheriff of Devon at Launceston. He was to receive this money – silver pennies packed into canvas sacks – and transport it to Bridgwater where it was to be kept until further order.

Also in 1234 Henry III gave custody of Bridgwater and its castle to one Richard of Wrotham. In 1235 he was replaced by Hugh de Virona who was styled 'Head of the Honour of Bridgwater', and tenants were ordered to obey him 'as their Bailiff.' These facts are known from the king's orders known as Letters Patent. Bridgwater is next mentioned in 1242 when William de Cantilupe was told to render £64 0s. 10d. yearly for 'the manor of Bridgwater' with its appurtenances.

Possibly Henry III dealt leniently with this case of wardship, as Magna Carta said overlords should. The succession turned on the marriage of William Brewer's sister to Reginald Braose, an alliance with a very powerful family. They had a son, William Braose, who married Eve, daughter of William Marshal. When William Braose died, he left four daughters – all royal wards. The Braose inheritance was divided but only two daughters, Maud and Eve, became involved with Bridgwater. Maud married Roger Mortimer (Fig. 5) and was given Bridgwater Castle plus one-third of the town's revenues. Eve married William Cantilupe and received two-thirds of the revenues. The Cantilupe connection was short, for William died in 1254 and was followed by his daughter Millicent, who married Eudes la Zouche. This family connection lasted many years. The Mortimer connection also lasted for a long time, eventually passing to Edward IV. The divided lordship and shared revenues continued, although the variable amounts were replaced by a fee farm (a fixed annual sum) in the 15th century.

5 Seal of Lady Maud Mortimer. The Mortimers were lords of the town in the late Middle Ages.

Court of the Castle and Haygrove

The oldest surviving court rolls from Bridgwater are for the castle and Haygrove Manor, 1371-72. The borough court met at the Gildhall or 'Hall of Pleas' as it was frequently called, and the other court met at the castle. It had less business than the borough because it dealt with a smaller population. It records the sale of rods from the park, and reeds and thorns from the castle moat. Cases include damage to crops by cattle or horses, giving the court a distinctly rural flavour, as might be expected. Many cases were similar to those in the borough court; amongst these were offences against the Assize of Ale. In October 1371 five men were involved who were probably charging above the standard rate. Two were fined 6d., one 4d., and one 3d. The fifth man was 'at mercy', i.e. they kept him guessing. Each was also fined another 1d. for giving short measure. They did not appear before the next court in January 1372, but were in court that April and fined 6d., 4d., and three at 3d. These offences comprised one-fifth of all cases heard.

One-third of the cases was for trespass closely followed by those for failing to scour out water courses. As Durleigh Brook followed a man-made channel to drive the little mill, the lord needed to keep it strictly under control. Sharply reprimanded offenders included the friary warden who was responsible for Durleigh Brook where it went 'round the garden of the Friars Minor'. Since the brook was the borough boundary it is curious that the lord's authority also extended over Hamp Brook which belonged to the Abbey of Athelney. The abbot was reprimanded for not scouring out the brook at Moorwall and the hayward fined 1d. for not making him! The abbot was told to do it before the next court. Apart from the marginal note that he was 'attached' nothing seemed to happen the second time and this was repeated in April 1372. Nothing more than this appeared to happen to other offenders: Thomas Carpenter and Nicholas Croute, who were responsible for the brook 'between Twenty Acres and Moorwall', nor to those responsible for Durleigh Brook including John Turlyt and John Hughes at Townsend, and Nicholas Croute at Westwayer (the horse pool near the Friary).

The only officers mentioned are the hayward and a reeve. Several cases are recorded of animals being held. There was a pound in the borough but no cases of strays were heard. The castle court heard about Thomas Duffiles' cow and some unknown person's horse; both were kept for three weeks. They also heard about Robert Croil's three sheep which should have been in custody, but were not there.

6 Seal of the Reeves. Before the Mayoralty was granted to Bridgwater in 1468 the borough was governed jointly by two reeves.

The Lord's Income

The Mortimers were sole lords of the castle and the manor of Haygrove but owned only one-third of the lordship of the borough. They employed two officials called reeves of the borough, who were elected by the townsmen to protect their rights and collect their share of the various dues (Fig. 6). Every year these two men drew up a yearly balance sheet.

The lord's income from the borough was derived from three sources: burgage rents, various tolls, and profits of the borough court. The balance sheet for 1386, chosen by Dilks, in *Bridgwater Castle & Desmesne towards the end of the 14th Century*, as being typical, is as follows:

A. INCOME

		£	s.	d.
Balance in				
1.	Burgage rents	9	6	0
2.	Tolls:	10	17	1¼
	River		3	9
	Market		10	2
	Fairs:			
	Ascension			8½
	Whitsun			4
	Michaelmas		5	0
3.	Profits of Courts	24	11	6

B. EXPENDITURE

1.	Allowance to Officers (i.e. Reeve & Beadles: each has ⅓ reduction of his burgage shilling)		1	4
2.	Loss of Rent (empty properties)	1	18	2¼
3.	Stewards expenses		8	7
4.	to the Castle Reeve	3	14	9¾
5.	to the Receiver (i.e. the Lord's Treasurer)	9	6	0
6.	Balance carried forward	9	2	7
		24	11	6

Dilks concluded that, since the annual share of burgage rents paid to the Mortimers was £10 to £11 a year, the total for the whole borough was therefore less than £33. Since burgage tenures paid 1s. each this might suggest a total of 650, but did not mean that there were 650 houses because a burgage tenure might relate to no more than a small plot of land.

Rent was not normally collected from empty houses ('in decay') but some plots may have been rented as gardens. The population might have reached 2,000 before the Black Death but would have dropped dramatically after 1348. Tallage lists from 1445-6 show about 300 houses. The various market tolls do not feature in the Borough Archives and the lord's right to collect customs on exports is not apparent until 1380 when a jury of 12 men found that a leading merchant, John Cole, had been avoiding payment for the last 12 years. The officers claimed he owed £20 duty on corn sold to foreign merchants in the harbour and another 20s. on sales of iron, fish, salt and wine. The court added extra for good measure and compelled Cole to pay £22.

Another attempt was made in 1386 to flout the lord's power by avoiding the port of Bridgwater. The conspirators were three burgesses and the vicar of Otterhampton who avoided paying import duties by persuading incoming boats to unload at Combwich. Over five years it was estimated that loss of customs revenue was £100.

Further income came from the manorial lands, including Castle Field and the opposite bank, as far as Saltland. The area still called 'The Parks' was the lord's park and the lord owned many of the meadows between Haygrove and Hamp Brook. On much of this land men still held their lands in villeinage and owed manorial dues as well as attendance at the court of the castle.

An area which presents problems is Castle Ditch. Dilks identified it west of the castle, in the neighbourhood of Angel Crescent. This area was treated as a ward of the borough in the 15th century. Evidence of settlement outside the moat on the north was found following a limited investigation in 1972.

Whatever the exact amount of settlement it was always paid a fixed sum, £4 4s. 6d. A further complication is that the term 'Castle Moat', when used in an agricultural sense, covered lands stretching from the Moat towards Saltland.

The various rents of free tenants and the demesne lands were £14 7s. 4½d. and those of the villeins £5 2s. 4½d. There was also a horse mill paying £3 8s. 0d. The rents of the common oven and the watermills were shared, the lord receiving one-third as they were in the borough. This, together with other property, would have brought in a total of about £50.

The only surviving roll of the manorial court is for October 1371, and January and April 1372. The total perquisites include the sale of rods from the Park together with reeds and thorns from the Moat. The average total of about 15s. is too high to be typical if the Court met monthly. The borough court shows a total income of £12 19s. 3d. for the year 1378-9, and £10 16s. 4d. for 1379-80. These totals include revenue from other courts such as Durnday and Piepowder (a summary court held at fairs and markets to administer justice among itinerant dealers) as well as the Fair tolls.

By the end of the 14th century various changes had occurred. The first document written on paper (1396) is an account kept by the 'Bailiff of the Community'. The Gild Hall was now usually called the Common Hall. There was a common clerk and a mace was carried. A common seal was used and a charge levied on those wishing to use it on important documents. From market and river-side there is mention of levies for moorage, use of the common plank and the common bushel. The community had become well established, taking more responsibility for its affairs. Eventually a fixed annual payment, a 'fee farm', was agreed.

On the death of Edward, Earl of March in 1425, the last of the Mortimers in the direct male line, the castle passed to the House of York. In 1454 it was held by Richard, Duke of York but the borough was in a state of decay and unable to pay the fee farm. The Duke appointed two of his officers to hold an inquiry and his receiver reported a shortage of 75s. of which the Duke's share was one-third. In 1460 Richard died at the Battle of Wakefield and was succeeded by his son Edward who assigned the fee farm of Bridgwater to his mother. The burgesses presented a petition stating that the Yorkist fee farm of £9 0s. ½d. payable to Lord Zouche was unbearable. In 1461 the Duchess of York reduced her share to £8 0s. ½d. In 1468 the town declined further and the sum was reduced to £3. On the death of the Duchess the fee farm was to rise to £10, probably meaning it would revert to its original amount. She died in 1495.

In 1556 a dispute arose when the Crown demanded payment of £16 per annum. A commission appointed by the Court of Wards and Liveries took evidence from some of Bridgwater's leading citizens. Apparently the fee farm had passed to Lord Daubeny, Earl of Bridgwater, who sold it to the 'Earl of Somerset' who sold it to Lord Zouche. Some of the burgesses still held receipts and satisfied the Court that after 1540 the decay of the borough was such that the fee farm had been reduced to £10 16s. 8d. and should remain at that figure. In 1563 there are receipts from the Zouche family and one from the Crown with whom they now shared the farm.

King Edward VI and his sister dealt kindly with Bridgwater. In 1563 Mr Haskyns was paid 6s. 8d. 'wch he layd oute in the Escheker for the dyscharge of the £10 wch was geven to the town by Kynge Edward the Syxt'. Queen Mary had also given £10 to the town, and two men had certified to the exchequer in 1559 that it had been spent in this way:

To the poor	£2 0s. 0d.
Repair of highways	£6 13s. 4d.
Repair of decayed houses	£1 6s. 8d.

In 1554 Queen Mary had granted the town the annual rent charge of 14s. arising from lands in East Stower which had formerly provided a light and an obit (i.e. an anniversary) in the parish church, the gift of John Colswayne, a former vicar who died *c*.1474. To this she added houses, gardens, and land formerly belonging to the Chantries here. The lands at East Stower were not sold until 1949. 'The Chantry Lands' were given their own section of the town rental for many years; they yielded £8 15s. 0d. in 1563.

The town also benefited from the will of John Colford, a former mayor of Bridgwater. 'The Colford Lands' too had their own section in the town rental, bringing in £11 3s. 10d. in 1562. Lands were a better gift than houses as medieval buildings were often flimsy and readily deteriorated; consequently their upkeep often cost more than they were worth.

Unrecorded Changes

It is obvious from the wording of the charters that after 1200 Bridgwater was an important free borough, but it is also clear that the lord's power was still considerable. His steward presided over the borough court and his officers still functioned, but were elected by the townsmen and not imposed on them. The decline of the lord's power was slow and gradual with no clearly marked steps. In 1200 the lord was collecting the burgage shilling, which was his by right, to replace the various labour services which had been performed on the manor. In the mid-19th century the borough still collected the burgage shilling but it was no longer handed to the lord of the manor.

The continued existence of lordship was prolonged by the large amount of property he owned in the town together with the separate court of the castle and the manor of Haygrove. Thus a shadowy deference to lordship lingered; it might be called 'the manorial element' in civic affairs and it was still present in the 18th century but impossible to quantify. The mayor had become the chief officer and there is no indication that the lord's steward ever showed any sign of interference.

A survey of town property made just before 1701 was produced under the heading 'Manor of Bridgwater'. More surprising is an entry in the Sessions Book in 1736 which records the business of Quarter Sessions, the court belonging to the borough and not the county. The entry says: 'We present all persons who have not attended this court [i.e. those who should have attended] and do amerce every such person one shilling.' Since those concerned were unnamed it is difficult to believe that anything was done about collecting the fines.

The same document states that four men, John Trott, Matthew Mills, Nicholas Mills and Jonathan Vinnicott, were solemnly admitted as members of the court on paying a fee of 1s. each. Surprisingly they were not called 'members of the court' but admitted as 'tenants of this manor'! The clerk used Latin for these entries: 'Johannes Trott admissus est Tenens hujus Manerii.' In practice the court of the castle ceased to function before 1730 and after then large parts of the area occupied by the castle were sold. There is no further mention of the lord of the manor and the 'manorial element' became extinct.

Amongst other changes which took place was the end of the gild merchants – the institution which had taught the town the art of self-government. Before establishing the mayoralty in 1468, the two stewards of the gild merchant were the common stewards who, like Roman consuls, presided jointly over town affairs. The gild merchant must have ceased to function *c.*1500 and would have been taken over by craft gilds but there are no records concerning their development. They are mentioned 200 years later as the 'Companies' of various trades participating in civic processions during the 18th century. At that time the craft gilds were still attempting to enforce the rules of apprenticeship and the borough was trying to help them to keep control of trade in the town.

3

THE CASTLE

The castle, built between 1200 and 1210, covered over eight acres to occupy about a quarter of the available building space in the western half of the borough. William Brewer was granted the licence to build in 1200. The plan adopted comprised an inner bailey (or upper ward) and a lower bailey (or outer ward) divided by a strong stone wall. The lower bailey was rectangular and probably regarded as impregnable. The east wall was parallel with the edge of the river.

Cartloads of red sandstone from Wembdon were brought in for the walls; other stone came by boat, upstream from the Polden Hills (Downend), and downstream from Ham Hill via Langport (Pibsbury). Probably a quay was built to handle this. About 150 feet of the east wall remains (Fig. 7), enabling its original height to be estimated by visualising the crenellation (battlements) on top of the wall. The water gate still exists in the east wall (Fig. 8) where three semi-circular Norman-style stone arches support the 13ft. thick wall above.

The lower bailey, its eastern face protected by the river, had strong circular towers at its four corners. In 1984 the south-east tower's location was discovered and a segment projecting north into a building site was thoroughly and professionally excavated. A larger segment lies under the steep roadway at the bottom of Chandos Street and was excavated after the demolition of Peace's warehouse (Fig. 9). The

7 Portion of the castle wall on west quay, exposed in 1970 on the removal of several old sheds.

portion of the tower uncovered stood several feet high and was impressive as it had been very carefully constructed by skilled workmen with every stone cut on a curve. The stone of the bottom courses was limestone, not lias, to withstand the lapping of the tides. Above was a course of Ham stone, chosen for its aesthetic appearance. The tower base was eight to nine feet high; local red sandstone would have been used for the rest but Ham stone for crenellation and other distinctive features such as arrow-slits.

The inner bailey, for centuries known as 'the bailey', occupied the higher ground to the west of the river. The dividing wall ran along the eastern side of what is now King Square. There was a great gatehouse here which survived until the end of the 18th century. Facing west, the direction from which any attack might be likely to come, were two large semi-circular towers. Its appearance is known from two sketches made by John Chubb. The building had been occupied in the early 18th century but Chubb's drawing shows it roofless and without the south tower (Fig. 10). His second drawing, possibly as late as 1800, shows how the other tower has collapsed to reveal an early Gothic door (Fig. 11). Both drawings show evidence of alterations made in Tudor or Stuart times to turn it into comfortable domestic quarters – the windows are reminiscent of the Elizabethan part of Kenilworth. Collinson thought the Harveys had done a lot of rebuilding. In both drawings the north side of Castle Street appears in the background.

In 1971 workmen digging a trench in Crowpill Road exposed the footing

8 The Watergate in the castle's west wall and providing access to the river. The wall above is 13 feet thick and was constructed by building two stone faces and then filling the space between with rubble set in an orange-coloured mortar.

9 Base of the tower at the north-east corner of the curtain wall exposed by excavation in 1985.

10 The castle gatehouse, no longer habitable, drawn by John Chubb during the latter half of the 18th century.

of a substantial wall constructed of blue lias and Ham stone. It was part of the wall which, with the gatehouse, divided the inner and outer bailey. Similar wall footings were discovered in Queen Street in 1973. Excavations in 1964 behind the Post Office before it was rebuilt only exposed a large rubbish pit containing pottery dating between 1350 and 1688. Much was Donyatt ware including bowls and candlesticks together with a range of glass bottles.

The outer bailey was irregularly shaped with its main entrance, a drawbridge, opening on to the Market Place. Since the western wall spanned the width of the castle there would be at least two more large corner towers making five or more towers in total. The main entrance would have been dominated by a tower, or towers, and there were probably semi-circular towers at intervals around the castle's perimeter.

When the drawbridge was renewed in 1387 a dozen oak trees were felled in the royal forest of North Petherton and much other timber came from elsewhere. The drawbridge was extremely heavy and enormous stone weights formed a counterbalance which required solid masonry in the two gate-towers. This gatehouse was located at the entrance to York Place where an 'elbow' in the street gives a hint of a barbican. It is impossible to be sure if any outwork was there because there is no documentary evidence. A 'Delvys Tower' is mentioned and it was not unusual for a special tower to be given its own name in the Middle Ages. This tower was probably not circular but built above the gate. It probably had machicolation (portals through which molten lead, stones, etc. could be dropped upon assailants) to menace any attackers who reached it.

Surrounding the castle was a moat with water supplied on its west by springs which now no longer run. Near the river the moat's eastern ends would be filled by spring tides. Since Fore Street slopes appreciably, weirs possibly retained the moat and similar arrangements probably applied on the west side. A boat, the

11 The castle gatehouse, also drawn by John Chubb but some time after the previous sketch.

gift of the constable, was used on the moat *c.*1400 but presumably on the north side to cut reeds. Using a boat normally precludes weirs yet one was discovered when the moat near the north-east tower was excavated in 1984. However, this weir, near the end of the moat close to the river, would have made it easy for a man to cross to the butts which were maintained for centuries at that corner outside the moat, which was 20 feet wide here.

Before erecting new buildings behind the Westminster Bank (York Buildings) in 1971 workmen discovered a 20 ft. deep depression filled with soft red earth, presumably traces of the moat. Another portion of the moat was investigated in 1972 before Bridgwater House was built in Northgate. Whatever the moat's original width, it was 65 feet wide here and the centre almost 25 ft. deep. Occupation layers on the south (i.e. town) side dated from the Norman times and on the north contained late medieval pottery; there were post holes from buildings on both sides. The moat had silted up over many years to leave three feet of blue mud, 10 feet of black mud, and a five-ft. layer of rubble, stone, clay, ash, charcoal and cinders. On the north side a sheer vertical cut may have been made before the siege of 1645.

When the moat had been filled in a ditch remained on the north side. The court of the castle was fining people for tipping rubbish here in the early 18th century. In 1946 this ditch was found filled with glass, rubble, and pottery kiln wasters from the adjacent Somerset Trading Company, most dating from about 1830 by John Browne.

If there were means of crossing the moat close to Fore Street, then the quay need not have been kept for use by the castle only. When the water bailiff's office began he had to reach the bridge, kept closed by a chain, to collect tolls. Strachie's map (*c.*1730) shows a curious angle where the moat must have joined the river at the south-east corner of the castle which could be the vestigial remains of a loading bay.

Documents suggest that the town cellar or official warehouse was on the west quay and eventually other private warehouses were built against the castle wall. Theoretically boats and goods, either arriving or being loaded under the nose of the castle authorities, would be subject to close supervision but cases of withholding payment of the lord's customs suggest that this was not always effective.

The outer bailey was not an empty yard but contained several buildings; the names of many are known but their sites are unidentifiable. Documentary sources providing information about the castle are the Ministers' Accounts for 1347 to 1413; most are from the period 1380 to 1400. The Mortimers, who owned the castle, never seem to have lived there nor is there reference to any garrison. One of the larger buildings was called Mortimer's Hall but was no longer a residence; it was full of hay in 1391 when the roof was renewed with fresh timbers covered with lead.

The Constable needed substantial living quarters which may have been provided by conversion of the gatehouse. Accommodation would also be required for servants and other workers. There was presumably a large kitchen since there was an oven which needed repairs. The castle had a chapel dedicated to St Mark where mass was said daily by two brethren from the Hospital (see also Chapter 6). The manorial dovecote, roofed with slate from Rookscastle, stood in its culverhay (pigeon yard) and supplied fresh meat in the winter. There was a barn for storing wheat and a horse-mill for grinding it. Accommodation would be needed for visitors such as the lord's chief auditor, or his chief clerk, or his receiver general, or even Sir Thomas Mortimer himself (in 1389). None would have travelled alone and, on one occasion at least, the chief auditor carrying a large sum of money from Winchester *en route* for Wigmore, was accompanied by a special guard. Five horses were kept at the castle so there would have been stables. One building served as the prison and its locks were purchased in Bristol. Like some of the other buildings it was usually full of hay. There was a pound for stray animals, and gardens – one was let with the horse-mill for £3 10s. 0d. a year.

There was a very large well with stone steps leading to the bottom. Its site was known early in the last century, and it was close to the river. There must have been other wells within the enceinte (enclosure of a fortification). It is not known what buildings, if any, were constructed in the inner bailey.

The accounts depict ordinary manorial life. One steward, assisted by a messor (the hayward appointed to supervise repair of fences and enclosures and to look after livestock), controlled the castle and Haygrove Manor. There were castle lands on the east bank of the river starting at Castle Field, and on the west bank the meadows of Saltlands. Peasantry on these demesne lands seem to have been quit of labour services. All paid the lord a tax known as chevage.

The castle was both a visible symbol of lordship and an administrative centre for other Mortimer demesnes at Odcombe, Milverton and, for a time, North Newton. The man put in charge performed the duties of three distinct offices: Constable, Steward and Receiver. His duties involved keeping the castle in repair and in a fit state for defence, presiding over all meetings of the manor

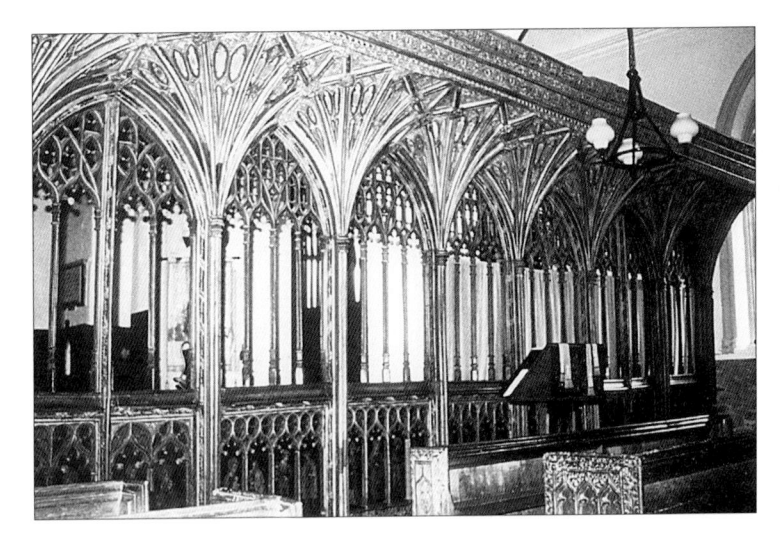

12 The choir screen in the parish church of Plaintree in Devon. This was given by the Countess of Devon in memory of her husband following his 'execution' in Bridgwater on 17 August 1469.

court, and being responsible for finance. He received a stipend of £5 a year. Theoretically an unskilled labourer in full employment and paid by the day could earn the same money so it is reasonable to assume that there were substantial perquisites.

When the last of the Mortimers died childless in 1425 his inheritance went to his sister Anne, who married Richard, Earl of Cambridge, son of Edmund, Duke of York. In 1454 her son, Richard Duke of York, possessed the Mortimer lordship but was killed at the Battle of Wakefield; his son became King Edward IV. Bridgwater was fortunate to avoid fighting during this period of the Wars of the Roses. It seems to have been a period of economic depression for the town, which found it difficult to pay the fee farm Edward had granted his mother. In 1461 the Duchess appointed a commission of four to investigate the matter. Despite the demands of her receiver it was reduced by £1.

The most dramatic event of the period was the death, in 1469, of Humphrey Stafford, Earl of Devon, who was well known in Bridgwater, held property in Enmore, and was a friend of John Kendale (*see* p.26). Several manuscripts in the Bridgwater archives refer to him between 1461 and 1467. He was only an earl for the last few months of his life so the Bridgwater documents call him Lord Southwick; bread, ale, and chickens for his visit in 1461 cost 7s. 10d.

In 1469 Edward IV was in difficulties, having quarrelled with the Earl of Warwick, head of the Neville family. Humphrey Stafford, Earl of Devon, was one who marched against Warwick in the midlands to suffer defeat; he then returned to Bridgwater. According to the older historians he was beheaded on Edward's orders for deserting the field at the Battle of Edgecote but the story is a fabrication derived from Holinshed. Contemporary sources make it clear that he was taken and executed by the common people of Bridgwater on 17 August. This was obviously a successful intrigue carried out by the Nevilles. The choir screen (Fig. 12) in Plymtree parish church was given by the earl's wife to commemorate his life.

4

The Borough

'Charter' is a technical word used for a certain type of document dealing with a grant but not necessarily issued by the monarch. Should an original charter be missing, its complete wording may appear many years later in an Inspeximus ('we have inspected') issued by the king as Letters Patent (i.e. an open letter). The text of Bridgwater's first charter granted in 1200 is known from an Inspeximus of 1318. The full text and a translation is in Volume 48 of the Somerset Record Society. Charters dated 1318, 1371, 1400, 1488, 1539, 1554, 1587, 1614, 1628 and 1683 are held by the Bridgwater Charter Trustees. Other charters granted have disappeared.

King John was short of money and was persuaded relatively easily to grant a charter. William Brewer obtained a document providing the community with a base on which to build. Not all towns could maintain borough status and some neighbouring vills, such as Nether Stowey, Stogursey and Chiselly Mount (i.e. Downend), endowed with some type of borough status in the 13th century, failed to survive.

The charter of 1200 granted certain specific commercial privileges with the right to collect the attendant tolls. There was to be a weekly market and a Midsummer Fair lasting for eight days. To be 'quit of toll throughout the kingdom' was the most coveted of privileges sought by merchants. These privileges were never granted to individuals but always to a group, and this grant implies that Bridgwater had a gild merchant from early times. London was always excepted from the 'freedom from toll' clause. Behind all the grants were the significant words: 'that Brugewalter be a free borough'. The phrase defies definition but has great importance.

The change from manor to borough meant a rise in legal status. Every townsman was now a free man and in no degree servile. He held his tenement by burgage tenure and, 'by paying one shilling yearly, or sixpence if he only held half a burgage', was quit of all labour services and payments in kind for which he had previously been liable. When he died any property acquired could be left as he wished and not simply to his legal heir.

The lord was not empowered to establish some sort of local government but still held considerable rights, power and property. Nevertheless, the seeds of change had been sown and the gild merchant, comprising the wealthiest members of the community, steadily increased its influence until it had virtually grown into the town government. The original charter was renewed twice without change but certain rights existed, undefined, until the reign of Edward I.

Among the powers granted were the pillory, which was kept in repair for the next 500 years, and the tumbrel – the terrifying cucking stool, usually a chair in which the offender was fastened then exposed to the jeers of bystanders or even taken to a convenient pond, stream, or river and ducked. Those punished included scolds, disorderly women and fraudulent tradesmen. Two other powers were the Assize of Bread and the Assize of Ale. Dating from 1266-7, the former gave the civic authority the power to set the price of bread in relation to the cost of corn and the latter the price of ale relative to the cost of malt. Bridgwater did not have 'withernam' (a form of distraint including a process of distress or arrest for debt used in the Cinque Ports and some other towns) nor 'wreck of the sea' (rights of cargo or goods thrown on land from a wrecked, stranded or foundered vessel).

The privilege of having a gild merchant to control trade was reconfirmed as late as 1468 by when it had in effect become the local government. Membership was compulsory and involved the levying of fees. The burgesses had first choice of all merchandise coming into the port during a period of 20 days.

Bridgwater was first represented in the Parliament of 1295 and returned members regularly after that. Members were called on to supply the king with money, an onerous duty rather than a privilege. In 1369 the king ordered that each member was to be paid 2s. for every day of each session, but few of these accounts survive and the earliest date from Elizabeth's reign. They suggest the rate had remained unchanged despite inflation in Henry VIII's time. In 1571 John Edwards received £6 16s. 0d. for attending on 68 days. In 1602 Alexander Popham was paid £6 for a session of 60 days.

Normally outsiders could only trade in food except during Fair time, and Nicholas Deveras of Waterford was fined 3s. 4d. in 1443 for selling salt fish and other things 'without license of the Community'. Since salt fish is food the fine was, presumably, for the 'other things'. In a general sense a man who paid his burgage shilling might be considered a burgess, but those who held privileges had to satisfy various requirements and 'buy their freedom'. Whatever the original rules for admission, during the 14th century a man who was master of his own craft could become a member.

In the 13th century the gild merchant was dominant but the Ordinance of the Burgesses (c.1280) is the only surviving document from inside the organisation. The members would meet inside their Gild Hall, although this building is not mentioned until 1354. In 1391 they made a new key to 'the stores of the Halle', suggesting that the Common Hall as it was now called was an upper chamber probably supported on pillars. The Ordinance made members agree not to make malicious accusations against fellow members by calling a man a thief or a native (meaning base-born or serf). If a member sought legal action against another member outside the borough, he had first to try to settle the dispute before the other gildsmen. Offences against these rules involved a fine of 12d. As late as 1550 Phyllype Farmer paid 6s. 8d. 'for brekyng of the lybertes'. The Ordinance stated that the officers, elected annually, shall be two Stewards assisted by a Bailiff. Their duties were unpaid but anyone elected refusing to accept office was fined 6s. 8d. Other duties were performed by those made Wardens of the Chantry of the Blessed Virgin Mary, the Chantry of the Holy Cross or of the town bridge. The gild merchant controlled these institutions, which each had to submit annual accounts. More general regulations forbade sale of meat and fresh fish before 9 a.m. and were intended to ensure that sales were above board, in broad daylight, and in open market. Medieval law prescribed heavy penalties for secret deals, or deals made privately or before the market opened.

13 Seal of the Commonalty (a self-governing community). This is an early form of the Bridgwater town seal.

The Stewards could fine all who broke these regulations. They had financial power. They apparently levied a tallage (a tax on un-free tenants usually paid at Michaelmas) on the whole parish, not just the borough. They authorised payments for repairs to the church from the common chest which had to be made by the Receiver, a borough official. After the gild merchant became the town government the borough officials were always named separately, except at the head, where the Stewards of the Gild Merchant were also the Stewards of the Commonalty (Fig. 13).

When a gildsmen made a bargain it had to be witnessed by two brother merchants, who shared his profit. Local merchants only could engage in retail trade within the borough except at Fair time. Neither of these rules appear in the Bridgwater document but they were common to all such bodies.

In theory, once a charter was granted under the Great Seal it was unnecessary for reconfirmation or reissue, yet the privileges it contained were so vital that the townsmen believed it was worth the cost of having it confirmed. Quite possibly they went to this trouble after the accession of every monarch. The charter of 1468 is of outstanding importance for it is the Charter of Incorporation. From this time onward the town has a corporation. The two Stewards of the Commonalty no longer act as spokesmen for the borough and the town is governed by a mayor assisted by two bailiffs and an unspecified number of burgesses. In 1557 the list of burgesses who paid cash and gave arms for the relief of Calais contains a complete list of the members of the Common Council. There were 24 and included an official element the two chief customs officers: the Customer and the Searcher. If they had been named as such the Town Clerk and the Recorder would also have been listed. There were also three women councillors: Isabel Hamond, Alyce Benett and Agnes Wallys, who would have been burgesses in their own right and possibly there in place of husbands who had died.

In 1559 the Rental of Town Lands (a balance sheet of income and expenditure) records: 'Mr Mullins for renewing the Charter and His fees as member of parliament and to Mr Shycom [i.e. Shercom] being mayor £35-11-4.' In 1588 they pay 'Mr Gyles our counsellar for the coping out of our charter 20s.'

Queen Elizabeth's charter of 1587 confirmed the borough's constitution and stipulated that the Common Council should comprise 18 members. As well as two bailiffs three other officers are mentioned: a Common Clerk and Protonotary, two Sergeants-at-Mace and a Clerk of the Market. It also authorised an additional fair, the Lent Fair, to be held the Monday after Shrove Tuesday and the four following days. Elizabeth also confirmed the charter granted by Queen Mary in 1554 which did not concern administrative or legal matters but a gift of land and property to the town. The land, at East Stower in Dorset, originally paid for a light and an anniversary in St Mary's church and belonged to the borough until 1949. The property comprised houses in Bridgwater formerly belonging to the chantries.

The charter of Charles I, granted in 1628, increased the number of burgesses in the Common Council from 18 to 24, specified the judicial powers of the Mayor, Recorder and Aldermen, and made provision for a Deputy Recorder. It also included a clause making the borough's boundaries identical to those of the parish. This clause was restated in 1683 so it may have been ignored. Inhabitants of the outlying hamlets are not found on surviving electoral lists, and Hamp was not included in the borough until 1835. The charter granted by Charles II in 1683 confirmed everything previously granted and introduced an annual fair to be held in the High Street on 28 and 29 December.

It is impossible to say how much a new charter cost. In the accounts of the Stewards of the Community for 1467 £1 2s. 8d. was paid to John Kendale 'for the renewal of our Common Charter'. John Kendale represented the borough in Parliament so it was easy to entrust him with the task, but the renewal of the charter of 1200 on the eve of a new and important charter in 1468, for which Bridgwater had petitioned Edward IV, is strange. Kendale was the town's first mayor.

A quittance or receipt dated 25 June 1559 gives some indication of what took place when Robert Mullens M.P. visited the Court of Chancery to renew the charter. Like most documents of this nature in the town archives it does not identify the charter concerned:

The charges of the patent renued the 2 day of June anno 1559	
In primis the Vyilam[1] and Capten letters[2]	10s.
the writynge	20s.
the yn Rolment	26s. 8d.
the Axamynacyon	10s.
to too masteres of Chauncery to syne the letters patentes	8s.
for the great seall	21s. 4d.
for wex & sylck lace	4s.
to Mr Andros to be amene[3]	

to my lord grate seall for sessynge[4] of the Fyne	10s.
the fyne to the Qune	£8
Summa	£13 10s. 0d.
Payd to Attwood for settyng owt of our letteres patentes to the pype	3s. 4d.'

[1] Vellum (i.e. the whole skin used for the charter)
[2] Capital Letters (i.e. the elaborate heading of the document)
[3] i.e. to be amenable (Mr Andros having the ear of the Lord Chancellor)
[4] Assessing

Several things can be learnt from this document. Drawing a large capital letter (reminiscent of Mary's 1554 Charter (Fig. 14) which had a large opening capital containing the Queen's portrait) required a special artist which cost 10s. whereas writing out the entire charter was only £1. Various Chancery departments were visited and each charged a fee: £1 6s. 8d. to enroll the document; 10s. to check the wording; £1 1s. 4d. for the use of the Great Seal; 4s. to cover the cost of wax and the silk ribbon; and it was important to give a 10s. tip to Mr Andrews otherwise something might go wrong! The odd 3s. 4d. paid to Attwood seems to have been completely forgotten.

Additional information on the back of the quittance includes 15s. 4d. commission for the town, 20s. for Lord Zouche, and Mullen's fee: 39s. for 30 days. The total was £17 18s. 8d. including another 11s. paid under the Act for sealing cloth. Apart from these details it shows Bridgwater paid to have its Charter renewed early in the new monarch's reign (1559), nearly thirty years before requesting a new charter in 1587.

The 1468 charter established two new courts, a Court of Record to meet weekly on Monday morning to try cases of debt and other offences involving less than 40s., and Quarter Sessions for which a Recorder, a man skilled in the law, had to be appointed. He and the mayor acting as Justices of the Peace kept the peace and also enforced the Statutes of Weights and Measures, the Assize of Bread, etc. The reversion of the farm of one-third of the borough was also given to the town. It is unclear when these payments ceased. For many years the town paid a small fee to the hundred court at North Petherton, but a receipt dated 1611 shows £37 15s. 4d.

14 Drawing of Queen Mary Tudor at the head of the charter she granted to the town in 1554.

paid to the Crown for lands originally belonging to the Hospital of St John, a substantial sum.

The charters were in constant use since they were frequently needed for consultation. This meant they had to be taken to Taunton or Ilchester or London, and this activity continued long after the last charter had been granted. In 1612 John Leaky, Receiver of the Borough, went to London carrying the charter in a leather case made for 1s. 6d. On finding the right office, he says: 'Mr Pitt's man charged a fee for telling our money and of xij d. more lost in tellinge 2s. 0d.' One Giles Langdon who accompanied Leaky received 10s. for his services 'for carryaige upp of £80 and for retourynge Downe £40'. '3 Councellors Fees' were £1 10s. 0d. and another money bag cost 5d. Leaky also wrote: 'for my owne expences and my horse meate in that journey for 13 Dayes £2 5s. 6d. My horse hier the same 13 Daies 15s. 0d.' Although the most important business was payment of the £40 fee and the other charges were incidental expenses the £40 is not entered in the accounts.

In 1617 the town paid 16s. 'for engrosing the Charter and englishing the same'. Presumably this was Elizabeth's charter and copying and translating were done locally.

In 1682 Charles II defeated the Whig attempt to exclude his brother James from the succession to the throne and pressurised 'Whig' towns to surrender their charters in exchange for new ones. In 1683 Bridgwater surrendered its charter and received a new one containing a clause giving the king power to dismiss at will any member of the corporation and to appoint another. There are no 'official' records of these developments in the borough archives but in 1719 the King was petitioned to revoke the 1683 charter on the grounds that the surrender had been made 'in a surreptitious and clandestine manner' against the will of the majority in the Common Council, who they also asserted that 12 out of 22 members had been removed by James II, arguing that both surrender and the new charter were void.

The only evidence of interference by James II is a letter of Decmber 1687 in which he removed seven men from being capital burgesses (i.e. councillors) and nominated their successors: 'We require you forthwith to elect and admit: John Gilbert Senr, Robert Balch, Roger Hoare, Thomas Turner, Samuell Pitman, John Francklin and William Bicknell to be one of the Capitall Burgesses & Towneclerke.' James had no intention of doing any more than obtain a compliant organ of local government and most men named were Presbyterians, who dominated local affairs until the Occasional Conformity Act was passed in 1711.

King George III granted the last charter in 1764 and it is unusual in being addressed to the Sheriff of Somerset. It says that the Mayor, Aldermen, Burgesses and inhabitants of Bridgwater are not to be molested in anything contrary to the tenor of their royal charters. Thus it confirmed all preceding royal charters granted to Bridgwater.

5

THE MEDIEVAL STREET PLAN

The medieval town was clearly defined: its perimeter followed Durleigh Brook on the south; a ditch fed by springs on the west led to the northern boundary by following what is now Mount Street to join the Castle Moat at Northgate. Eastover was also bounded by ditches. The King's Council in 1269, by Letters Patent, made 'to the good men of Bridgwater, at the instance of Roger Mortimer (their lord)' a grant of murage (a tax for maintaining a town's walls) for five years. Fortunately Bridgwater never built the walls as they would have been a constant expense.

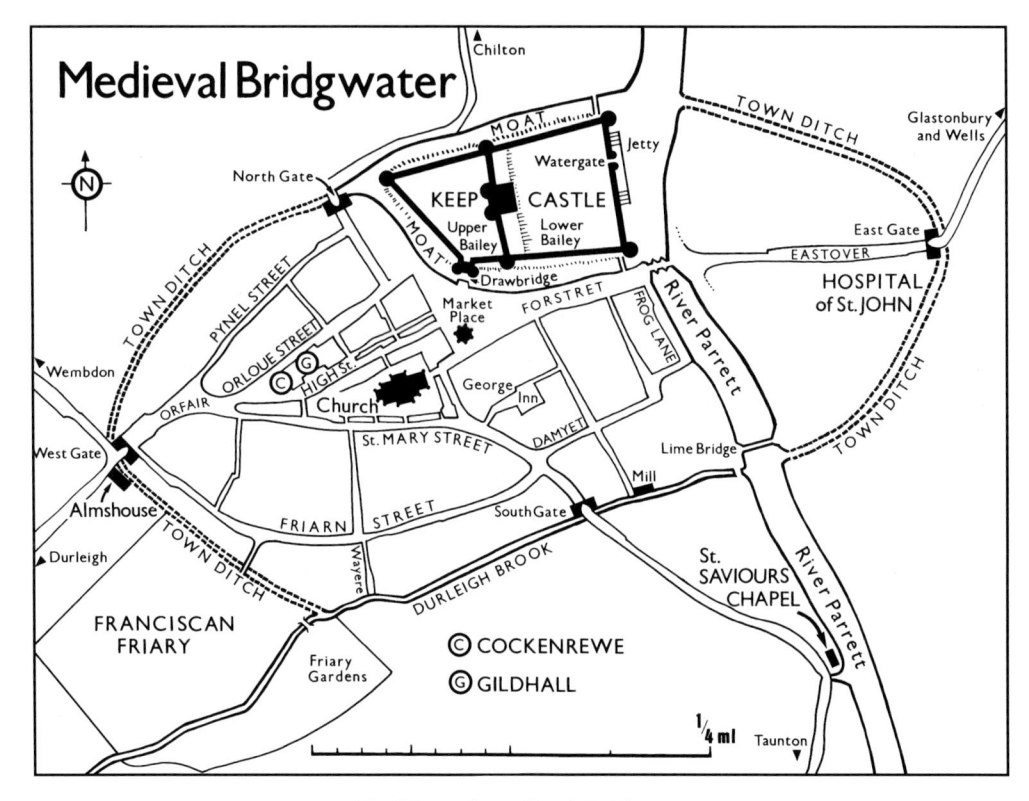

15 Map of medieval Bridgwater.

These boundaries may represent the original borough and this area remained almost unchanged as Bridgwater's nucleus. In 1468 the borough encompassed a wider area, from 'a certain cross called Kelyng Crosse' on the east (where the A38 and A39 meet) 'to a certain bridge called Lymebrigge on the south'. This bridge crossed the river near the town side of Durleigh Brook and the boundary followed the brook 'to a certain field called Mathewes felde on the west', then 'to a certain place called Cropile on the north'. It is still called Crowpill and situated where the Crowpill Rhine joins the Parrett. Over the river the boundary returned to Kelyng Cross (Fig. 15).

By 1468 houses outside the West Gate extended to form West Street and there were some houses along the road to Wembdon making North Street. Beyond the East Gate there were enough houses to justify the appointment of someone to collect their dues for the borough. Eastover is low lying and the Eastover section of the town ditch would be brim full at high tide. There was also 'a dyke three feet broad' which was covered 'where necessary' (1286) and dug to let the tide remove sewage from the Hospital of St John.

Although the town ditch was deep, at least round the castle, it is impossible to know how far west the water reached. Near the West Gate it was probably beyond tidal reach and depended on local springs. A document of 1302 refers to 'The Wall on the Town Ditche' near the West Gate, which was probably an extension of the gate fortification. Here the ditch was fed by a spring near the bottom of West Street which still ran in 1800.

The town could only be entered by one of the four gates. The East Gate stood near Eastover's junction with Broadway; the North Gate alongside what is now called Northgate House; the South Gate where St Mary Street crosses Durleigh Brook to become Taunton Road; and the West Gate where Penel Orlieu joins Broadway. Built of red sandstone quarried in Wembdon, it was the most elaborate of the four town gates. In 1299 Richard Maydus had been allowed to build a house over it which was still there and being repaired in 1599. In the lease the town reserved the right of entry to ensure the fortifications were not weakened. No trace remains of any of the gates and their locations are only approximate.

The town had only one main street: 'The fairest streate and principale showe of the Toune ys from the West Gate to the Easte Gate' Leland wrote in 1539. Its three sections acquired separate names: 'Eastover', 'Twixt Church and Bridge' (first called 'Forstret' in 1367) and 'High Street'. The road between the Market Place and the Orfair, a second market place inside the West Gate, is now Penel Orlieu.

The road from Taunton ran through the South Gate towards the Market Place. The western edge of the Cornhill followed the edge of the churchyard but, apart from the High Cross, first mentioned in 1367, permanent buildings were on the site of the present Market House. Four documents written between 1365 and 1370 mention 'the street leading from the east stile of the church towards the Gildhall' so there was a passage here at right angles to the High

Street. This passage, shown on Strachie's map of *c*.1730, had been built over before the first Ordnance Survey map of 1803. This section is always regarded as part of the 'High Street south side, which can seem strange. For instance, the *Swan Inn* appears to be in the Cornhill but a 1656 lease mentions 'a tenement lyeing on the south parte of High Street called by the name of the Swann'. This inn stood on the site of 6 and 7 Cornhill, with its carriage entrance opposite the east end of the church. The *Swan Inn* is first mentioned in a castle rent list of 1553 where a lord's rent of 4d. was accepted in lieu of '4 iron horseshoes and 38 iron keys'. The rent in kind indicates the medieval origin of the *Swan*, which was still standing at the end of the 18th century.

The East Gate and South Gates would often be busy since they covered routes from London and Taunton respectively. The highway was paved for about a mile outside the South Gate. The road through the West Gate was also busy as it not only led to the town's open fields but also to local villages. In times of flooding outside the South Gate travellers used the West Gate and travelled over the hills to Taunton, this particular route being considered part of a long distance highway to the south west. In 1675 John Ogilby advised travellers from London to Barnstaple to use this road. Minehead could also be reached via this route, the alternative being the road through Wembdon to Watchet. The North Gate (Fig. 16) was never busy as the road led only to houses outside the Castle Moat and then to Chilton Trinity.

16 The North Gate drawn by John Chubb in 1790 on the eve of its demolition.

The town centre was dominated by the castle, with its main entrance located in the north-east corner of the Cornhill or Market Place, first mentioned in 1361. The High Cross stood here, its footings exposed recently during town centre improvements. The fish stalls, the stocks and churchyard's east stile were located in the south-west corner. The common oven, used by the many householders without an oven, stood by the east stile. In 1391 John Cole bought a small house which was flanked on one side by the church stile and by the 'communum pistrinum' (literally common bakehouse) on the other.

The east stile, probably on the present churchyard gate site, was a gateway with a small room above. Something similar survives at Feock in Cornwall. The Bridgwater version was let to John Champayne as his tenement until it was demolished in 1556. Robert Bishop bought the roof lead for 18d. and two labourers paid 'to make cleyne the strett at 6d. the daye for 1 daye'. It was rebuilt in the 17th century, and at an unknown date 'Roger Hoan holds by lease, all that chamber over the passage going into the East Gate over the churchyard.' Later it was held by Thomas Hemons, and described as 'chamber and cockloft over the passage going into the churchyard'. He surrendered the lease in 1691 and it was taken over by Matthew Luff, whose family continued to hold it for many years.

St Mary's churchyard was gradually encroached and hemmed in with houses which by the 19th century had become a row of tiny, insanitary cottages occupying the entire south and east sides. Some cottagers caused trouble by breaching the wall to gain access to the churchyard. It took many years to eliminate these buildings. The 1887 Ordnance Survey shows four still standing west of the churchyard's main entrance.

The pillory possibly stood near the stocks outside the east stile but no direct evidence supports this hypothesis. In the early 18th century it stood near the fish shambles in the High Street. In 1378 'the old Pillory' was still standing and 'the stump', on which women scolds were forced to sit, may also have been near the east stile.

Encroachment on streets was always a problem in medieval towns. Bridgwater acquired a row of small buildings in the middle of the High Street, dividing it into 'North Street' and 'South Street' and making it narrow and inconvenient until their mid-19th-century removal widened the stretch between the *Mansion House* and the *Old Oak*. It retains an extra-wide pavement and corresponds with 'the Shambles', so called because the butchers formerly occupied this area. In 1379 eleven were fined 6d. each for selling meat unfit for human consumption. The slaughterhouses were behind in present-day Clare Street, which medieval documents called 'the Back' or 'the Common Back' but later often 'Back Lane'. It was an unpleasant area because, apart from the slaughterhouses lining one side of the road, all kinds of rubbish was dumped here, including rotten timber and old mill-stones. Property owners at the western end insisted on naming it 'Orloue Street', and by the 18th century it had become 'Penel and Orlew Street' (with many different spellings) although 'Back Street' still lingered.

The Medieval Street Plan

There is no indication that Mansion House Lane had a name in medieval times, although after 1500 it was obviously a passage alongside the Church House that was difficult to negotiate because of obstructions. The Church House had an external stair and, at the High Street end, a well complete with collar, windlass and pent-house cover. Old Oak Passage was called 'Godwin's Lane' then but, earlier in 1345, 'Godwyneslane' after the Godwin family who lived in a house at the High Street end. In the 16th century a few new houses were built amongst the butchers' houses and called 'Chapman's Row'.

Men of the same trade gathered in the same area which became known by the name of the trade. Though no law stated that this must be so, it was unwise to defy custom and in 1379 five men, Walter Brere, Nicholas Pridye, John Govere, Walter Foy and Robert Collinges, were summoned to answer: 'Why they made a market for cloth other than in the accustomed place?' This case, unfortunately, gives no indication where cloth was normally sold. The bakers seem to have been free to establish shops in different parts of the town. In 1379 Walter Baker, Richard Fourner, John Everard and John Baker were all outside the West Gate, whilst another John Baker and Philip Buclonde were outside the South Gate. They had no loaves on sale when the Sessions were being held and were fined 3d. each. Three had already been fined for not having bread on sale on Whit Sunday and Whit Monday.

The Gildhall and Tolsey were probably where the present Town Hall stands. Beyond was 'the Cockenrewe', a row of cooked meat shops and another example of a few houses on the north side of the High Street being given their own name. At one time these buildings were called the 'Via Cocorum' (street of the cooks). A second market place was located between High Street and the West Gate. Eventually pigs were sold here and it became known as Pig Cross, the name first appearing in 1610. Two documents from 1399 and 1403 describe this market as being 'near the West Gate'. Then it was called 'the Orfair', probably meaning 'cattle market'.

'West Street' is first mentioned in 1335. Its width suggests it was yet another market and was certainly used as the sheep market until 1935 when a new site opened in Bath Road. Street level here was low and the north side pavement, with iron railings, stood high above it. On market day the sloping verge was divided into sheep pens by hurdles. Redevelopment during the second half of the last century resulted in pavement and roadway appearing to be on the same level. Following the demolition of old cottages in North Street in 1962 before Westgate House was built, borings showed medieval levels were 11 to 14 feet below the present surface. There was no trace of the town ditch or town wall, nor of the West Gate, but construction of a new road alongside the Classic Cinema in 1973 revealed a section of ditch about 16 feet wide. This was probably a Civil War defence dug on the line of the medieval ditch; it followed the south side of Mount Street but, before reaching North Street, turned towards the West Gate. Further sections of the town ditch were discovered in 1986 in Mount Street before the Angel Place shopping precinct was built. Every section showed a 'V'-shaped profile almost 20 feet across.

The stone moulding outside 45 High Street was originally above head height but is now only 30 inches tall (Fig. 17). The extent of rise in street level varies from place to place. The area around the parish church seems to have been kept clear of debris through the centuries, leaving the ground level constant, but the astonishing rise in ground level near the top of Castle Street must surely be due to demolition of the castle.

The Cornhill was originally designed as a large rectangular area, presumably clear of buildings, but, as 14th-century records show, an inn was erected there together with a group of buildings. The neat plan of a large town square was apparently sacrificed to mercantile interests jockeying for display place in the front rank. Simultaneously the line of buildings on the north side of the High Street crept closer to the moat and the main gate of the castle, almost blocking access to the North Gate.

17 Remnant of medieval stone work in High Street. Now only 30 inches tall, this pier would originally have been above head-height. A similar one can be seen at both ends of the Marycourt.

'Forstret' was so called in 1367 although its more usual name 'Between Church and Bridge' persisted until the beginning of the 19th century. The present Fore Street follows the medieval street line but its size and appearance were very different then. The castle moat, with the high wall of the castle behind, ran along its north side, not below the present buildings but further back, in line with the yard of Castle House and following Queen Street. A watercourse (*cursus aquae*) followed Fore Street's south side, presumably fed from a spring near the Cornhill. In 1966 the former Congregational Church site revealed some medieval pottery, a hearth and some bones.

Fore Street ended at the bridge and 'Beyond the Bridge', first called Eastover in 1357, began. It had something of a separate life and in 18th-century rate lists, although one of the borough's wards, is referred to as 'Eastover and the Franchises'. This must indicate some degree of overlapping jurisdiction with one of the manors beyond the East Gate. The only example of any disagreement is in the council minutes for 1732 when a committee was appointed to talk to Mr How, 'Lord of a manor in the Franchise of Eastover, concerning an incroachment made by Samuel Tucker in setting up pales before his door'.

'Back Quay', now Binford Place, is not named in medieval documents but Frog Lane, a favourite medieval name for a wet place, began there. 'Froggeslane' in 1260 went from the quay, where there was certainly a slipway before 1456, as far as Frog Lane Bridge which spanned Durleigh Brook following the line of the main path in Blake Gardens. Nearby was the South Bridge, a larger structure traversing the river to a place near a limekiln and hence often called Lime Bridge. Named in the Royal Charter of 1468 as one of the borough limits, it was never mentioned again except in an instruction 'From Lime Bridge to St Saviour's Chapel', concerning use of the river bank many generations after one had collapsed and the other had been abolished.

Dampiet Street ran from Frog Lane to St Mary Street at a point where 'Mill Lane' was not yet named. 'Damyate' – spelt in a variety of ways including Damyetstrete, Damyate, Dameyate, Dameyete, Damyet, Damyete, Dampnyate, Dampyate, Damyhete – clearly meant 'the way to the dam'. Eventually Dampiet supplanted the rest with an intrusive 'p' for ease of pronunciation. The dam was a stone step across the stream which increased the height of the fall to the wheel paddles below.

Friarn Street, often spelt 'Frerenstret', means 'the street which led to the Friary'. The Horse Pool is still recognisable despite its degradation. 'Silver Street'

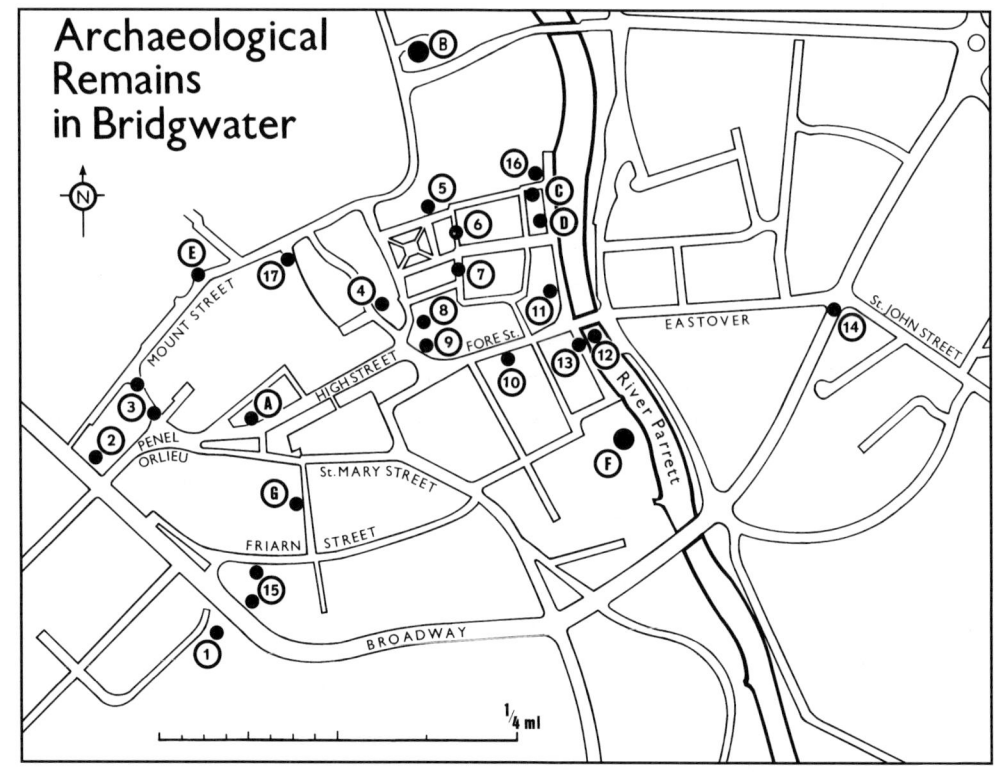

18 Map showing the location of archaeological remains discovered during the 20th century.

was not so named until about 1730; in the 14th century it was the street which led 'from the parish church to the church of the Friars Minor'. Excavation in 1989 on the site of a demolished house, No. 43, revealed the town ditch running north-south in line with Friarn Street. After passing the site of the house it turned south-east towards Durleigh Brook, proving that the Friary lay outside the town defences. The location of archaeological remains is shown in Fig. 18.

Several streets were named after men who once lived in them. Pynel Street is first mentioned in a conveyance drawn up for John Pynel in 1352 which distinctly says that the house has two courtyards, one of which is called 'Rome', alongside the North Gate. By 1415 it had become a garden called Rome and it was still there in 1473. Pynel Street corresponds with Market Street and is closely associated with Orloue Street. The name of one or the other, usually Orloue, was used as the name of a ward. A description of a house in 1352 shows it stood on the corner of Pynel Street and Orloue Street on the east side of Penel Orlieu. By the 18th century Market Street was known as 'Prickett's Lane' and Orloue Street had become 'Penel and Orloue Street'. At that date Penel Orlieu was always known as 'Pig Cross'.

John Crouile lived in Dampiet in 1349 and 'Crouiles's Lane', impossible to identify, was named after him. 'Pekesplace' in 1386, 'without the South Gate', presumably had a similar origin. 'Blind Lane' outside the West Gate means 'blind alley' and it ended before reaching St Matthew's Field. It was later called Roper's Lane and then re-named Albert Street in Victorian times. The name George Street was not used in 1380 although the *George Inn* stood there; it was described as 'in Damyete'.

When rates were collected and the town was divided into wards most took their names from streets. There were usually about a dozen. Those named in 1557 were Eastover, Twixt Church and Bridge, Orloue and Pynel Street, the High Street north side, the High Street south side, Damyet, Castle Ditch, St Mary Street, Friarn Street, and Without the West Gate.

A 1378 list of wards included North Street (called Without the West Gate towards Kidsbury), Without the East Gate, and By the Were. 'By the Were' is included with the hamlets in 1366 as though it were outside the borough, yet records from 1449 show 'a street called the Were' included with the town wards. The name must refer to the fish weir at the north end of the east quay. A 1616 lease speaks of a meadow well behind the gardens on the north side of Eastover 'on the east side of the water Parrett called the Great Dam'. Originally this dam must have worked a tide mill. In Elizabethan times rent for the dam meant rent of the field, usually 8s. For many years it was let to Bernard Redbeard, written 'Barnarde Radburtt' in 1576. During the 17th century, however, although repairs were usually concerned with posts and fencing, and the field gate lock, it seems that the meadow was connected by a strip of land to Eastover. A building in the street used to hold meetings became an inn in the 18th century and the dam site was converted into a dock for ship building.

The Medieval Street Plan

Two wards, first included in 1446, are missing from the 1557 list: 'On the Quay', which probably refers to East Quay, and 'The Hundred Acres'. Dilks thought this was by the river north of Eastover but the only evidence is a section of an early 19th-century Ordnance Survey map printed for a special purpose and showing it to be in the vicinity of Polden Street. Reasons for wards appearing or disappearing from medieval lists could include their degree of prosperity but a catastrophic fall in population could wipe out a ward.

When collecting church rates outlying hamlets also included North Bower (now called East Bower), Chilton, Dunwere, Haygrove, Hamp and Horsey.

Crosses

Crosses were erected to proclaim peace and as a reminder of Christian values in streets where markets or fairs were held. The five Bridgwater crosses served as useful landmarks for visitors.

In about 1480 there was 'an old cross' outside the West Gate where the width of the street made it suitable for holding a market. Inside the West Gate there was undoubtedly a cross on the site later known as Pig Cross. In 1769

19 The High Cross which stood on the Cornhill, drawn by John Chubb towards the end of the 18th century. Originally built in 1367, it was re-built between 1567 and 1569 at the great cost of £90. It was demolished early in the 19th century. Bridgwater's other crosses were simple, comprising a slender shaft on a stepped base. Pig Cross was surmounted by a sundial.

a handsome 18th-century cross surmounted by a sundial was moved from St Mary Street to here, where it replaced 'an old cross'. The High Cross in the Cornhill, first mentioned in 1367, was a covered market cross where traders could stand protected from the weather. Later it was put to many other uses and was a building of great architectural value which stood for more than 400 years (Fig. 19).

St Mary Cross is not mentioned until the 18th century when it stood in the street outside the south-east entrance to the churchyard. Strachie marked it on his town map *c.*1730. St Mary Street's width from the bottom of Friarn Street to this point suggests trading may have taken place here before the Cheese Market was established in 1681. Eventually so many crude shelters clustered around the cross that it became a nuisance and was moved to Pig Cross in 1769. Other fairs and markets were held in various streets with permission from the Common Council but without any cross being erected.

Keling Cross was presumably given by the family of that name in the 15th century. Well beyond the East Gate, it marked the borough limit and stood where the Bath Road joins the Bristol Road built 400 years later. A summer fair to sell horses was held in Monmouth Street throughout the 19th century.

6

THE HOSPITAL OF ST JOHN, THE FRIARY AND THE LEPER HOSPITAL

Towards the end of King John's reign (*c*.1215) William Brewer founded a small religious house known as the Hospital of St John. It did not belong to any specific religious order although contemporaries sometimes described it as Augustinian – not totally inaccurate as members were canons regular and not monks. This small independent community had their own Rule drawn up for them by Bishop Jocelin in 1219. Initially there were seven brethren.

They possessed the same 'liberties and customs as any house or brethren of a hospital or similar religious order have' and had to wear a habit such as brethren of a hospital ought to wear 'but with a cross of black or blackish colour impressed on their cloaks and outer garments'. Their chief duty was care of poor, infirm and needy persons. Their income must always be devoted to 'the sustenance of Christ's poor' and never diverted to other uses; for instance 'no rich men or powerful are to lodge or stay in the hospital at the charge of the house'. Amongst the sick they had to take care not to admit those suffering from lunacy, leprosy, or contagious diseases. Pregnant women or suckling infants were also excluded. The brother in charge of the infirmary could admit two or three suitable women 'not noble – but of good conversation and report', to help to nurse the sick.

For maintenance they were granted 100 acres of land in Bridgwater and the churches of Bridgwater, Northover (at Ilchester) and Isle Brewers (near Ilminster) and their tithes. However, they had to pay 100s. yearly to the monks of Bath and serve Bridgwater castle's chapel, celebrating mass daily. The lord provided books, vestments, vessels, lights, etc. but the hospital kept all gifts and oblations 'without dispute'. Later more churches were added to these possessions: Lanteglos (near Fowey) in 1283 by the gift of William Boynton; Wembdon in 1284 by the gift of William Testard; and Morwenstow (north of Bude) in 1285 by the gift of William de Monkton. Further gifts included land in Dorset, at Toller Porcorum (about nine miles north-west of Dorchester) and at Bridport.

Following this increase in endowments, the Bishop in 1298 ordered certain changes. The monks had to admit six chaplains who would celebrate daily, bringing the complement of the house to thirteen. They had also to maintain 13 poor scholars in the house 'habiles ad informandum in grammatica' (fit to learn Latin), and give a daily meal from their kitchen to seven poor boys sent from the town school by the rector.

Further gifts were made by Richard de Wiggesbere in 1327, including Chilton Trinity church, and chapels at Idstock (between Cannington and Otterhampton), and Huntstile (near North Petherton). Endowments made in 1333 enabled the monks to serve a chantry in Wembdon. However, in 1336 the hospital was excused from paying the tax known as tenths 'on account of its poverty' and in 1350 Bishop Ralph of Shrewsbury offered Indulgences to persons caring to contribute towards its rebuilding. The 'Valor Ecclesiasticus' (1537) reported that hospital endowments for almsgiving amounted to £32 5s. 8d. but as two of its estates maintained 13 boys and a third seven almsmen only £1 13s. 0d. was available for general distribution.

In 1463 Bishop Beckington sent along Hugh Sugar because the Master, John Holford, was so slack. Sugar compelled the community to build a prison complete with stocks and fetters. In later medieval times religious life failed to attract men as it had done earlier, and in 1445 when Thomas Yle was nominated Master of a similar hospital in Wells the house had only two members! Some years later, in 1497, when John Holford was elected, Bridgwater had only nine brothers and one of them was about to retire.

No buildings have been identified but they stood near the East Gate. In 1958 some houses in Eastover were demolished on what is now the south-west corner of the Broadway and Eastover junction in preparation for a new road. The bases of walls, which enclosed an open yard belonging to the hospital, were exposed. It lies below the northbound lane extending to the central reservation. The only finds were some oyster shells, possibly used as palettes for mixing colours, and a human skeleton.

The hospital had a door outside the Town Gate enabling late travellers to gain admittance when the Town Gate was locked. It occupied a large area, comparable with that of the nunnery at Cannington where the medieval precinct wall still stands. The enclosure held a church, which William of Worcester says was 112 feet long, and an infirmary which was probably an aisled hall with, possibly, the women's quarters attached. There would be a day room with a dormitory above, a chapter house and cloister. The hospital would have had a sizeable kitchen, refectory and parlour and enough space within its boundaries for a garden, a fish pond and a graveyard.

On 5 February 1539 hospital life was abruptly terminated when the Master, Robert Walshe, elected in 1525, surrendered the house to Henry VIII. There were only eight brethren including the Master. Why the drastic decline in numbers occurred is unknown, but perhaps the Black Death was a factor. The meekness of the brothers' surrender enabled them to enter the secular world with modest but adequate pensions: Robert Walshe received £33 6s. 8d.; Thomas Goggyn, Richard Kymrydge, John Colde, John Wyll and Robert Fyssher were given £4 each; John Wood and John Mors received £2 each. On dissolution the hospital's income was £120 19s. 1d. well below the £200 limit set by Parliament, so the commissioners treated it as a smaller house. However, nearly 150 years earlier the wealth and power of the hospital provoked the hatred of the townsmen. The events can be followed in the Calendar of Patent Rolls 1377-81.

A rebellion in 1381 resulted in two days of violence. On Wednesday 19 June a crowd in the Market Place was harangued by Thomas Engilby supported by Adam Brugge, a leading townsman, Nicholas Frampton, the vicar, and John Blake. Then, carrying a banner with the royal arms crudely displayed to indicate that no treason was meant, they marched over the bridge to stop and hammer on the hospital gate. William Cammell, the Master, asked what they wanted. They demanded money, certain documents (bonds) and a promise that the vicar should receive his tithes in full, threatening to burn the hospital if it did not comply. The Master had no choice, documents were handed over and burnt, Nicholas Frampton got his rights, and 200 marks in cash were handed over.

The mob's fury was undiminished and they went to look for various agents and legal advisers of the hospital. First they sought John Sydenham, destroying his houses at Sydenham and stealing goods worth £100. Various court rolls and deeds were also taken and burnt. Next they turned on Thomas Duffeld, the town's leading lawyer, wrecking one of his properties before burning it. Then they marched along the river bank to Chilton Trinity where Walter Baron lived. The angry mob killed him and then returned with his head on a pike which they placed on the bridge.

Next day the townsmen made for Ilchester to take Hugh Lavenham, who once had been in charge of the king's prison there but was now a prisoner himself. It is not known why the men of Bridgwater hated him nor how John Bursy was implicated but Bursy was collected at Long Sutton and taken to Ilchester. Here the mob broke open the gaol, a small building on the bridge, and freed the prisoners. Lavenham was seized and John Bursy compelled to execute him. The mob then returned to Bridgwater bearing Hugh Lavenham's head to display on the town bridge. This seemed to assuage anti-clerical passions and the rebellion was over.

Within four days the King's Council proclaimed Bridgwater to be 'contumacious' (wilfully disobedient to the order of a court). When eventually a general amnesty was declared, Bridgwater together with five other towns was excepted and therefore one of the last places to be pardoned. Nicholas Frampton, who had been outlawed, surrendered in London in February 1382. Thomas Engilby, also a fugitive, was condemned to forfeit land to the annual value of 40s. together with farm produce and stock to the value of 50s. In March 1383 he was given a royal pardon and allowed to go to Ireland in the king's service. He returned within a year and lived quietly in Bridgwater.

Most western European towns had experienced severe social strains during the 14th century and outbreaks of violence were common. In Bridgwater, as at St Albans in 1381, local agitation was concentrated against a religious house. The Church had become wealthy and sluggish, and the English nation had become cynical as it watched a long succession of French popes ruling from

Avignon. In 1378 Urban VI returned to Rome but, unfortunately, the French cardinals had withdrawn their allegiance and supported a rival pope in Avignon. The Great Schism had begun.

Nicholas Frampton was made vicar of Bridgwater by the papacy, which claimed the power to over-rule the local patron. Parliament had made such action illegal in the 13th century but the king never seriously attempted enforcement. After 1378, since only certain countries supported him, the Pope lost much revenue and so was unlikely to relinquish a power bringing him fees paid by any vicar he had appointed. In Bridgwater the aggrieved patron, the hospital, had shown resentment against a vicar 'provided' by the Pope by withholding some of his revenues.

The Master of the Hospital was the most powerful ecclesiastic in the neighbourhood. In 1349 the hospital acquired as a single gift: '16 houses, a shop, a solar, 2 stalls, a garden, and 23½ acres of land'. After the Dissolution a father and son, both called William Hodges, compiled a catalogue of 69 Bridgwater houses formerly belonging to the hospital, each with a garden, which they proposed to purchase from the Crown. As the hospital had grown rich and powerful, appointing vicars to many churches, drawing rents from farms in the neighbouring villages, and owning houses in nearly every street in the town, its wealth and power excited envy and fear. Its agents drove hard bargains, made stringent conditions and set everything down in writing, and by the 14th century an institution which had been founded with benevolent intent, and entirely praiseworthy aims, had become the object of suspicion and of hatred.

Day-to-day running of the house was probably lax and in 1325 Bishop Drokenford held an inquiry, but little happened. In 1348 the Black Death affected the Bridgwater area badly. In a superstitious age the sudden epidemic, which possibly killed over a third of the population, must have created a psychological climate of fear and mistrust which would take more than a generation to die out.

Attacks on the hospital happened three times in 1380, once in February and twice in July. There are three lists of persons indicted and seven names appear on two. Only six trades are mentioned: tanner, webber, sheather, carpenter, hosier and hellier. Several bear well-known family names of the period: Marys, Black (or Blake), Croneyle (surely Crouile), Bruwere, Criche, Tanner and Sely. Only two names of the leaders of the 1381 rising are listed: Thomas Ingilby and Adam Brugge.

The hospital seems to have antagonised William de la Zouche, lord of the borough (a title he shared with the Mortimers), who brought an action in October 1380 against men who prevented his steward holding a View of the Frankpledge, a Saxon system whereby tithing members were bound to stand security for each other's good behaviour. The View was the inspection by the authorities to ensure it existed. William Cammel, Master of the Hospital, heads the list of the men involved, and the others are obviously his supporters. Further names of the 'Clerical Party' appear in an indictment of March 1381 brought by John Blake, who became one of the ringleaders in the events of June. Names include Michael of Perry, and Michael of Sydenham (both landowners), Hugh Goldsmith, John Cerveys (Chaplain), William Hole (a Chamberlain), William Webbe, John Palferyman and Thomas Duffeld. It can only be surmised that Lord de la Zouche supposed that the Master of the Hospital was becoming a rival to his own power and influence in the town. The rebels must have known this.

Another fact that defies explanation is William Coggan, lord of the manor of Huntspill, seeming to have supported the rebels. It is just possible that rural connections (the castle still had customary tenants outside the borough, and the hospital held farms in several villages) indicate some agrarian problems but, as far as Bridgwater is concerned, the term 'Peasants Revolt' is a misnomer.

The Friary

The arrival of the friars, 'Pellegrini et Peregrinantes' (Pilgrims and Wanderers), was one of the most remarkable events in the whole of medieval history. In the early days, from 1210 to 1240, the life of St Francis inspired young men to rebel against the materialism of the age and renounce all wealth. Those doing so, largely the sons of the affluent merchant class, experienced the 'Franciscan Joy', a feeling of elation and release from worldly cares.

On 8 September 1224 the first group of nine brothers landed at Dover and headed for Canterbury. The group then split and in ones and twos tried to get a foothold in large towns, starting with London and Oxford. Their success was phenomenal and within a few years they were holding a provincial chapter and dividing England into custodies. Bridgwater was in the custody of Bristol which contained nine houses.

It is remarkable that the Franciscans came to Bridgwater in the very early days. Leland was told they arrived in the time of William Brewer II, which would mean *c.*1230. Thomas of Ecclestone says they changed their site sometime after 1240, probably meaning they arrived that year. The Friars always asked for a useless piece of land or a building that nobody wanted. Undoubtedly this is what they were given in Bridgwater, but clearly they disliked it because in 1245 the king ordered the lord of the manor, William de Cantelupe, to find a friendly place fit for the Friars Minor to erect a church and other necessary buildings. In 1246 the king wrote to the town bailiffs ratifying the assignment of land made to the Friars Minor. Almost certainly this site gave its name to Friarn Street. Grants of oak from the royal forest of Petherton, six trees in 1250 and another six in 1284, suggest that building had commenced.

In 1349 they were given six acres of land 'for the enlargement of their dwelling place'. The Ministers' Accounts of the castle in 1359 refer to nine burgages 'where the Friars Minor used to dwell'. The date when such entries were first made is unknown but it is tempting to suppose that between 1349 and 1359 the friars had crossed the town ditch and erected new buildings outside the town defences. In 1984 archaeologists investigating the land at 43 Friarn Street found the town ditch followed a line close to the edge of Friarn Street and did not go round the friary buildings as was previously supposed.

There was no stock plan for a friary, and friars were constantly on tours of duty so no fixed number lived in the house. Possibly the nine burgage plots occupied in Friarn Street were all on its south side; one document mentions a 'close wall' (a precinct wall) on the south side of the buildings. Presumably the church was somewhere along that line. In 1352 Silver Street is described 'as the street which goes from the parish church to the church of the Friars Minor', and in 1361 a house inside the West Gate was said to be 'in the street leading from the West Gate to the church of the Friars Minor'.

After the community moved beyond the town ditch the friary gate was approached over a plank bridge. Perhaps the name 'Friars' Gate' went with the friars, but it certainly described a house in the Churchwardens' Accounts for 1489: 'Reseywyt of rente at freren zete 20d.'

In 1445 their church had been completely re-built and was consecrated by Bishop Beckington. From dimensions given by William of Worcester, it was a fine building 200 feet in length and 50 feet wide. Unlike early Franciscan churches it had aisles about 12 feet wide and, a feature common to churches of this order, a crossing passage 'between nave and Choir'. One end of this passage usually opened to the street and the other led inside the precinct.

William of Worcester copied a list of names from the martyrology shown him by the friars. Some were famous locally and some nationally. Many were buried here, including Sir John Trivet (d. 1394) who left 800 marks for building a new bridge in Bridgwater; Thomas, Duke of Lancaster (beheaded in 1382); Sir John Kemys; Lord Richard Tiptoft; Brother Geoffrey Pollard (d. 1440); Sir Matthew Gornay (usually spelt Gournay) (d. 1406), and his wife, both connected with Cannington; Lord William de Cantelupe who held the manor and castle of Bridgwater in 1245 and was described as founder of the church; William de Bytton, Bishop of Bath and Wells (d. 1274); and Roger Mortimer. Alice, daughter of the Earl of Warwick and wife of Sir Matthew Gournay, was buried in the middle of the quire. The arms of both Trivet and Pollard are on floor tiles at Cleeve Abbey.

A famous Franciscan, Brother John Somer, a mathematician and astronomer mentioned in Chaucer, was a Bridgwater friar. He died in 1419 or 1420 and was buried here. Robert Crosse, provincial minister of England after 1280, who had probably been a Bridgwater friar, was also buried here. One important tomb in the church had an iron grating around it but it is not known whose it was. In 1720 John Cannon wrote that no buildings survived, only the cemetery and churchyard, yet long before the 19th century no tombstone was standing. Surprisingly, not one grave has been uncovered.

All available evidence suggests that the friars enjoyed Bridgwater's respect and confidence. In 1409 the Warden issued a Letter of Confraternity to William Dyst and Joan, his wife, admitting them to the benefits of the order, meaning that the brethren would pray for them. Other townsmen paid for a fixed number of prayers to be said. Nine Letters of Confraternity were issued and there were requests for burial in the Friary church. William of Botreaux had the bodies of his children, William and Anne, transferred from south-east Somerset to the friary in Bridgwater.

Documents produced at the Dissolution mention six buildings: the church, 'the second house' (probably a misreading), the chambers, the frater (i.e. refectory), the kitchen and the buttery, but give no precise details; the area covered and number of brothers accommodated are unknown. The house was not wealthy and its income only £53 4s. 5½d. in 1538. It was surrendered on 13 September, the deed of surrender being signed by eight friars including the Warden, John Harris. All were summarily evicted without pensions. Next year the five bells were sold for £40, lead from the gutters for £12 10s. 0d., and 'certain elm trees growing round the aforesaid friary' for £10. Eleven laymen, including Hugh Poulett, John Cuffe, William Portman, Alexander Popham and William Michel, enjoyed fat pensions paid from the house's former revenues.

When Leland visited two years later, he noted that 'the Accustomer of Bridgwater (Customs Officer) hath translatid this place to a right goodly and pleasant dwelling House'. This was John Persone, who enjoyed the house together with six acres of orchard and gardens for an annual rent of 2s. In 1544 the site was granted with other properties to Emmanuel Lucar, a London merchant.

In 1934, workmen excavating Friarn Avenue for a new council estate uncovered the bases of six piers in a line, obviously part of an aisled building. Each was solidly constructed of stone blocks with smoothly dressed faces and measured 6½ feet by 5½ feet. Unfortunately the levels were not taken and depths unrecorded. However, each base appeared to be about three feet high and ground level about eight feet below the 1934 ground level. The bottom section of one pier was *in situ* on top of its base and left in place when the trench was filled. A similar pier section dug up on nearby allotments was taken to the Admiral Blake Museum. It still retained its medieval lime wash.

The site engineer believed it was the Friary church and local historians agreed. However, provided no feature forced a change of plan, churches were carefully orientated, and the excavated building axis ran from north-west to south-east. The line of the outer wall (the only wall found, to the north east) suggests an eight feet-wide aisle – smaller than the church dimensions but consistent with an infirmary having beds placed in the aisles and its central 'nave' kept clear. The building's limits could not be ascertained but its distance from the street suggests that it may have been sited for quiet and seclusion.

A few yards to the south were the remains of two walls sited at right angles to each another. One, with buttresses, was about 15 inches wide, well built of Ham stone and about 20 feet long. The other, nearly 30 feet in length, was much thicker, 36 inches wide and built of limestone rubble. A small but well-constructed drain was associated with this building. The remainder of the area was not fully examined but it is remarkable that the dual-carriageway

Broadway, opened in 1958, was cut across the friary site without discovery of any further artefacts.

Several medieval tiles were found near the stone drain in 1934 and are exhibited in the town museum. They are typical Wessex designs and similar floor tiles have been found at Glastonbury and Cleeve. Most are about five inches square. Several date from the 14th century but others with deeply inlaid pipe clay designs and trowel-cut keys on the back may be earlier. The heraldic designs are the Royal Arms of England (Fig. 20); the Arms of Richard, Duke of Cornwall and Count of Poitou; the double-headed eagle used by Richard of Cornwall after his election as King of the Romans (he would have been the next Holy Roman Emperor but his election was disputed) (Fig. 21); the Arms of Clare, and the Arms of either Warenne or St Barbe (Fig. 22). There is also a fragment of a large two-tile design showing Richard I in single combat with Saladin, and several conventional designs typical of the medieval period. No trace of any kiln was discovered. The only other objects recovered were a medieval metal purse top, similar in size and purpose to the top of a woman's handbag, and two door keys.

20 One of the medieval tiles found on the site of the Friary; this example shows the Royal Arms (Plantagenet) of England as borne by King Henry III.

The Leper Hospital

Leland wrote, 'There ys an hospitale yn the west part of this towne, of the building and foundation of menne yn the towne; but it is endowed with little or no lande', which past historians thought meant a leper hospital. Leland probably made a mistake, as a later recollection of his Bridgwater visit refers to the same institution as 'Ann almose house made by the town. It hath little or no landes.' The hospital was the Hospital of St Giles, and if it existed in the 1530s Leland should have known its dedication. If there was a leper hospital it would have been founded and built by the lord of the manor and not by the town. Moreover, the West Gate almshouse existed in the 1530s and Leland must have seen it.

The only evidence for the leper hospital's existence is in an early 14th-century document, probably produced between 1303 and 1334. It only exists as a copy printed in 1634 and its accuracy cannot be guaranteed. Originally it was part of a collection of legal documents called a Registrum carried by a medieval attorney as part of his stock in trade. Following the invention of printing these Registra were published as law books. A writ referring to the Hospital of St Giles contained, within three dozen lines of Latin, every known fact about the hospital. It is addressed to the Archdeacon of Taunton

21 Another example of a medieval tile from the Friary site, this one showing the double-headed eagle borne by Richard of Cornwall, son of Henry III, as 'King of the Romans', a title he hoped would be followed by 'Holy Roman Emperor'.

but later proper names are abbreviated to the initial letter. A reasonable assumption is that 'B' means Bridgwater, one of ten parishes in the archdeaconry having this initial. The hospital is under the control of 'M' or 'Marg', which could mean Margaret Mortimer who was widowed in 1303. She had a son called Roger, and this agrees with 'R' in the text. Her husband's name, however, was Edmund and the text gives 'I'. Assuming this is an error of either copyist or printer, then the writ dates from between 1303 and 1330. It says that the hospital was founded by 'the ancestors of R', i.e. the Mortimers, which could mean the date of its foundation was before the 14th century. Most leper hospitals were earlier, and none was founded after the Black Death.

The writ is a Writ of Prohibition in which the King tells the Archdeacon the hospital is not an ecclesiastical institution and the church courts have no right to intervene. It was issued following a complaint from three male hospital inmates, 'R of S, R of K, and J of B', who were dragged before the church courts and now suffered excommunication and other forms of oppression. The plaintiffs may not have been lepers, the writ stating explicitly that the hospital was founded for the maintenance of lepers 'and other poor and infirm men'.

22 This medieval tile from the Friary site shows the Arms of Warenne or St Barbe (the shield chequy). The family has no connection with either the Friary or Bridgwater.

7

THE PARISH CHURCH

Churchwardens' accounts leave no doubt that the church was the single most important factor in the community's social life. Every year meticulous preparations were made for the great festivals. In 1420 the Easter candle needed 19lb. of wax which cost 5½d. per lb. 'Painting the picture for the Resurrection on Easter Day' in 1418 had cost 2s. so two years later only 2½d. was spent 'preparing it'. In 1432 3d. was paid 'for peyenting of the 3 Kynges on twethe day'.

The sepulchre had to be prepared at Easter (pins and needles cost 2½d. in 1432) and William Ellis earned 8d. for 'keeping it' and ensuring the light kept burning. The item: 'for a carpenter to mend the sepulcher – 2d.' suggests it was a timber structure and buying nails for the sepulchre is mentioned frequently; perhaps it was a processional object, hence the use of wood rather than stone.

An unusual entry in 1429 is for 'boring of the banerholys yn the lofte – 2d.', followed by 'mendyineg of the baneres – 1d.' Clearly several banners were displayed on the rood screen in connection with one of the festivals, perhaps Corpus Christi, a major occasion with processions through both church and town. An elaborately ornamented litter called a 'ferter' was prepared which enabled the Host to be borne with great honour. A new ferter cost 2s. 4d. in 1429.

The Lenten Veil usually needed attention and entries include 'a pulley bought for the Lenten Veil – 4d.' in 1420. The veil was a curtain suspended by riddle rings (from French *rideau*, a curtain) hung on a rod stretched across the chancel. It was probably violet and concealed the altar throughout Lent to emphasise the mournful nature of the period. 'Lenten Cloths' were used to cover images.

In 1445 24 lbs of wax was needed for two torches and the light before the High Cross at Christmas, which cost 11s. The churchwarden, John Paris, allowed himself 4s. for '12 days labour of mine against Christmas and Easter, Whitsunday and Corpus Christi day'. It was customary to hang a star from the roof at Christmas, so in 1449 'for a man hired to hang the star together with nails bought for the same – 1½d.'

Numerous tapers and smaller candles were needed besides the main candles and moulding these lights must have kept men busy every week. The church was much darker than it is today because the roof was several feet lower, the present roof and clerestory being mid-19th-century alterations. The gloom was offset by applying lime to the walls and freshly whitened walls together with many candles must have made the burgesses proud of their church. Money was even spent paving the floor.

The church buildings were subject to constant care and attention. There are charges for repairs to the tower, glazing the windows, mending the roof and so on, but there were three outstanding achievements: casting a bell, building the spire and the rood screen.

The bell was cast in 1318 before regular churchwardens existed, and to pay for it four lay wardens were appointed: Richard Maydus, Philip Crese Erl, Gilbert Large and Richard Dunster. Parish collections produced some money and much scrap metal from old jars, plates, basins, ewers and mortars, all brass and weighing 180 lb. An old bell weighing 425 lb. was included. The lay wardens then bought 896 lb. of copper, 40 lb. of brass and 320 lb. of tin and had a new bell cast. It weighed nearly 16 cwt. 'and there remain 80 lb.' It cost £19 of which the bell-founder, called the Master, received £3 16s. 6d.

The pit in which the bell was left to cool for several days may have been dug in the nave floor. Such a pit was discovered in the Royal Free Chapel at Cheddar in 1961 but the likelihood of a similar discovery at Bridgwater is slender as in 1967 several yards of the nave floor were exposed while removing two rows of pews at the eastern end. Below a false wooden floor were open vaults divided by brick walls and a coffin in each compartment which appeared to date from the 18th and early 19th centuries.

The account for building the spire was kept separately by the Borough Receiver, William Tanner. He names 16 wardens from the borough but no wards or streets. They raised the enormous sum of £118 7s. 9½d. Outside the borough but within the parish were the hamlets of East Bower, Haygrove, Hamp, By the Weir, Dunwear, Horsey and Chilton which produced £18 14s. 6d. by levying a special rate. Another £6 11s. 2d. came from gifts and legacies, making a grand total of £143 13s. 5½d.

A Robert Crosse presumably directed operations for the church as he was paid a 40s. fee and employed a clerk. The spire was built by Nicholas Waleys of Bristol, who received £90 7s. 4d. The timber came from Petherton Park but the slates used were cut from Ham stone. Many craftsmen are named. John Aleyn, William Blacche and John Betere were all paid 'by indenture' like Nicholas Waleys, so they were probably master masons. John Western was a quarryman, and Walter Ruddock an ironworker who received 35s. 8d. but supplied his own iron. John Churcheye and Richard Deye were carriers of stone (their thick leather gloves costing 9d.), and John Godhyne was a carpenter.

There must have been several crises during this huge task. John Turlit was paid 24s. 8d. for 'a cord called a cable'. 'A tool called a crowe' was fetched from Downend where it had been used, perhaps, for quarrying lias and 15d. was spent having it repaired. Something very serious must have happened to send William Crese to fetch Nicholas Waleys from Bristol at a cost of 18d.

Building took less than a year, being completed in 1367 and the result was a masterpiece. Any kind of spire would have been unique in this neighbourhood

23 Seal of the Chantry of the Blessed Virgin Mary.

but the Bridgwater spire is about twice the height of the church tower. It is a landmark visible for miles across the flat countryside and for centuries featured in sailing instructions guiding ships up the river. Perhaps the burgesses had this use in mind when they decided to create such a prominent landmark.

The rood screen is first mentioned in 1415: 'paid William Thomas for trimming timber for the rood screen (pulpitum) 1s. 4d.' In 1418 the churchwardens bought a great oak from Robert Tanner for 20s. and then paid 8d. 'in carriage of 2 parts of the same to the lodge', and another great oak from William Thomas for 13s. 4d. The screen was erected 'before the High Cross' in 1420. The crucifix hung from an iron hook for years, and still remains *in situ*. Money was paid for scaffolding and bringing timber from the lodge. Two masons were hired 'to set up the said rood screen' and to bore holes in the pillars, and they had a man to assist them. Other men were hired to empty the charnel house and clear up when work had finished. All of this plus extra materials such as nails, boards and refreshments cost £1 1s. 8½d.

The main roof was built of lead-covered wooden boards but the chapels may have originally projected at a lower level since they were roofed with stone tiles. By the 15th century, with one exception, all were under one roof. The Lady Chapel or Chantry of the Blessed Virgin Mary is the earliest recorded (Fig. 23). It probably belonged to a religious gild or fraternity and was placed in the choir, presumably behind the high altar. The only light here came from the east window (replaced in Victorian times) as there were blank walls both sides; the side windows were inserted in 1851 using Bath stone, all the medieval windows being made from Ham stone.

Two drawings made in 1828 and 1832 (Fig. 24a & b) show the original appearance of the church. Fig. 24b shows a projecting section of wall surmounted by battlements and with 16th-century flat-topped windows on the right of the south porch; the wall is now level with the rest of the nave wall and the window is pointed in the Decorated style.

The original south transept roof remains and has a large circular boss carved with the figure of a king wearing his crown and seated on a throne. There were probably two chapels in this transept, a south chancel chapel being created later which remains in use. Originally it may have been the chapel of Holy Trinity 'made' in 1415 for £4. A similar arrangement existed in the north transept. The organ now occupies a former chantry chapel site, probably that of St George, for a 1551 will refers to the north aisle as 'sometime called St George's aisle', which confirms a note of 1445 headed 'in the north side of the church' and naming five men who sit in the Chapel of St George. All the costs of maintenance seem to have been borne by the churchwardens, who repaired

The Parish Church

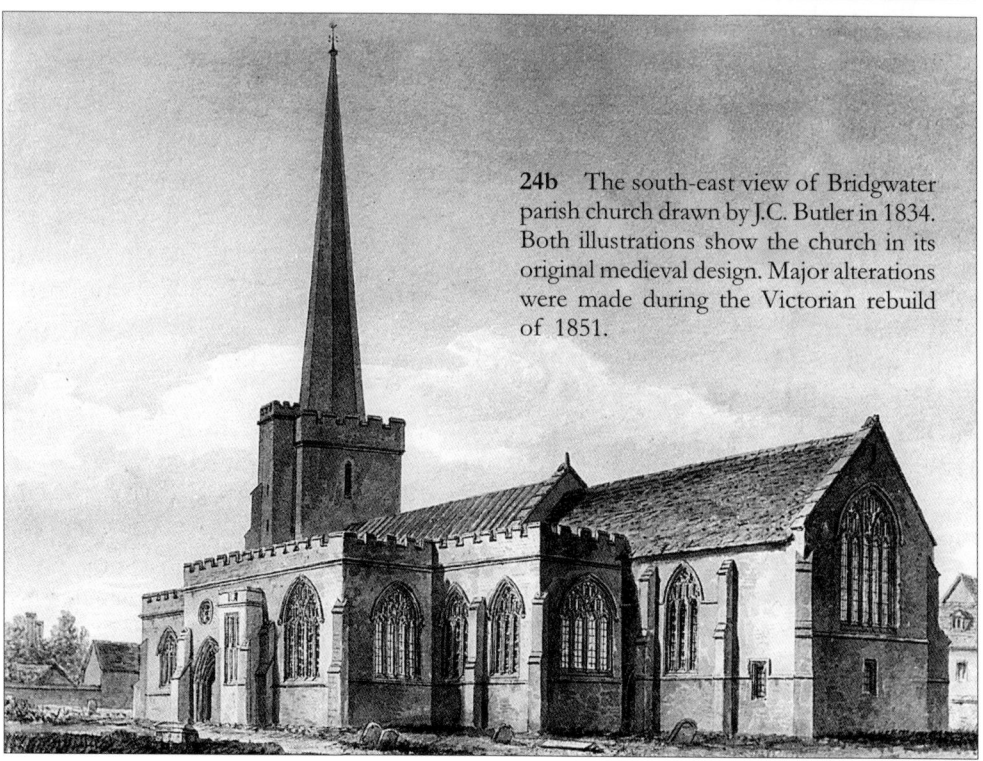

24a The north-east view of Bridgwater parish church drawn by J.C. Butler in 1828.

24b The south-east view of Bridgwater parish church drawn by J.C. Butler in 1834. Both illustrations show the church in its original medieval design. Major alterations were made during the Victorian rebuild of 1851.

the roof and the paving in the chapels of 'Trinity and Blessed Mary'. An entry in 1448 shows two tilers and their servant were paid 'to tile the Chauncell by Seynt George Chapell 12d.' and repairs to St George's Chapel were also done by Henry Plummere (i.e. plumber) for 3s. 9d., plus lathes costing 2d. and 10 lb. of solder priced at 20d.

The charnel house was probably a small building in the churchyard with a Chapel of the Holy Cross above it distinct from the Chapel of the Holy Cross within the church. Previously it was assumed that the boiler house, below ground level, was the charnel house and the chapel above was in the north transept. Such a buiding was essential in medieval cemeteries where bones frequently surfaced from shallow graves; these were collected and put in the charnel house.

Over the centuries the north transept has been altered beyond all recognition. The 'Clerks Room' was above the north porch and a mullioned opening with wooden shutters in the porch wall was originally a squint enabling the clerk (three of whom were attached to the church) to look through two further openings, one in the transept wall and the other in the chancel wall, for the moment of the elevation of the Host and to ring the Sanctus bell. Later alterations of the transept did away with this arrangement.

Two other chapels appeared in the 14th century, All Saints and St Catherine's; at first All Saints was an altar alongside that of St Mary. The building of a Chapel of the Holy Trinity in 1415 was foreshadowed by a gift in 1403 made subject to a condition that it could be revoked if royal licence had not been obtained within 10 years – necessary under the Statute of Mortmain which forbade the alienation of lands and property held by a corporate body, usually the Church. Not only was the chapel created but in 1416 the king described the gild merchant as being 'of the Holy Trinity'. Apparently the most powerful institution in the town was giving the new chapel the esteem it had formerly bestowed on the Chantry of the Blessed Virgin Mary. The property of the Blessed Virgin Mary was held by the burgesses collectively.

Numerous documents refer to chantries, most being conveyances transferring property to them or wills adding to their endowments. In 1482 John Smith gave his anvil in return for the right to be buried outside the entrance to the Chapel of St Anne. Eventually all the rents and profits of his estate were to go to this chantry. John Kendale's (1489) will directed that he was to be buried in the Chapel of St George. The chantries derived most of their income from property and land thus granted but it fluctuated because some grants were for a limited period, such as the donor's life, and houses they acquired could fall into disrepair. Chantries ceasing to pay their way went out of existence. Disposal of their remaining assets was not recorded but the powerful gild merchant probably resolved this.

Over the years eight chantries were associated with the church. The following dates give the earliest reference to each: the Blessed Virgin Mary or Lady Chapel (1267); Holy Cross (1267); St Catherine (1384); All Saints (1385, although a simple altar dedicated to All Saints alongside the altar of the Blessed Virgin Mary is mentioned in 1310); Holy Trinity (1415); 'Holy Cross above the Charnel House' (1415); St Erasmus (1455); and St George (1475). Altars without chapels which are mentioned were being dedicated to St James, St Gregory and St Sonday.

Accounts kept by the wardens of the Blessed Virgin Mary in 1372 show its chaplain's stipend was £4 6s. 8d. (13 marks). Oil for the lamp burning continuously in the choir cost 11s. 8d. Special wax candles for the Feasts of the Assumption and of the Purification cost 6s. 0d. Other incidental charges included Chief Rent to the Lord (4s. 8d.), 3s. 0d. to the clerk who drew up the balance sheet, and 4d. to the clerk who lit their candles. In 1372 expenditure was £11 5s. 6d. By 1387 the chantry had serious financial difficulties but as its two wardens were appointed by the gild merchant and answerable to its stewards most difficulties could be resolved. It must have been a formidable crisis which caused them to close an old foundation and then re-found the chantry. The king levied a £20 fine under the Statute of Mortmain because it had to be re-endowed and directed the town to pay 40s. of this to the queen, and her receipt is dated 1394. The re-endowment document was drawn up by the gild merchant and sets out the chaplain's duties in great detail. He was to be a priest appointed by the Gild Merchant's Stewards and present every day at the canonical hours accompanied by his clerk. Thus he had to don his vestments and take a service every three hours during the day. He had to pay his clerk out of his own pocket and ensure that a lamp burned continuously in the choir. Detailed instructions

25 The Old Vicarage. The front wall, north facing, is composed of lath and plaster (wattle and daub) and is obviously of considerable age. The upstairs timbers of the open roof appear to be 16th-century in date.

described the numbers of candles, tapers and torches which had to be lit. By ancient custom, the chaplain and the vicar shared the wax left over after every funeral. He had to find a man to keep the church clock in repair unless he did this himself. The churchwardens formerly paid the Keeper of the Clock a salary, one mark (13s. 4d.) being mentioned in 1385. He had to live in the house where the chaplain had always lived – 'the house next to the Vicarage on the west side'. During the late 18th century the vicarage was the present 47 St Mary Street (Fig. 25), which was probably the medieval vicarage, the chantry house of the Blessed Virgin Mary standing alongside. Robert Northover, who was appointed is the same person mentioned as chaplain in 1387. The bishop confirmed his appointment. The rules and duties drawn up by those governing the town were far more onerous than those normally attached to a family chantry where the chaplain only celebrated once a day, praying for the souls of past family members, and was then free to do as he pleased.

Medieval gilds often supported a priest and provided a chapel for him to pray for gild members' souls. There is no strong indication that Bridgwater merchant gild was formally dedicated to the Blessed Virgin Mary or if the dedication changed between 1387 and 1415. A will of 1408 mentions 'the fraternity of Holy Trinity' as if this were also a gild, and a lease of 1418 refers to 'the fraternity of Holy Cross in the Charnel House'. In 1429 one Stephen Cok left his 'best cup called a macer' to his wife but on her death it was to go to 'the fraternity of St Catherine'. Another document, in 1486, refers to 'Holy Roode gelde or chapel', and John Kendale's will of 1489 mentioned 'the Gylde of St Anne'.

Funeral arrangements in wills frequently stipulated that each priest present should receive 6d. and each clerk 3d. but how many claimed is never noted. Several documents show there were three parish clerks but the number of priests is less easily determined. They were supposed to attend a yearly service on a special church anniversary called the 'Year's Mind' and in 1456 the vicar and chaplain of the Blessed Virgin Mary attended and both received 2d.; five other priests present were paid 1d. each but not all the clergy were there. The Bishop's Register compiled for Bishop Beckington in 1449 begins with John Wheler 'parochial chaplain', and then names eight chantry priests called 'anniversary chaplains'.

Modern historians try to distinguish a chantry from a gild but our ancestors may not have done so. Officially those connected with St Mary's church were chantries and all except one were under the church roof. In 1523 John Yuckar (also spelt Jugker), then aged 38, became chaplain and he was still in post aged 63 when the chantries ceased. On appointment he was invested 'for life' with the endowments providing his income. Although the rents' value is not stated they generated a net income of £9 14s. 8d. in 1548, so Yuckar was wealthy. His duties included praying daily for 'the good estate of the King and the Kingdom, and for the mayor, bailiffs and burgesses, and for the souls of Richard Bruton, William Gascoigne, William Powlet and his wife Eleanor, John Poulet and Constance his wife, and all her boys, Thomas and William Gascoigne [a clerical error?] and all the benefactors of the aforesaid chapel'. The list is similar to that written in 1455 for William Magot when he gave three houses to support the chaplain. Prayers were to be said in perpetuity for the souls of those named.

A document *c.*1483 lists the goods in St Catherine's aisle including a mass book with silver clasps and a 19½ oz. chalice together with various vestments, towels and altar cloths. There was 'a cloth to self before Seynt Kateryn in the lent tyme', either an image or a picture of this saint.

The Court Roll of the Chantry of Holy Trinity held on 9 November 1473 exists. Attended by the Mayor, the court was composed of all tenants of chantry lands and houses and its business concerned rents, entry fines and repairs. One man was given until the following Easter to repair his tenement and faced a 20s. penalty for non-compliance.

The cost of maintaining the whole church from 1383 to 1387 averaged about £10 per annum. The Chantry of the Blessed Virgin Mary, which encountered difficulties in 1387, would have remained solvent had its income remained a steady £8 per annum. The Chantry of Holy Cross (Rood) cost less than £1 per annum as its only cost was the lights. It had no separate chaplain and the two wardens were always the two lay churchwardens. In the 15th century separate accounts for the Rood Chapel ceased.

On dissolution there were three chantries: Holy Trinity with a net annual income of £9 4s. 8d., the Blessed Virgin Mary with £8 0s. 8d. and St George with £6 2s. 6d. There was additional income of 14s. from Stower Eastover in Dorset which provided a light and an obit (i.e. an anniversary). The document drawn up by the Commissioners noted 'the inhabitants petition to have a free Grammar School erected there' but the request was ignored. A further note adds that the vicar's income was £12 6s. 8½d.

Inventory of Valuables

A 1447 inventory of 'the goods of the Church' lists valuables. Three works of art stood on the rood loft: a simple silver-gilt cross mounted on a copper-gilt shaft and foot and each side two silver-gilt statues, one of St Mary, the other St John. Suspended from an iron hook above was the Great Cross, always called the Holy Cross or the High Cross after 1300, which was presumably a crucifix carved in wood. Only metal objects were listed as valuable, so when Thomas Goldsmith gave 2d. to the church funds in 1441, inspired by 'the best cross', he probably had the silver cross in mind.

No gold is mentioned but there was an impressive quantity of silver: a monstrance, two censers, three chalices, some cruets, a chrismatory, two cups, two candlesticks and a 'ship', a boat-shaped vessel for keeping incense. A relic of St Stephen was encased in silver and a box contained broken silver. Two crosses, two candle sticks, one box for use at the sacrament and one holy water sprinkler made of latten were also listed. Latten, an alloy of copper, zinc, lead and tin, was evidently prized. Its appearance is dull, much like pewter, and this may be why the two crosses were gilded.

Part of the inventory lists 14 service books: three mass books, two graduals, two processionals, an epistolar, a colle (presumably a Collectar or book of Collects, i.e. short prayers), a book of antiphons, a breviary, a manual, an ordinal, and a book naming deceased church benefactors. In 1545 somebody gave the church 'a book called an antiphonary Psalter costing 40s.'. After the Reformation pages from service books were used to wrap the Bridgwater Water Bailiffs' Accounts. They were not from the parish books, nor from Glastonbury as was once supposed as they do not follow the Benedictine form of service. They probably came from the friary or possibly the hospital and are kept in the town's museum.

The Chapels

There were four chapels in medieval Bridgwater. Horsey (dedication unknown) was presumably a dependent chapelry of St Mary's church and Horsey inhabitants paid for its upkeep. The survey preceding dissolution of the chantries noted that the vicar of St Mary's provided a priest to celebrate mass there every Sunday. As a priest was living in Horsey in 1086 the chapel's origin could be very early. Its site was excavated in 1903 and the report of 1906 says it was 45 ft. by 13 ft. 6 in. in size. The west wall was four feet thick and other walls about three feet and sketches suggest that the masonry was very rough. The only objects found were fragments of green pottery. There is no further evidence of its use after 1548.

The Chapel on the Bridge, St Saviour's, was served daily by one of the Friars and was presumably a late foundation for it was not mentioned by William of Worcester. Leland was told that it had been built within living memory by a merchant called William Pole. A small oratory outside the South Gate for travellers' use stood on the river bank somewhere near Old Taunton Road. In 1564 two workmen were paid 16d. 'for mendying see walls', mention of river defences which seems to confirm Leland's description that the chapel was on the bank. In 1581 Robarde Slovenes and Robarde Swayne were paid for four boat loads of stones 'for the causeway'. The derelict site was evidently being used as a 'highways yard' for the repair of Taunton Road which had a metalled surface for about a mile.

All three chapels, together with that dedicated to St Mark at the castle, must have closed at the Reformation. Apart from Horsey they were probably simple oratories.

8

The Medieval Port of Bridgwater

In the official sense the word 'port' means an area administered by a Collector of Customs and not necessarily a single harbour. Bridgwater was originally included with the Port of Bristol but by 1348 had become a port in its own right covering 80 miles of Somerset coastline from the Devon border to the mouth of the Axe.

When shipping first came to Bridgwater is unknown but if the pre-Conquest word 'Brycg' meant a jetty rather than a bridge then boats would almost certainly be moored here. Unfortunately little is known about the port or its ships before the 14th century. In 1306 Gascon merchants were shipping lead in a Bridgwater vessel, the *Sauneye*, whose master was a William de Wyght. A Bridgwater ship was present at the siege of Calais in 1346. During this period other Bridgwater boats were transporting cloth, the *Blome* loading at Dartmouth in 1349. In 1375 one of 36 merchantmen captured and sunk by the French in the Bay of Bourgneuf was the *Saint Marie* of Bridgwater. At 170 tons she was an exceptionally large vessel and was valued at £810, a huge sum. Ships then were usually small and shipping activities very limited.

The power to collect lastage, a duty on imported goods, was granted in the original borough charter, which implies but does not prove that the town was already being used as a port. Ships for Edward I's military expeditions in the 1290s were taken from Bridgwater, and State Papers (Domestic) show that Bridgwater had become a regular collecting point during the Hundred Years War, when the Crown requisitioned shipping.

The town's prosperity in medieval times was linked with agriculture, broadcloth production and the presence of a port. Port equipment was simple. There was a wooden crane which frequently needed the carpenter's attention as well as strong rope and a supply of train oil. Canvas bags were purchased for loading goods and 'Bushel Baskets' were brought from Bristol, their bases strengthened with iron plates. The crane was probably on the quay near the bridge, where a loading bay would be convenient for handling goods going into the town or across the street to the Langport Quay. A warehouse known as the 'Town Cellar' was nearby which probably looked similar to the one preserved near Poole Harbour in Dorset. Such cellars were not necessarily built below ground level.

26 The Town Bridge drawn by John Chubb towards the end of the 18th century. The alcoves provided shelter for pedestrians from passing wagons.

The appearance of the medieval bridge with its three gothic arches spanning the river is known from John Chubb's sketches (Fig. 26). The earliest bridge was probably made of wood, as is implied by the town seal, but no documentary evidence exists to support this. There was a tradition, reiterated by Leland in 1529, that a stone bridge was erected by William Brewer in 1200. The Letters Patent of 1286 authorising the Hospital of St John to dig a dyke to the river refer to 'the great bridge', a phrase which may indicate the existence of a stone bridge at that date.

In the undated 13th-century Ordinance of the Burgesses 'custody of the bridge' was a duty burgesses had to be prepared to perform. The bridge was also regarded as an adjunct of the port. A merchant and shipowner, Dennis Down, left a pipe of woad 'for the reparacion and maintenance of the bridge at Bridgwater' in 1304. Timber bought for the Great Bridge in 1394 was probably needed during repairs. In 1395 Sir John Trivet gave 300 marks (£200), an enormous sum, to build a new stone bridge. This bridge lasted four centuries and had the Arms of Trivet (Fig. 27) sculpted on the parapet.

The charter of 1468 authorised tolls on carts crossing the bridge to cover repair costs and suggested using stones cleared from the river bed. In 1484, towards the end of the Wars of the Roses, a special appeal was made to the public to save the bridge which was being destroyed by the constant passage of military vehicles carrying heavy guns and by tidal action. The reason for

27 Two versions of the Arms of Trivet, the family who gave £200 for a new bridge in 1395. The more elaborate version is based on a tile at Cleeve Abbey. The Trivet Arms were apparently carved on the bridge parapet but there is no record of which design.

the military traffic is unclear and the only evidence of a major repair is from a much later account in 1532. This work cost £5 10s. 4d. and lasted about nine weeks, most of it being done by two dozen labourers. The material used included stone from Pibsbury and Puriton. The Master of the Hospital, 'My Lord of St John's', lent wagons and gave sand, accepting only meat and drink for the waggoners. Lime was purchased at 10d. a quarter to mix with the sand and gravel was dug from St Matthew's Field, the man who dug it being paid 8d. Its carriage to the bridge cost 6d. and a boat was hired for four days for 3s. To pay for the work an organised collection was made by Collectors with books in the country parishes but money in the town was the responsibility of members of the crafts. Several payments due to the town, such as fines for freedom, were diverted into the bridge fund. A collection of broken silver sold in London realised 25s. 4½d.

During the reign of Henry VI customs officials were properly organised, with an official called the Customer heading a team comprising Controller, Searcher and Surveyor, and Tide-Waiters at Combwich. In 1558 an Act classified ports, such as Bridgwater, and their sub-ports or creeks, which included Minehead and Axwater. In 1671 further reforms were attempted, the Controller becoming Chief Officer and the Customer dealing only with coastal trade. The officers drew small salaries and charged fees but overriding this, and defeating all attempts at reform, was the practice whereby the officer appointed drew the salary and then paid a deputy to do his job. Smuggling was rife until far into the 19th century.

Bridgwater was an important cloth town and Weaver, Tucker and Dyer common surnames in the 15th century. These occupations are frequently given with witness names in legal documents. The Tallage Lists (c.1443-50) are also evidence that 11 weavers operated in the town in six different streets. The surface of medieval cloth was felted by fulling, and a cloth-producing area needed fulling mills. The one reference to a mill in Bridgwater is in the late 14th century. Fulling mills needed fast-flowing streams and pure water, so the Quantock Hills were an important part of the economy. The volume of broadcloth exported during the 15th century varied widely from year to year. It fell dramatically after the invasion of France in 1413, recovered after peace was made in 1453, but slumped again in the 1460s. From 1472 recovery was sustained and in 1476 a record 494 pieces were exported, only surpassed in 1481 when 964 were sent out. Bristol exported a much greater volume, over 6,000 pieces in 1401.

One unpleasant feature of medieval trade was the problem of disputes between towns. In 1450 J. Vessey, a merchant of Bilbao, sold nine tuns of wine at £2 a tun to two Bridgwater men called Founs and Hill. They agreed that should the cargo be seized by pirates the buyer would not be the loser unless the pirates were English. Apparently it was seized by Bretons. Founs said that he left 16 pieces of cloth worth four marks each with a man called Perrons and complained that Vessey had conspired with Perrons, seizing the cloth to pay for the lost wine. Vessey's story was that three Bridgwater men, one of whom was Founs, came to Bilbao and borrowed 200 marks (£133) from one John of Subarra. They defaulted and were imprisoned, but two escaped. Vessey claimed he was imprisoned in Bridgwater in retaliation.

In 1475 Bridgwater made peace with Youghal in Ireland. There is no explanation concerning the cause of the trouble but it had led to the comment: 'Riots and disturbances have been done both by you and us.' In 1497 the Water Bailiff rode to Combwich to meet the Warden of Youghal so presumably the peace was maintained.

There are many 16th-century records of payments for clearing mud and silt near the quay. With one exception they concern drains close to the crane. An instrument called a 'wormer' was used to clear a pipe and in 1495 William Sibley received 3d. for 'scouring the dock of the filth driven down with the great downfall of rain'. The word 'dock' could suggest ship-building but there is no other evidence to support it at this early date. However, expert naval opinion always supported the view that the Bridgwater area was suitable for ship-building despite the Parrett's navigational hazards.

28 Map showing the medieval coasting trade of Bridgwater based on information derived from the Water Bailiffs' Accounts.

29 Map showing Bridgwater's medieval foreign trade based on information in the Water Bailiffs' Accounts.

9

THE END OF THE MIDDLE AGES

During the 16th century the castle's defences were probably neglected. Its 1553 rent list reads like that of a prosperous manor: the lord's income was £34 11s. 6d. Court fines provided £11 2s. 3d.; tenants 'on Castle Ditch' paid 16s. 4d., and on Haygrove, 109s. Several acres of meadow were let, none below 1s. an acre. Peter Stoket, who had the common oven, paid 5s. 3d. A horse mill called Castelmyll with 12 acres of land was charged at 40s. and 13s. 4d. was paid for three parts of the watermill called Litlemyll.

The medieval church always attempted to enforce certain standards of behaviour, especially sexual morality. In 1519 Wolsey was Bishop of Bath and Wells, and his consistory court dealt with one John Moon of Ditcheat, who was married to Alice Servington but living with Joan Browning. He would keep her as his wife, he said, 'in despyte of the churche'. Eventually he submitted, signed a letter of abjuration and was warned to keep away from Joan Browning and ordered to go on certain days to certain places with bare feet and legs, bearing a bundle of faggots on his shoulder and a paper inscribed in large letters, 'I have deluded the holy sacrament of matrimony', in the manner of a penitent. His punishment began on 12 May at Bridgwater Market Place, and was followed by visits to Wells, the churches at Ditcheat, Bath and St Mary Redcliffe at Bristol. Post-Reformation cases heard during the 16th century were similar to this: although punishments excluded standing barefoot in the Market Place, public penance was certainly exacted.

The West Gate Almshouse
The almshouse is first mentioned in a Bailiff's Account for 1455: 'for repair of the almshouse without the West Gate this year 10s. 10d.' In 1546 John Bentley, a shoemaker, left a legacy providing the residents with 5s. 4d. yearly and paying 2s. 2d. to the mayor to ensure they received it. Bentley also wanted his legacy administered by a trust of six men. After a few years the town took over the endowment, payments were reduced to 5s. and appeared in the Town Rental, and the mayor lost his fee. Bentley's name had been forgotten by 1630 and the 5s. apparently came from 'an old gift paid at All Saints'. Five shillings was insufficient to feed four people for a year but the town never paid more although cloth for clothes was provided. Occasional gifts included from private

sources a blanket and a sheet to each of the four poor men and women, a legacy from Elizabeth Prowse in 1555. The inhabitants apparently lived in small, separate houses and, whenever a new threshold was provided, the occupant was named.

Money was frequently spent repairing the building but the most common request was for new rope for the bell, which usually cost 1d. or 2d. and occasionally 6d. The bell needed a new gudgeon in 1611 and had to be re-hung in 1616. In 1562 a new bellcote had to be built which cost 2s. 6d.

Church Ales

In the early 14th century Bridgwater was probably the first place in England to levy a compulsory church rate. Parishioners continued to raise money voluntarily, though, usually by holding church ales. Fresh ale was brewed and cakes were baked, and after the service feasting began, participants paying for their food and drink. In fine weather trestle tables were erected in the churchyard or the church nave was used. These were very jolly occasions so the church authorities eventually discouraged the activity.

In many parishes inhabitants moved beyond the archdeacon's jurisdiction by using a building outside the churchyard, usually with a downstairs kitchen and an upstairs room for feasting and dancing. Such buildings were eventually known as church houses and became a feature of almost every Somerset parish although they are virtually unknown outside the West Country. Cannington, Crowcombe and Chew Magna have examples.

30 The *Mansion House Inn* in High Street. By 1537 this building was the Church House; then the upstairs became a schoolroom and housed the Free Grammar School in 1722.

Bridgwater obtained its church house in 1537 by purchasing a building in High Street. The conveyance appears identical to that for an ordinary transaction but two copies were made, one in English and the other in Latin. On the back of one is a title written in a later hand: 'Dobull dede of the churchowse in Bridgwater'. Doble was the man who sold the property to John Hammond and John Walsh. Following Hammond's death in 1554 his son Hugh transferred it to James Boyesse (Boyce) and several others. It was then formally described as the Church House. It is now the *Mansion House Inn* (Fig. 30).

Church ales were held only on the great church festivals but the hall was let for other purposes. The building's first recorded use in 1540 has: 'Item payd for wyne on Corpus Christe day for prestys and clarkes and the Sunday after to the Church howsse ... 8d.' In 1565 this was given as: 'pd Mr Foskewes man which playd at the Church howse ... 2s. 0d.' Repairs costing 13d. appear in the fragment of a churchwarden's account *c.*1547. In 1592 the tiler and his man repaired the roof of both church and church house for £2 7s. 8d.

Early in the 17th century the royal judges discouraged church ales as they were a source of disorder. Together with changes in social outlook, this led to the church house's ceasing as an institution. New uses were found for redundant buildings such as a school, poor house or inn. Bridgwater became a schoolhouse but was still called the 'church house' well into the 18th century. A corporation minute of 1743 refers to the Free School as being in 'the chamber over the Church House'.

Entertainment

Entries concerning Corpus Christi refer to a procession provided by the gilds, when mystery plays were performed. An entry in 1495 specifically refers to the Shepherds' Play: 'to the schipperdi's pagent on corpus cristy day ... 10d.' A Franciscan usually organised the pageant, which accounts for the gallon of wine 'to the greyffriers' costing 8d.; the Hospital received two gallons, and in other years the church clergy were also gifted wine.

Besides travelling actors a bearward occasionally visited and his arrival was greeted with pleasure. There are examples in 1540, 'to the berewarde Harry ... 2s. 0d.', and *c.*1542: 'my lorde Markys of Dorsettes berwarde ... 18d.' In 1582 the Queen's Bearward arrived and was given 3s. 4d., 'in my absence' said the mayor. There are references to bull baiting but this took place in a field outside the East Gate, described in 1687 as 'one close of pasture containing 1 acre' and let to Sarah and John Read. It was still known as Bull Baiting Acre in 1836. Hooking a porpoise always caused great excitement. Besides being rewarded the man could keep his catch to sell. The reward was 12d. in 1504 but 3s. 4d. in all subsequent examples.

Butts are referred to between 1483 and 1487. At a later date, 1562, two labourers, Hucklebrig and Richard Tyilar, were paid 9s. 'for the makyn of the butts'. Strachie's map of *c.*1730 places them on the west river bank just beyond the house called 'The Lions'.

Visiting Performers

Much borough entertainment was for the chosen few, such as the mayor, members of the Common Council and invited guests. Between 1495 and 1547 minstrels visited frequently. They were usually personal servants of a noble household, which prevented them from being treated as vagabonds. Their reward was occasionally only 12d. but sometimes as much as 6s. 8d. During the reigns of Henry VII and Henry VIII the King's Minstrels visited Bridgwater eight times between 1495 and 1540, whilst 'my lady the King's Mother's Minstrels' came in 1495 and 1505.

Other visiting groups included those from the Earl of Arundel, and Bristol, in 1495; from Lord Derby and Lord Shrewsbury in 1504; Lord Audley and Lord Northumberland during 1525; and the Lord Admiral and the Earl of Bath in 1547. In 1532 the minstrels of Lord Fvarryn (i.e. Fitzwarenne) were paid 16d. and money was also spent on their patron: 'for a gallon of wine to welcum my lorde Ffarryn and my lady … 12d.' Clearly this was an official visit when Lord and Lady Fvarryn brought their minstrels with them. During the first year of Queen Elizabeth's reign an entry states: '1559-60 my lorde Robart Dudlys plaers … for a reward … 13s. 4d.' A most unusual visitor in 1555 was the Queen's Jester, who received 3s. 4d.

The grant to travelling entertainers was a long-standing tradition which was probably meant to start a collection after the entertainment but it is difficult to know who comprised the audience. Some plays were performed in a large enclosed courtyard, such as that in some inns; others were indoors, either in the common hall, or the hall of a large house. In 1535 an entry has, 'payd the Kyngges Players the Saturday after Mathosday at the Sarsons hed … 3s. 4d.' *The Saracen's Head* was a famous inn but its site is unknown. 'The Earl of Bridgwater's players that played at Master Meyrys house 5s.' in 1540 suggests that the mayor, Richard Terrill, lived in a hall house that could accommodate a large gathering, though in fine weather the performance may have been in the courtyard. In the same year 'the erle of Bathys players for a rewarde and dede notte play … 2s. 0d.' Perhaps bad weather was the reason.

There is no continuous record covering every year but from existing documents it seems that a group of actors visited the town every year and some years more than one group came: in 1593, exceptionally, there were four groups.

Preachers

Travelling preachers began visiting during Edward VI's reign. In 1552 the unnamed preacher was given a bottle of wine costing 4d. Another came in 1566. There are two separate entries, the first reading: 'for a brekefast for the precher, for a gallon of secke, a gallon of Whitt wyne & one pound of suger … 3s. 10d.; for horse mitt for prechers horse … 18s.' At the end of the Water Bailiff's Account Richard Fyshe has written, 'and so remayneth 65s. 11d. whereof paid to Mr Mulleyns layed owte by hym upon the preacher … 31s. 8d.' There was obviously some special business involving more than entertaining a preacher staying just one night; the amount of food provided for the horse seems to indicate that a meeting was held.

In 1573 the vicar of Westonzoyland was paid for preaching, his 40s. being entered on the Rectory Account and not the general Town Accounts as were payments to travelling preachers. That same year one Gryffyn, an itinerant preacher, was paid 6s. 8d. together with wine and sugar costing 12d. He visited again in 1593 but how often he was here is unknown. On 18 April 1592 was paid: 'by Mr Mayores order for a denar bestowed uppon Mr Frye & the reast, Frye the preacher ... 10s. 0d.' and the same year was paid 'a strange preacher ... 5s. 0d.'

The congregation must have demanded sermons because some preachers were retained the whole year: 'Mr Barklye, Mr Frye & Mr Hewes preachers for one yeare then endyde ano 1592 ... £20 and the vicar ... £13 6s. 8d.' By way of a change were 'Mye L of Wostares playeres the 15th of September ... 13s. 4d.' In 1601 a preacher named Jones was given 10s. An unexplained note in the same year says 5s. was paid on 11 October for 'half a preacher'. In 1603 an anonymous preacher was given 5s. but Edward Holcombe received 20s.

The popularity of sermons suggests the growth of Puritanism but that did not stop the performance of plays. In 1601 Lord Hereford's Players visited and received 13s. 4d., and in April 1602 Lord Sandwich's Players were paid 13s. 4d.; an unnamed group performed in July.

The evidence given here does not show a spate of visiting preachers but must be seen against the background of the rectorial grant. When this was made by Letters Patent, the duties of the two clergymen paid by the Town were not defined, but a Preacher was to receive a stipend of £20 a year suggesting Elizabeth had anticipated a demand for sermons and taken steps to meet it. The other cleric, the minister, was regarded as 'having the cure of souls' and his stipend was 80 marks, or £13 6s. 8d.

The fact that wandering preachers were welcome that suggests the official preacher did not satisfy demand. The following century a strong body of Puritan support developed, and Bridgwater came to be regarded as a Puritan town. The Puritans supplied the real strength of the opposition to Charles I, and in a town such as Bridgwater, open to trade with the Netherlands, it is not surprising that families like the Blakes became staunch Protestants.

Official Visitors

Royal judges on circuit were regular visitors. Frequently a royal messenger, a Crown official called a Pursuivant, delivered a writ or other important document. Since even the Water Bailiff was regaled with wine on presenting his accounts it is not surprising that most visitors were similarly treated. Only once is detail of food given: in 1495 'John Perry of Huntworth bringing a buck to the mayor & his brothers [from the Lord Chamberlain who had been hunting in the royal forest of Petherton] ... 3s. 4d.; pd. to Clement of Haygrove to make pasties of the same venison ... 4d.; more for making the venison ... 8d.' In 1536 the corporation sent 'a pottel of seke [sack] and a pottel of Clarrat wyne to the Vyseters at Syne Jonys ... 10d.' These were Thomas Cromwell's men preparing to dissolve the Hospital of St John and, probably, the Friary.

Investment of a new Recorder was an important occasion: 'for Master Recorders dynner and hys men whanne a toke hys othe and for my lorde Syne Johnys [i.e. the Master of St John's Hospital] and the abbot of Athelney & other strangers & for wyne ... 7s.'

At Christmas 1542 was: 'payd to the playe at Master Mayors [John Newport] yn cryssmas hollydays to Gybbys & his Company ... 2s. 8d', possibly resembling entertainment nowadays provided by the local pantomime society. A Richard Gibbs was paying 5s. per annum rent for a house belonging to the town, and in 1558 a Richard Gibbs was a member of the Common Council.

The highest expenditure listed was for entertaining the Bishop of Wells plus his household and servants in 1563:

> Charges bestowed upon my Lorde bishope at his laste beinge here as folowithe
> Item in primis brede and beare for supper and brekfaste – 12s. 0d.
> in gasconne wine whitt and clarette – 4s. 8d.
> a gallon of secke – 19d.
> 2½ lb of sewger – 3s. 4d.
> in mittone [i.e. mutton] – 6s. 8d.
> a breste of veale – 10d.
> 3 capons – 4s. 0d.
> a dosen chekyns – 3s. 0d.
> 22 pygeons – 20d.
> 2 cople of rabbattes – 12d.
> yowre spices – 12d.
> in frute – 8d.
> in beffe at brekfaste – 4s. 0d.
> in horse meate – 7s. 0d.
> At his retorne backeward from Mr Coles
> Item in wine and suger at his diner – 6s. 8d.
> summa 58s. 2d.

By contrast, in 1540, 'the Earl of Bath at his coming home to Master Mayor and Master Davy the week after Relicing Sunday ... 6d.' Relic Sunday, or 'Feast of Relics' was formerly observed on the third Sunday after Midsummer but now on the Sunday after All Saints Day.

False News

In 1555 public rejoicing was ordered following news that Queen Mary Tudor had given birth. It was well known she was desperately anxious to have a child. There was free wine for everyone on the Cornhill: 'for a hodgsyde of wyne unto Robert Mavnsell wch was drucken at the hey corse [High Cross] when it was sayde there was a prynce borne ... 36s. 0d.' Then guns were fired: '4 lbs of gunnepowder at the newse of the qvynys grace ... 5s. 4d.' Alas, it was all for nothing. The news was without foundation and Mary Tudor remained childless.

10

THE BURGESS HALL
AND THE HIGH CROSS, 1557-1602

The Town Hall was called the Gild Hall in the 14th century, the Hall or Common Hall in the 15th century and later the Burgess Hall. There are references to the Gild Hall (la Gyldhalle) in medieval times which indicate it stood on the present Town Hall site but building accounts are unavailable before the Elizabethan period. Most relate to roof repairs and suggest that the original medieval Gild Hall was still being patched up. In 1567 repairs to the rainwater gutter required 17½ lbs of solder, indicating a metal rather than wood gutter. The name of Patrick the Tyler (1565) suggests the use of kiln-fired roof tiles. On occasion ridge tiles were used which were probably locally made. A 1565 extension, the 'House of Accounts', involved 16 days work by builders and nine days by their labourers at a cost of £1 16s. 4d. Roof repairs in 1573 required 3,500 slates ('helyng stones'), and 7,300 laths at a total cost of £3 8s. 3d. Three years later nine tons of stone and 1,000 slates were used, then in 1579 further work on the gutter and windows required another 1,000 slates and 13 loads of stone.

In December 1580 a virtual re-build of the Common Hall commenced which continued until 19 May 1581. Finally William Blacke (probably Blake) mended two locks on 26 June for 8d. The final cost, about seven marks, comprised:

Materials:	£1 16s. 10d.
Labour:	£2 16s. 7d.
Total:	£4 13s. 5d.

Builders' wages were 8d. a day for the master and 7d. for his men. The masters were named Jasper Castleman, Robert Stevens, John Collins, Jeffrey Hurt, Dapsey, Greenslade, John Adams, Richard Nell and Richard West (spellings modernised). The work lasted 90 days but only certain details are described: Margaret Stone 'maken klen the Hawlle' which she did twice for 4d. and 6d. respectively; she also counted stones for 3d. and Richard West, a glazier, charged 4d. to repair a window. The materials suggest a typical half-timbered Elizabethan building. The slates came from Boscastle. The wattling rods were either hazel or withies. Much old material on site would be re-used but the absence of sand is curious.

One day's work was 'to specke & parge', i.e. to make reinforced plaster work. An extraordinary entry states that Richard Chubb was paid 8d. 'for the waste of whet had to the Haulle to mack the outsures wthall'. It possibly means that he made a shed, or outshat, from surplus materials. Greenslade was paid 3d. 'for tellyng of the stares for the Haulle' (i.e. counting them), but his fee also included mending a hole in the church chancel.

In 1582 200 laths and 1,000 slates were used and another 1,000 laths and 1,000 slates in 1583. In 1586 the entrance was re-plastered and William Wallis paid 3s. 4d. for 'drawing the lables' in the Hall, which may mean making 'honours boards' with lists of names. The Town Court required 300 slates in 1592 costing 15s. plus 1s. carriage. Two shillings was spent making a place to hang the town crooks which were used to pull burning thatch off roofs. Further repairs in 1595 needed 3,500 nails, 5,000 slates, and involved mending side timbers. The £4 16s. 6d. bill also included whitewashing both Hall and Church House.

The Fire of 1597

The Hall was considered a safe place so gunpowder was usually stored there, but in 1597 there was a serious fire at the time of Sessions, presumably in September. Fortunately this was not a disaster, but repairs were needed. Volunteers who had helped were rewarded, as three quarts of sack were 'bestowed upon them wich were taking pains about the fire at Sessions' (2s. 6d.). Two other men, Clay and Richard Eddy, were paid 16d. for 'watching the fire at the Sessions for a day and a night'. Greenslade and his boy spent four days re-tiling the roof. Glass was replaced by Richard Newman, a glazier, who charged 10s. to supply 20 feet of new glass for the Hall windows, and the office window. Another six feet of glass cost 2s. plus 2s. 2d. for fitting it and repairing the wall.

A new Powder House was created above the north porch of the church. Payments made included £3 10s. 0d. to Christopher Salmon for gunpowder ordered by Richard Stradling. The amount can be estimated from a bill of 3s. 3d. for 3lbs of powder. The labourers who moved some gunpowder to the quay and then eventually back to the Hall were paid 6d. for 'heaving the powder into the cellar' and then 'heawlng it up into the loft above'. Later they received 8d. for carrying powder from Mr Michel's loft on the Old Quay to the Hall again. Eventually one Hacking was paid 20d. for carrying the powder from the Hall to the Powder House.

Charges for the Powder House included a pair of hinges for the door on 20 October, and another pair for a door over the little window costing 3s. 4d., as well as a further 9s. 4d. for the timber. There was also some extra work in making good the walls and plaster. Three locks were fitted to the Powder House door.

Rebuilding the Burgess Hall, 1601-2

In 1601 the Hall was completely rebuilt. The materials cost £18 9s. 4d. and labour £6 9s. 3d., a total of £24 18s. 7d. Some 147 days' work was done, mostly by six men, four boys and one labourer. Two men, Yawe and Robyson, were paid 2s. for building a wall, and a man called Parker earned 6d. The chief workmen shown in the table were paid 1s. a day, the man 9d., Rowell's son 8d., and the boys 4d. Work was normally done only in daylight but on one occasion Williams, who employed both a man and a boy, spent 4d. on candles, presumably to enable him to complete an urgent task.

Rebuilding was mainly reconstruction of the existing half-timbered building. The roofing materials were re-used, only three rafters being purchased and 1,000 tiles, which cost 10s. 7d. Only 12 ridge tiles, called 'Cresses', were replaced. 'Cresses' is usually taken to mean 'Crests', a word still used, but by the 18th century ridge tiles were known as 'creases' and probably made locally in small quantities in the same way as pottery. Since the tiles are never called 'tile-stones' it is likely they were kiln-fired and not slates.

Timber was cheap and plentiful, so expenditure of £6 7s. 1d. implies a large quantity. Most would be used for a strong frame and the rest for interior work. Five hundred double laths were needed, probably for the floors. Ordinary laths cost 6s. 8d. per thousand and initially 1,800 were purchased, but a further 18s. was spent, presumably on another 2,650. Much boarding was needed, probably for partition walls. Little is known about the plan of the building except that it was galleried at one end as boarding for this cost 9s. Four new doors were purchased for 2s. 6d. each.

The local smiths must have been busy making nails as 9,000 were used. Lath nails were bought by the thousand. Board nails were not always specified. 'Spikes', very large nails, were sold by weight, 4lbs for 12d., but not many were needed. Ironwork costs, £4 1s. 5d., were high. At least eight new locks were needed, a lock with two keys costing 3s. 4d. One new lock was for the door of the Armour House. Another, much smaller, which only cost 8d., was for the entry wicket. Doors require various accessories such as hinges, usually called 'gemasses'. Some had bolts and there were 'justs'. At least two doors had rings, two costing 18d., and presumably operated latches by the method still used. These were called 'karalaches', a word derived from the medieval Latin *carola* meaning a ring. Another type of hinge fitted to some doors was called 'a hook and twist'; it is still used but called a 'hook and ride'. The new Hall also included a prison and its ironwork alone cost £1 15s. 8d. It took four days to limewash.

One feature of the Hall was a very large window – the frame cost 4s. 6d. and glass another 9s. The total cost of glass for the Hall was £2 1s. 10d. Amongst the furnishings only two new forms were made costing 8s. There was also a mill, probably a hand-mill for grinding flour, one of which type was repaired and then taken to a workhouse in 1620.

Important aesthetically and as a symbol of royalty was a new Lion, which cost 20s. 6d. The town also employed an artist from Wells called Bemen to create a royal achievement which was probably placed on the wall behind the Mayor's Chair. It cost 13s. 6d. to fetch Bemen from Wells with his 'tubell', an earthenware vessel presumably used for preparing paint. When complete the achievement had to be transported from Wells and Bemen was paid £2 3s. 0d. including carriage for what was described as 'dra[w]ing the Kynges Armes'.

The overall appearance of the new Hall is unlikely to have been 'black and white'; more probably the timbers were allowed to retain their natural colour, which is restrained and very beautiful. On one occasion, at least, the accounts distinguish between oak boards which cost 24s. for 300 and the cheaper elm at 5s. per 100. The materials used for filling in the walls of the timber frame suggest that essentially mud was used. Clay was bought for 13s. 3d. and mixed with hair. One bill for hair was 10s. 2d. but another 15 bushels was used and no price given. The builders also used 32 sacks of lime costing £2 12s. 0d. Thus the walls were cob rendered white, though a little additional yellow ochre was acquired: 'for ocker to colie [i.e. colour]: 8d.; skrees & yole oker 5d.', which is not enough to colour much wall. Some wattle and daub is mentioned but there were no large purchases of wattling rods.

Surprisingly no new tools were needed, but two old bisgeys were repaired: 'layinge a besskewe 4d.; new ma[k]inge of a besgew 2s. 0d.'. The word 'bisgey' is still used in Somerset's rural areas to describe a two-headed metal implement, one head like a pickaxe and the other like a mattock. It is fitted with a metal pickaxe-style handle.

Rebuilding the High Cross, 1567

The High Cross on the Cornhill is first mentioned in 1567 when one of the leading townsmen, Geoffrey Shercomb, was entrusted with re-building it. The accounts give no details of materials used nor name the workmen, and the cost seems extraordinarily high. There are two sets of accounts for 1567, those of the Receiver, Richard Castleman, and those of the Water Bailiff, John Wilkins (Wylkyngs).

The Receiver gave Shercombe two payments towards the making of the cross and 'towardes the byldynge of the Crosse': £59 and 42s. The Water Bailiff also made two payments to Shercombe: £3 on 25 April 'for to by stones for the Crosse', and £5 in August 'in monaye for the Crosse'. The town had also borrowed money which was repaid in 1568: £13 on 23 April to the new churchwardens and £8 on 23 January to a private person called Humphrey Murell (Owmfrye Mwrlle) who supplied a sword girdle costing 14d. needed for the muster in 1569. These entries seem to prove conclusively that John Chubb's 18th-century drawing of the High Cross shows an Elizabethan structure (Fig. 19), although the Elizabethan rebuild may have been a reproduction of the original design.

In 1568 the Cross was equipped with two hooks to hang beams (18d.), and some weights (3d.) which came from Taunton. 'The beam for the Cross' (i.e. a steelyard) cost 8s., whilst a hook and chain cost another 6d. 'Ropes for the scales' cost 8d. and further small items were recorded, such as 'spikes for the Cross', i.e. spike nails, at 2d.; nails 5d., laths 8d., and lath nails 2d. Another 10s. was paid to Robert Stevens for keeping an eye on the work and recorded as 'Robart Styvenes for Waytten at the Crosse betwyx Wyttswndytt & Myhellmas'.

In September 1568 the town spent £2 10s. 0d. 'in too the lowttrye'. The nature of this lottery is unknown but it could have been an attempt to raise money by avoiding levying a tax.

11

Bridgwater under Edward VI, Mary and Elizabeth

The archives between 1546 and 1559 contain several references to Richard Hyatt, age unknown, a contemporary of James Boyce (b. 1508), William Gold (b. 1510), and Geoffrey Shercombe (b. 1516). Hyatt's life reflects the lifestyle of the Tudor middle class and provides the only clear written evidence for the existence of a tidemill in Bridgwater.

In 1546-7 Richard Hyatt served as Water Bailiff, an irksome duty paying a fee of one mark (13s. 4d.). He must already have paid 'for his freedom' and been admitted as a burgess. In 1548 he was described as a yeoman and owned 'Hyatt's Barn' so perhaps, like many merchants and tradesmen, he was also a small farmer. Hyatt rented a large garden from the town for which he paid 12d. in 1539. In 1558 he sent six barrels and two hogsheads of herrings to Taunton, and in 1562 supplied wattling rods to builders. To maintain his various enterprises he probably employed labour.

31 Salmon butts in the River Parrett at Stretcholt, a few miles downstream from Bridgwater. Nowadays these are the only ones permitted and are operated by one family.

32 A salmon trap. The butts shown in Fig. 31 comprise several of these wide-mouthed wicker funnels attached to posts.

The document calling him a yeoman is a lease permitting him to construct a fish weir above the bridge. This was on the river bank in Salmon Parade between the Town Bridge and the present hospital, which in 1548 was near Hyatt's Barn. The lease was for 21 years and the rent 3s. 4d. a year plus one salmon. In 1550 the Receiver noted that Hyatt was 3s. 4d. in arrears. At low tide the fish weir was to measure 14 yards towards mid-stream. It did not comprise nets stretched between posts but resembled traditional salmon butts with long wide-mouthed wicker funnels attached to posts and facing upstream. These are still used at Stretcholt a few miles downstream (Figs. 31 & 32).

Hyatt was a churchwarden in 1550 and became mayor in 1557 having only just been made a Capital Burgess (a life member of the Common Council), and in 1561 he was one of the two bailiffs. In 1557 he lived in St Mary Street in what must have been a large house because his wife, Margaret, in 1540 invited travelling actors to perform there.

Hyatt was reasonably wealthy and in 1557 he had to contribute 2s. in cash together with military equipment consisting of 'a bill, a jack and a skull' to a levy funding an expedition intended to recover of Calais from the French. Another levy made in 1569 to purchase corselets and calivers (i.e. breastplates and small guns) required him to pay 3s.; only nine other townsmen paid more.

The Tidemill

The 1548 lease states that the fish weir was to occupy a space where there was once a mill 'and nowe be certayne stakes in the ryver named Perott between myle tayle and a barne named Hyatt barn' on the east bank. This must refer to a tidemill which had gone out of use. Power to drive floor or grist mills was in great demand and the tidal fall in the Parrett was more than adequate for a mill, although this advantage was counteracted by the rapidity with which the dam entrance could silt up. It is not known how many tidemills were constructed.

Downstream, where the north side of the bridge meets East Quay, was a parcel of land recorded in 1553 as having been purchased 'to the Chamber of Bridgwater since the others', 'the others' apparently referring to Chantry Lands on which the corporation was charging rents. This land was described as 'j tenement in Estover in the tenewer of Barnarde Radbarde wth his apportinances & j colse [close] of grounde comonlye called the Dame a the rent … 27s.'. The rent was reduced to 8s. and remained unchanged for the rest of Elizabeth's reign. The name 'the Dame' suggests that it, too, had been a tidemill. In the 18th century a dock was constructed here by an enterprising man called Trott who let it to a ship-builder. In the 19th century Carver's dry dock was built on the site.

Legacies and Gifts to the Town

Following the accession of Edward VI the town paid 20d. in 1549 for 'a Book of Communion' which was presumably the first prayer book. This was soon followed by another Book of Communion and four psalters costing 12s. 8d. including carriage from London. These entries hint at the difficulties facing a government attempting to establish a new national church. A surplice using 6½ yards of dowlais was bought and made for R. Gregory, which cost 3s. 4d. to buy, and another 6d. to make. Thirteen pew rents were collected (Fig. 33), probably the total number of seats in the church then, and Hugh Smith repaired the clapper of the great bell for 5s. Geoffrey Shercombe was paid 14s. as nine months' rent for the parish anvil.

Following dissolution of the chantries their property rents seem to have been paid to the town. A report detailing the property of the three surviving chantries was unenthusiastic about its value: 'Memorandum that all the foresaid tenements and cotages belonging to every the saide chantrie bene sore in Decaye and a great parte of them at the poynte of utter Ruyne.'

Between 1551 and 1553 three important wills were proved. All used the traditional formula, 'I bequeath my soul to Almighty God and my body to be buried in the Church …', but each left money to the poor: 'to the Poor Men's Boxe' (Elizabeth Prowse 1551-2), and 'to the Poor Men's Coffer' (J. Thomas and J. Colford 1553), suggesting that a Poor Box had been installed in the parish church.

In October 1551 the Vice Admiral of Devon and Somerset came to meet the mayor and 12 'lawful men' in order

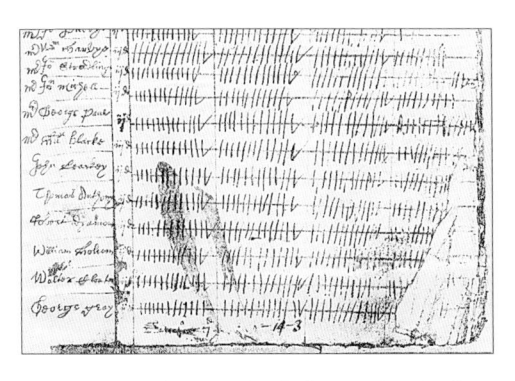

33 Part of a makeshift notebook for collecting pew rents. 'Mr' indicates a counsellor.

to collect information concerning ships and sailors. In the same year, Richard Tyrrell, who had recently been mayor, was discharged of his debts in consideration of his giving 'an iron beame to the Guyldhall, remaynyng yn the Common House'. This was a steelyard for public use.

In 1553 a barber, John Thomas, left gifts to his friends, including 10s. to William Jones, his tailor, a cap of scarlet to William Nicholles, shoemaker, and a pair of hose and a doublet to John Lawrence, butcher. To the town he left 30s. 'towards the reparacions of the highways' and 50s. to the poor. In 1551 Elizabeth Prowse had left a blanket and a sheet to each of the four poor folks in the almshouse and 40s. to the mayor, 20s. of which was for the poor and the remainder to repair highways.

Following the accession of Mary in July 1553 another important will, that of a merchant called John Colford, brought fresh gifts to the town. His lands were worth £9 6s. 10d. a year, and were dealt with in a separate section of the town accounts. Probate was granted in the first instance by the Manor Court of Bridgwater Castle with Haygrove, and then the matter was sent to Westminster.

On 21 May 1554 Queen Mary, by Letters Patent, formally granted much of the chantry lands and properties to the town. These, too, occupied a section of the town accounts and, despite the adverse report mentioned earlier, were worth £9 6s. 10d. a year. In the 1555 report on 'lands of the Chantries' the item with the lowest rent was noted: 'Wm. Poles did holde j howse in the churcheyarde agenste the church dore … 6d.' This lean-to shed must have been an eye-sore and an obstruction to the free passage of parishioners and in the 1558 Rental of Town Lands, late the Chantries, it was given as: 'takyn downe … the howsse before the sothe churche dore'.

Nothing suggests that Mary had any ulterior motive in making her grant to the town. Church services had reverted to the Roman Catholic liturgy, as this entry in the Rental of Town Lands in 1558 shows: 'Chargys at master Colwayns & Mr Colvards derige & others for brede, wyne, chesse & ale & the prysts & clarcks & to others that dyd helpe & for the lyght … 5s. 8d.' Near the end of Mary's life she gave the town £10, which was spent thus: £2 for the poor, £6 13s. 4d. on repairing highways, and £1 6s. 8d. mending decayed houses.

In December 1556 the town received a demand from Lord Zouche for £16 per annum for the fee farm. The Court of Wards and Liveries appointed a commission to hear the case in Bridgwater. Evidence for the Town was given by James Boyce (aged 48), Robert Mullens (aged 40), Geoffrey Shercombe, merchant (aged 40), William Gold, mercer (aged 46), and others who produced receipts to support their case. In February 1557 the Court decided the fee farm should be discharged for £10 16s. 8d.

Arms and Defence

Arms belonging to the town were normally kept in the Armoury at the Guildhall and in 1591 comprised:

6 Corselets and Headpieces
11 long Pikes
3 Rolls for Bowmen covered in Red [protective cover for the left arm]
1 Alamain Rivet and a Headpiece [an alamain rivet being a certain type of breast plate]
4 Locks (?) of Mail covered with canvas
5 Bows and 5 Quivers of Arrows
13 Bills
9 Swords, 7 Daggers and Girdles
8 Soldiers Coats of red

Additionally 12 calyvers and nine powder flasks were in the care of John Bedow. In 1603 there were 12 barrels of powder over the church porch.

Care of the armour – cleaning, greasing and repair – became an annual charge: in 1578, 'Water Wyatt for Kepying of the armor for hys fee for 1 yere 13s. 4d.' However, routine work was not always adequate and in 1569 the town paid 3s. 4d. for cleaning two corselets. Other tasks were given to those with appropriate skills, and in the same year feathering two sheaves of arrows cost 2s. 6d., and William Thomas, the glover, made two arrow cases for 22d. Bill staves were supplied locally, Toogood of Durleigh providing a dozen in 1579. A more unusual entry in 1578 has 'Bowringe out a flare for a callyver ... 2s. 0d.' 'Mending touch boxes' is a more common repair than boring the touch hole.

Military equipment was expensive. In 1569 money to buy corselets and calivers was levied in the town and 77 burgesses contributed about £5. Next year four calyvers were bought in London at 18s. 6d. a piece, with four swords and four daggers costing 32s. Carriage added a further 22d. to the bill. Gunpowder cost 16d. per lb. and match 1d. Pikes when taken out had to be properly dressed and 'frenge for the peckes' was probably red. Drums were also important and kept ready for use. Drum sticks cost 4d. a pair. Edward Holcombe was paid 3s. 6d. in 1584 to hire a drum player for the muster.

Musters were held regularly, and the term 'trainers' suggests that some men were considered to be qualified instructors. In 1586 Mr Blacke (probably Blake) bought armour for the Hall in London costing £9 15s. 6d., and 'Powder and Match for the treners & for the general muster' cost 10s. 8d. Bridgwater musters were in Castle Field and afterwards the men were given dinner. At Taunton in 1596 shoes were provided. Steel morions, a type of helmet without a visor and lined with canvas and cloth, were worn. The muster bill in 1584 was 53s. for powder, shot and beer.

A curious entry in 1579 concerns one Darby Fowler 'for hys dagger & was not lowabull to sarve the same tyme ... 2s'. Later that year he was in a party sent to Ireland whose preparation included the purchase of 'canvase for the sawdyeres shurtes, breches & dublets', together with '3 Sorde blades, 6 daygar blades with hoetes & pumelles & haftes ... 20s. 6d.'.

Archery practice was always encouraged by the authorities because of the risk of the gunpowder supply failing. The government imported bow-staves from Italy, two bows in 1570 costing 10s. The butts were in a field on the river bank beyond the castle and approached either by crossing a stone sill across the moat near the castle's north-east tower or via North Gate and then walking beyond the moat. The butts needed constant attention. In 1577 two men worked for 2½ days at a cost of 5s. making new ones. A new post, probably supporting the target, cost 2s. 3d., and drink for the workmen 2d. The main expense was the turf for banks behind the targets which cost 26s. 8d. and was delivered by boat.

Tudor musters were notorious for serious disorder and lack of discipline and complaints came from the public who often suffered. Expensive arms and equipment were lost; bribery and corruption were rife; men wanting release were willing to buy it, and others vanished after the muster finished instead of returning to their lawful occupations. Despite these problems Somerset produced 4,000 foot, who in 1588 marched across England to reach the south coast when invasion was expected.

Local archives sometimes yield tantalisingly brief items. In 1584 was 'Pd to Mr Godbarde for that hee pd at Bargges for Syr Franses Drackes beyeng ther wth Mr Mayore … 19s. 8d.' Drake came here on official business and was properly entertained by the mayor, a merchant called John Holworthy.

Cappers and Tailors

The Elizabethan Council's attitude to commerce was erratic, and somewhat hypocritical in view of the Queen's grant of monopolies to courtiers. Cappers were harassed for exploiting cheaper methods of producing goods. Bridgwater's Common Council assisted the cap-makers by helping pay any fines incurred. In 1578 the cappers were paid 10s. 'for the wearinge of cappes' half the £1 fine imposed by one of the Acts concerning hats and caps passed in 1566 and 1571.

In 1562 Hugh Culverwell, a Bridgwater tailor, was bound to observe the Queen's proclamation 'touchynge hosen' by a bond of £40 which would remain void if he observed all the articles and orders in an Act expressing horror at the extravagant waste of cloth caused by the latest fashions. The document names all seven tailors working in the town.

The Elizabethan Church Settlement

The original grant of rectorial rights in Bridgwater was made in 1548 by King Henry VIII to the Earl of Bath. Later this arrangement was varied, probably by agreement between the town and the Earl of Bath, which explains why Bridgwater Corporation was collecting tithes before 1571 when this right was granted by Letters Patent. This entitled the town to collect all tithes in the area, including the hamlets, provided certain payments were made. The town could then expect a favourable balance to help with running costs.

The nine Rectory Accounts of 1568 show a gross income of £103 18s. 3d. and payments of £73 19s. 8d., leaving a balance of £29 18s. 7d. In 1579 gross receipts were £124 13s. 5d., payments £81 13s. 3d., and the balance £43

0s. 2d. The main source of income was the tithe of corn, which was collected half-yearly and in 1579 amounted to £18 for Haygrove, Chilton Trinity and the Town, £24 for Horsey, £33 6s. 8d. for Dunwear, £26 for Bower and £12 for Hamp. Ninety years later Haygrove paid £93 8s. 11½d., Horsey £63 16s. 0d., Dunwear £114 10s. 3d. and Hamp £79 11s. 3d. Although tithe was collected in kind, the only reference to this is in 1644 when the town paid £2 rent for a barn and another building to house tithing corn.

The town, exercising its rights as rector, was taking one-tenth of the parish's agricultural produce. Sheep must have been scarce as they are only mentioned once, in 1568, when John Goodman declared 42lbs of wool and paid 27s. 4d. Not all tithes were levied on agricultural produce, nor were they always a tenth. In 1568 tithes were collected on saffron (the only reference to its cultivation in Bridgwater) which was grown to produce colchicum, a remedy for gout. Turner's *Herbal* of 1568 says this plant grew near Bath so it is interesting that it was grown in Bridgwater in the year Turner's book was published.

The 1568 account mentions four orchards, 23 cows, 18 gardens, four hens, cider 13 and honey three times. A Haygrove man grew hops for which he paid 2d. The smallest orchard paid 2d. and the largest 3s. Of people keeping cows only two paid as much as 12d. Cider payments were small although a Haygrove man paid 14d. Most gardens were assessed at 1d or 2d. but four paid 4d. Keeping hens cost 1d. for each person. Two of the four beekeepers paid 12d., the others 2d. each.

The numbers paying tithe in Bridgwater and the hamlets were 158, and 91 were in Bridgwater. There were 21 in Hamp, 12 in Haygrove, five in Chilton Trinity and one in East Bower. Payments collected in Bridgwater ranged from 1d. to 12d. but were higher in the rural areas: from 10d. to 3s. 2d. in Haygrove, 1d. to 3s. 2d. in Hamp, 2s. 4d. in West Bower and from 3d. to 16d. in Chilton. Sixty-nine of the Bridgwater men paid a tithe noted as 'parsonabus', meaning a 'clear gain (on his labours)', but this payment does not appear in the hamlets. The amounts are small, usually 2d., 3d., or 6d. Another class of payments called 'part' (i.e. for possessions) was common in the hamlets but not the town.

There were four men in the borough who kept cows, three gardens and three orchards. The document describes a community in which the inhabitants lived modestly, with many keeping a few cows and hens. The absence of pigs is odd as poor families often kept a pig to fatten. In 1575 Robert Holmes of Hamp paid 6d. for cows, possessions 3d., garden 4d., and agistments 4d. Agistments were often paid on cattle but here presumably refer to pasture.

Tithe was also paid on male and female servants 'for their wages', suggesting the amount varied according to the wage paid. Payments for women were usually lower than those for men. The highest recorded is 8d. for a manservant in 1579 other payments for men ranging from 1d. to 6d. The total levied was 10s. 5d. for 35 entries. Payments for women ranged from 2d. to 4d. and totalled 7s. 8d. for 31 entries. At that date 60 to 70 families could afford a servant. William Godbeare (mayor 1591 and 1599) paid 6d. for employing John Stayner, and

Fabian Weech, the tanner, paid 3d. in respect of Thomas Foster. Geoffrey Shercombe (merchant, bailiff in 1548, mayor in 1559, 1564 and 1565, and 1583) paid 4d. for John Coleman. Margaret Falls (2d.) was employed by the Searcher, a customs official who is not named. Edward Hayne (4d.) was employed by the Millward.

The Port

During neap tides – a fortnight every month – vessels over 100 tons could not reach the bridge. Most ships trading in Bridgwater were 'picards' of about 15 to 30 tons, but there were a few larger boats called 'ballingers', such as the *William* (70 tons) which joined Drake at Plymouth in 1588. Port operation was controlled by the Water Bailiff, who also recorded tolls on carts crossing the bridge and boats travelling upstream to Langport and Taunton. In 1549 he was paid 13s. 4d. (1 mark) a year. The craneman was paid two guineas. The mayor at the time was paid £5, the Recorder £1 and the Town Clerk 13s. 4d.

In 1598 Alexander Hill of Taunton owed 15s. 9d. for lighters carrying 94½ tons of iron and coal that had shot the bridge and another 14s. 2d. pontage on 85 tons taken over the bridge then re-loaded on the Langport Quay. A barrier and chain across the bridge assisted the craneman to collect this toll. In the 18th century pontage and the craneman's job were farmed out. Only 88 examples of the Water Bailiff's Accounts have survived from 1495 until 1652.

Nature of the Trade

Prosperity depended on exporting undyed cloth known as 'Bridgwater' and one of Bridgwater's two M.P.s paid an annual fee to the Clerk of Parliament for the right to 'seal the cloth called Bridgwaters in Bridgwater, Taunton and Chard'. This valuable privilege was granted in 1556 by 'a nakt paste at thys present parlament', in the words of the Bridgwater scribe. In 1588 the fee was 40s. The port of Bridgwater was obviously an important outlet for a cloth-producing region which covered a wide area.

Bridgwater merchants exported much agricultural produce, particularly peas and beans. The chief import in early times was wine but others included coal, salt, iron and fish (mostly herring). The oldest coastal trade involved bringing coal from South Wales. The Irish trade was also important: Bridgwater imported fish, hides, wool, linen, timber, wax, tallow and linseed oil, while the Irish took coal, salt, iron, beans, peas, beer, hops and finished cloth.

Evidence from the 16th century suggests a prolonged period of slack trade. In 1588 the Collector wrote, 'For this quarter nothing inwards, neither outwards anything. God send boats!', a comment of possibly greater significance than the oft-quoted facts that the buss *Emmanuel* had gone with Frobisher in 1578 or that the *William* had joined the operations against the Spanish Armada in 1588.

That year Bridgwater was asked to produce one ship and one pinnace, and next year a barge, fully furnished for war. The town compounded for £447, later reduced to £333. Two townsmen, Robert Bucking, 'now mayor', and Robert

Stradling, were paid in 1593 'for servyes of ther shippe in ano 1588, alowed by consent … £26'.

In 1591 the mayor made excuses when a ship of 100 tons was demanded from Bridgwater and Ilfracombe. 'Our town depending heretofore altogether on trade,' he wrote, 'is at the present by reason of the want thereof greatly impoverished.' In 1596 the Collector resigned because 'the trade is so small it will not pay the fees'.

Hazards to Shipping

A Venetian vessel was wrecked in the river off Huntspill in 1547, probably caught by a rapidly ebbing tide which swung her across the river to break her back. The vessel was a danger to shipping and on 16 September 1548 the mayor authorised two Bridgwater graziers, John Page and Richard Davy, to remove 'the hulle of the Venycian shippe, latelie perished'. Both men gave their word in a bond of £20 that they would get rid of the hull of the ship.

Navigational hazards were considerable and many ships were lost on the Gore Sands off the mouth of the Parrett. The changing course of the river added to the dangers. In the early 18th century the Parrett had two extra mouths, one to the north at the foot of Brent Knoll and another opposite Huntspill. Straightening the river was often discussed but never undertaken.

Piracy was another danger. Lundy, the island off the north coast of Devon, was a nest of pirates in 1608. At later dates trouble usually came from privateers, either Dutch or French depending on the international situation. As late as 1808 a French privateer seized a sloop off the Welsh coast.

12

An Unusual Municipal Enterprise

For centuries wheaten bread was the staple food of southern England (some rye bread being eaten in the north) and so the life of every town and village depended upon a supply of millstones. The only area where genuine millstone grit occurs is near Swansea so most districts often made do with the best available substitute. In Cornwall granite was used, though too hard to be easily dressed whereas West Somerset stone was much too soft. Teeth were worn down by chewing bread containing grit from grinding stones. Calculations estimate that even by the 18th century a person ate 6lb. of pulverised sandstone every year of his life. No suitable stone occurs in the Bridgwater area but it could be obtained through Bristol.

There are several entries in the Water Bailiff's Accounts for unloading millstones before 1555 but that year a change occurred and there was a big increase in the quantity being handled, which included the winding of three lots of millstones, 14, four and 12 respectively, and two tons of grinding stones. Not all these were needed in Bridgwater, merchants having realised that many places found the journey to Bristol difficult and preferred to purchase millstones in Bridgwater. From this point the Receiver kept a separate account of trade in millstones and grinding stones, although after a few years the trade was recorded towards the end of the Town Accounts. Often the purchaser's name and place of origin were recorded.

It is not surprising to find that villages within ten miles of Bridgwater were being supplied but stones were also being distributed over a much wider area. Customers came from the whole of Somerset and distribution in the south-west reached the coast beyond Exeter to encompass much of Devon. To the south-east it extended to Dorchester, so that even obscure Dorset villages sent to Bridgwater for millstones.

A variety of stones were sold: millstones, horse mill stones (Fig. 34), grinding stones, mustard stones and quern stones. The greatest number were grinding stones but the most important sales were of millstones. These appear to have been bought ready-dressed since rarely is anyone paid to dress them, as in 1586: 'Thomas Morris packman to newe tryme 4 mylstones … 4s. 0d.' No example of the millstones seems to have been preserved although two mill pecks in the local museum are a reminder of the economic importance of the trade which

34 A few yards inside Blake Gardens there is this 'rather ugly little building' described as 'part of a horse mill called Frog Lane' when purchased by the Balch family in 1681. It was eventually used as a summer house and called 'The Turret'. Built largely of brick with some stone it shows many signs of repair. It may contain some of the earliest examples of locally made brick.

Bridgwater dominated for almost 150 years. A large profit was essential because of the risk of loss or breakage and once a stone was dropped into the river – it was recovered but the task must have taxed local ingenuity to the limit.

In 1578 Edmund Clowter was buying millstones for £1 each and selling them for £1 10s. 0d., whilst at the other end of the scale corn stones were bought for 2s. a pair and sold for 3s. These prices appear to have remained steady for many years.

Mr Blake (Blacke) visited Paul's Fair in Bristol in 1584 and was given 21s. 4d. for his expenses. There he was reported as having ordered '20 stones' at a cost of 40s. plus 10s. freight. In 1560 Richard Jones recorded the receipt of £51 14s. 2d. from the sale of millstones against costs of £31 7s. 10d. – a profit of £20 6s. 4d. The figures indicate the size of the financial operation. In 1565 sale of millstones realised £47 17s. 8d. with costs of £34 16s. 0d. The apparent profit of £13 1s. 8d. is modest, but the town had purchased 20 loads of grinding stones and six pairs of corn stones (small stones used by farmers for grinding mustard) at a cost of £13 9s. 4d., and sales only amounted to £7 4s. 0d.

From time to time there are lists of stones unsold at the year's end. In 1563 it amounted to 30 millstones, 91 grinding stones, six corn stones, three malt corns and 12 little grinding stones for cutlers. Nobody seems to have worried about the surplus since they were confident that buyers would be found. The transactions for 1586 can be tabulated:

	Total (including surplus from previous year)	Sold during the year	Unsold at end of year
Millstones	43	23	20
Grinding stones	111	32	79
Quern stones	6 pair	2 pair	4 pair

A few details sometimes illustrate the flow of trade. Special entries made in 1584 show sales at fair time: At the Lent Fair 13 stones were sold to the smiths for 38s, 13 stones were sold at the Midsummer Fair for 46s. 4d., and on St Matthew's Day eight were sold for 28s. 0d. No heavy millstones were included. An entry records the arrival of 64 grinding stones worth £7 6s. 8d. at the Midsummer Fair and also includes an unusual item whereby Edward Smith was paid £4 for four stones 'that came from Highbridge with Smith's boat'.

There was a possibility that stones kept for long periods might deteriorate. In 1586 the Receiver noted that the unsold stones were left 'upon the Kaye & in the strete wt some in the corte of the Common Hall'. Only the small stones were moved to the Hall and left in the open courtyard. On the other hand, in 1617 there was sold to 'John Scorse of Gregry Stocke, a myle stone of 4 foot 9 ynches being a refuse and hath layen hyer 14 yeares and upwards by report ... £2 0s. 0d.'. In the 1620s one Mrs Parsons was paid 3s. 4d. a year 'for standing of our stones agaynst her wall'.

The cost of a millstone was determined by its diameter. Measurements and prices must have been agreed when each contract was made. On 23 February 1597 John Pody suddenly called upon to act as Receiver proceeded with great caution. He introduced his account by noting that 23 millstones were left by Mr Stradling, and 10 had been bought by Mr Jones, then went on to say that he found 20 grinding stones 'besides one was lost before I came into office, as the crane man told me'. Then he had to deal with a dispute over prices. After completing an entry which he later deleted, he wrote, 'payd Mr Wm Kechme for the ij pere of mylstones wch were rd by Mr Jonnes wch were above the syse we dyd agree for, for wch we were to agre wth hyme ... 20s. for the stones were v fot & iiij inches & he demande the above the pryse of the rest 40s.' This entry is signed 'by me Wilim Catchmay'. John Pody was pleased with this and proceeded next to get personal receipts written into his book by the vicar, the preacher, the schoolmaster and others for their salaries, but the procedure was later discontinued.

Men named as selling stones before 1560 are Walter Tyler, William Welshman, and John Worley of Monmouthshire. In 1558 one Gapper was given 20s. when he went to Bristol for millstones. The family name appearing most frequently as supplier of millstones is 'Catchmay', variously spelt Catchmayde, Cacheme,

Catchmed and Kechme. It still appears after 1660. George Catchmay, in 1585, was described as 'of Bexwere', now known as Bigs Weir, in St Briavels parish in Gloucestershire, about 5½ miles from Monmouth. The records of 1561 include T. Tyler, and in 1562 'Fatheir Tyler of the forrest' is named. In 1584 there was John Tyler, and in 1596 Phillip Tyler. Other names which occur later are Tyrell, Glover, Brodley, Gethen, Reeves and Morse.

In 1594 the Bridgwater Receiver went to Bristol to see the stones loaded. The cargo of eight loads of grinding stones cost 18s. per load, a consignment being worth £7 4s. 0d. and costing another 8s. to have landed. The Bristol visit usually coincided with the date of one of the big fairs, either at St Paul's tide or at St James's tide. Frequently the only charge shown is for horse hire, but in 1561 18d. was spent on breakfast for Mr Catchmay and others at St Paul's Fair. It cost another 8s. for Mr Tirrell's man and the man who accompanied him to travel from Bristol into the Forest of Dean to choose millstones. Another 8s. was 'for my own charges riding to the Forest'. In September Mr Tirrell's millward was sent into the Forest at a cost of 3s. It is obvious that there were many incidental payments which added to the final cost of the stones.

In 1621 seven pairs of millstones costing £3 13s. 4d. a pair arrived in Bridgwater with one horse millstone costing 12s. The bill for these, £26 5s. 4d., was paid to Thomas Mundin, Mr Catchmay's servant, who was also rewarded with 11s. 'for his paynes for sending gud stones' and 1s. 6d. 'spent uppon him in wine etc.'. In 1603 the accounts open with the sale of 19 millstones (and one broken stone) for £33 0s. 2d., and 80 grinding stones for £21 4s. 4d. A new name to appear is that of Mansell, a Bridgwater man sent to the Forest for stones. In 1610 prices for grinding stones are quoted as 2s. 6d. for one 2½ feet in diameter, 4s. 8d. for 3 feet, and 6s. 6d. for 3½ feet. In 1619 a stone of 3ft. 5in. was worth 13s., and one of 4ft. 3in. cost 18s. 8d. Prices for millstones are not given, but in 1610 a millstone bought in Bristol for £2 10s. 0d. plus 7s. 6d. for carriage had a diameter of five feet and it was sold for £3 2s. 0d. A profit of 4s. 6d., minus landing costs, scarcely seems an economic proposition.

In 1611 there is a hint of something new when Mansell rides into Wales to see Mr Catchmay. Perhaps they were now seeking to obtain millstone grit stones from Swansea? This visit was followed by the purchase of 11 millstones and 12 grinding stones. In 1616 'a Welshman' was paid £5 for 20 grinding stones. In 1612 a newcomer called John Whittington arrived bringing 60 grinding stones (£22), and the town spent 10d. 'uppon the Marchant of the said stones in beer and wine'. The sum of 4d. 'spent on customers wch bought grynding stones' was also mentioned.

The trade probably continued through the Civil War but could not have been brisk. During 1659-60, the last year of the Commonwealth, it was badly managed. In spite of having 42 millstones unsold, the town bought another 24. Since only 19 were sold, the surplus increased to 47. The 19 stones raised £47 7s. 0d. so the town was apparently encumbered with a surplus of over £100 in capital cost. There was also a surplus of 323 grinding stones and 85 querns, which were being sold for 2s. 4d. each. The sale of querns is a reminder that some people were still grinding their own flour.

Mr Catchmay supplied grinding stones in 1660-1, but millstones came through a merchant called Perkins. The town paid a certain sum cash down, and the balance of £30 to Mr Catchmay at St John's Tide (24 June), and of £16 to Mr Perkins at St Paul's Tide (25 January). Next year Mr Catchmay received a payment of £40 for both millstones and grinding stones.

Between 1669 and 1672 several grinding stones were sold but there is no summary of stock held and it is likely that the trade ceased. During the years 1686-8 the only reference to millstones is a note that £1 10s. 6d. was paid for dressing them. There is no indication in the archives of the reason for the disappearance of this trade. The older authorities say that in the 17th century millstones were imported from France, so perhaps the superior quality of French millstones accounted for the loss of Bridgwater's position.

13

THE PROBLEM OF POVERTY

The problem of poverty became acute in the early 16th century when small groups of beggars roamed the countryside. The stock treatment was to whip them out of the parish, which was hardly a remedy, and as the depression continued other ideas were developed. London levied a poor rate in 1547 but few other towns followed and by the end of the century social conditions had deteriorated dramatically, forcing Parliament to act. From 1597 several statutes were passed culminating in the Poor Law of 1601. The 1597 Act was the first authorising a Poor Rate.

Bridgwater documents contain ten accounts entitled 'Collectors of a Special Stock for the Poor', seven covering 1597-1603 and the others 1612-13, 1614-15 and 1626-7. 'Special Stock' merely indicates a category of poor relief paid not from rates but from charitable gifts, legacies, rents of land and houses. The new title disguises the oldest form of poor relief – private charity.

In 1598 the first item of income, 40s., was 'the gift of Wm. Lancras, gent.', followed by 50s. derived from capital of £50 'given as a stocke by William Jones deceased to be let forth uppon use and the profit thereof yerelie to be distributed, among the poore of the said borrough at Easter yerliel'. Then 40s. was paid by the Receiver from renting Colford's lands, an ancient legacy, followed by 40s. interest on £20 donated by a man called Parry (Pare). Several houses provided rents, and a new pound given by Simon Saunders (Saunderes), which cost £5, could be let for 10s. a year.

In 1600 Humphrey Blake, Admiral Blake's father, left 'the yerelie summe of twentie poundes growing oute of the use and profitt of the said twelve score poundes'. His will said the interest was to relieve six or more poor people, and also for 'the cawcies [i.e. causeways or highways] within the parishe of Bridgwater'. It gave no guidance concerning intended proportions so Margaret Blake, the widow, was consulted and it was decided that £16 was for poor relief and £4 'for the Reparation of the cawcies'. Margaret Blake requested that four poor people should receive 'Twenty shillinges a piece yerlie so longe as they should live', naming four widows: Susan Price, Joan Bindon, Agnes Balhatchett and Joan Pawson.

Income from the Special Stock in 1596 was £22 16s. 2½d. and the Collectors (the fund treasurers) distributed £21 16s. 9d. amongst 146 people including, 'Fower

Almespeople ... 16d.', the four residents of the West Gate almshouse. The 1615-16 account shows that the revenue was £39 12s. 0d., and 'all the weeklie paimtes to the pore during the whole yeare as appeareth in the boke ... £27 0s. 2d.'.

Growth of the Rating System

The law required appointment of Overseers of the Poor, assisted by churchwardens, to supervise provision for the destitute. A 1599 document names four Overseers, Henry James, Christopher Salmon, George Paul and John Beddow, and two churchwardens, William Francis and John Champlin, which suggests that the policy was being implemented.

The idea of a poor rate was new but it presented no difficulties because the practice of assessing a neighbours' wealth was an old English custom, a citizen being expected to state the value of his visible possessions. Something similar was started in 1188, the Assize of Arms, to help determine what arms a man could afford to provide for the defence of the kingdom. According to Bishop Hobhouse, the earliest example in England of a local rate being levied was the Church Rate paid annually in Bridgwater from 1383. But once the Poor Rate had been adopted various other parish needs could be addressed, such as care of highways and the cost of constables.

A well-thumbed little book used by the Overseers when collecting the Poor Rate during 1616-17 has survived. The rates were payable weekly and handed over in 'the maiores Ile' (the mayor's aisle), probably the south aisle of St Mary's church. Several pages have hastily-made indiscriminate entries, such as 'given to ij pore fokes 3d. given to Avon Coromes 4d.', the last entry appearing on three occasions. Two such entries refer to food and fuel: 'wood & bacon 6d. Pork 6d.'.

'Special stock' income was £22 16s. 2d. in 1598, and £21 14s. 9d. was paid out to provide doles for 146 poor people. Amongst them were 'Fower Almespeople 16d.' Usually the entries relating to alms are more specific:

> Christmas 1614 – the almspeople without the South Gate 1s. 6d.
> Easter 1615 – the almspeople without the West Gate   2s. 0d.

but other doles might have been left by legacy. The total income in 1599 was £42 4s. 2d. The Collectors' account for 1615-16 is a little more informative: £39 12s. 0d. was collected, and 'all the weeklie paimtes to the pore during the whole yeare as appeareth in the boke £27 0 2d.' Since 120 payments of 1d. per week total £26 a year weekly doles were tiny. The alms folk who had each received 3d. in 1597 and 4d. in 1598 eventually received an annual grant of £5 4s. 0d. for four persons. They probably considered themselves very fortunate to have a small house rent free plus 6d. per week in cash.

In an extraordinary incident in 1601 a Bridgwater boat took so long to return from the Newfoundland fishing grounds that its cargo deteriorated. The town apparently took it over, selling the fish at a loss, but some was so bad it could not be given away. The entry relating to this reads:

The Problem of Poverty

> One thowsand of Newland fish beinge unsold wch cost £3 15s. 4d.
> Receyved of the sale of this fyshe 45s. 2½d.
> there remayneth yet ungiven & unsold 61 fishes.

The total income that year was £43 8s. 7d. and payments £38 18s. 3d. At the end of the document the clerk indicated the balance with these words: 'Soe remayneth Cleere in the Accountantes handes the some of £4 10 4 And threescore & one Newland fishe.'

Help from the Neighbours

There were other methods of providing relief, one being to board out children, and occasionally adults, in other people's homes. When sickness affected a family a woman was frequently paid to go and help:

> 1599
> for keeping the hoopers 2 children 5 weekes at
> 20d. the weeke... 8 4
> for keeping one of them 9 weekes for
> 10d. the weeke ... 7 6
> the widoe Toogood for 9 weekes for 2 children
> at 6d. the Weeke ... 9 6

This 1599 account also lists several payments for clothes for those boarded out and several grants for sickness:

> to releive Johane paxsy beinge sick ... 2d.
> to releive Robt Roberts beinge sioke ... 12d.'.

Yet another deserving case in 1599 was

> Thomas Comons whoe hath many children ... 12d.'.

Loans to Artificers

Bridgwater had a scheme known as 'Loans to Artificers', whereby a leather worker, say, in difficulties could be lent money to buy a fresh hide and thus gain the opportunity to start afresh. In worsening economic times the scheme would fail but in certain conditions it could work. A document from 1601 recording such loans lists 30 cases.

Names are grouped in threes; the first being that of the artificer or craftsman, and the next the two townsmen who guaranteed the loan. The number given to each case was followed by four columns stating the borrowed capital and the interest. Sometimes loans were made interest-free. The document gives the impression that the scheme was working.

Tinker, Tailor, Soldier, Sailor

The 1601 Poor Law made each parish responsible for its own poor but left several areas of the law unclear. Poor men looking for work or crossing the country to return to a home parish and needing relief carried a document signed by a magistrate, as a *bona fide*. These so-called 'passes' were easily forged and a Bath schoolmaster enjoyed a useful supplementary income from doing this:

'He doth usually make passes for Irish people,' was a comment made in 1649. An example from 1619 has: 'Andrew Crandon for so much geven A pore man wch had a passe and goinge into Devon shere is 6d.' Genuine passes had no legal validity and quickly gained the sanction of custom but illicit begging was cruelly punished:

> 1617 'Peter Blackmore for whiping of 4 vagabons 1s. 4d.'

Vagabonds were assumed to be rogues, and from James I's reign liable to be branded on the shoulder with the letter 'R'. No recorded instance of this happening in Bridgwater exists and cruelty could be tempered by offers of food and shelter, as in 1619:

> Whippinge of towe Boyes beinge Strandgers whereof one was a Tynkar is ... 8d.
> Thomas Sheppard for so muche desburst for the fore sayd towe Boyes And a woman for ther kppen [keeping] one nyght ... 6d.

When women were whipped at St Matthew's Fair the offence was rarely stated. On the one occasion when the Receiver was explicit his sentence is incomplete:

> 1617 'Peter Blackmore for whiping & woman that Lay with a ... 4d.'

Soldiers seemed always to be moving across the country and the Irish campaigns at the end of Elizabeth's reign and the settlement of Ulster under James I could account for much of this activity:

> 1616 'to a soger wch laid in the ward [i.e. he was in prison] 4d.'
> 1620 'Owin Bowen of penbrucke A soldar bond for london 1s. 0d.'
> 1622 'John Morgan and Wm Suthoot beinge soulders and for ther Relefe is 1s. 6d.'
> 1627 'Wm Day Baylife to two Irish soldieres is 6d.'

Sailors are as numerous as soldiers and often have more spectacular stories of ill luck, as the following show:

> 1614 'Ryngold flud a poor man that lost his ship by the pyraits ... 1s. 0d.
> Thomas Robenson a poor man that had his shyp cast away in fowl wether ... 4d.
> William Charles & Lowell in the 10 of aprall whom had lost the shipe & goodes by a piratt ... 4d.'

In 1646 there were 15 seamen given 4s., who were presumably travelling as a group. But not all sailors evoked sympathy: in 1619 'The Bellman for whippinge of A strandger being A Seaye farringe man out of Devon sheare ... 4d.'

Stories of ill-treatment at the hands of foreigners, especially if they were Turks or Arabs, found ears eager to listen. The earliest example, however, describes a brush with the traditional enemy:

> 1602 'paid to a Prisoner taken in Spayn towardes his relief in passing to London ... 1 s. 0d.'.
> 1617 'to a trayler [i.e. traveller] wch came out of Turkic ... 1s. 0d.'.
> 1621 'Richard Bruokington of milbrucke being takin by the Turkes and for his relefe is ... 8d.'.

There seems to have been no prejudice against foreigners and there are many instances of charitable treatment of the French and one of sympathy for two Belgians:

> 1619 'Sabastean Braune and his Brother beinge Wallons and travelers … 1s. 0d.'.

Apprenticeship

Medieval apprenticeship terms were from three to 10 years and the terminal rewards also varied, some being small amounts of cash, 6s. 8d. in one case and 20s. in another, others gifts of clothes such as a cap and gown. Apprenticeship originally meant leaving home and living in the master's house. Life was harsh and the standards of discipline would be considered cruel nowadays. After 1600 occasional clauses occur in contracts to say 'he is not to be beaten too severely' (a young weaver in 1602), or even 'she is not to be chastised' (a girl of 10 apprenticed to a housewife for 11 years in 1607). Boys entering the workhouse were expected to learn a trade such as weaving and spinning, although doubtless girls did spin, knit and carry out various chores.

In a harsh and brutal age examples do occur of good nature asserting itself. In 1598 the Hopkins family (often spelt Hotkins or Hockings) who lived near the river in Frog Lane were given 12d. instead of the usual 6d. In 1599 they were given clothes, Richard Hopkins a jacket using four yards of material costing 3s. 6d. and 8d. for the making the 'Hockinges blynd boy' a jerkin and breeches costing 4s. 1d. and 8d. for the making, and another brother, Simon, the same clothes, which cost 3s. 6d. and 8d. for the making. Later still 'the blynd hockenes boy' got two shirts for 4s. and a pair of stockings costing 14d. He faced a bleak future until somebody was inspired in 1601: 'Payd to Edward Edwardes to teach Blinde hopkins to play on the harpe for his better mayntenance 10s.'

In rural areas boys went to farms and girls into service, but it became increasingly difficult to persuade farmers to take boys so lists of employers were made and a rota ensured that each in turn took an apprentice. A greater variety of trades was available in the town. On 9 February 1579 Andro Laynge was apprenticed to Rafe Huntte, carpenter, for seven years at a premium of £10 paid by the town. On completion he would have 10s. in cash and tools of every sort. Premiums varied, often inexplicably. Laynge's was high in order to cover the cost of the tools which he would eventually keep. The conditions of service were set out in an indenture, and every indenture had to be recorded at the Gildhall. In 1599 eleven were drawn up at a cost of 12d. each.

14

TOWN LIFE UNDER THE EARLY STUARTS

A banquet in 1604 in honour of James I marked the new reign. The Receiver wrote, 'Mr Henry Jones for a banket at proclaminge the Kynge £2 0s. 0d.' In 1609 a new padlock and bolt were supplied to the Goldsmiths' Hall and in 1627 the roof was repaired for one shilling. References to Bridgwater goldsmiths are scarce but a few silver spoons exist with the town arms engraved on their handles. The goldsmiths worked chiefly in silver and silver gilt and gave Silver Street its name. In the 1930s a derelict building with a gothic-style door stood there which was probably once a silversmith's workshop. (Fig. 35).

Plague

The first record of plague in Bridgwater is in 1609, the year the name Pig Cross was first used. Plague was always called 'the sickness' and the Receiver's first entry says £8 14s. 1d. was spent on the sick people. This was followed by another for 20s. and then Matthew Borde was paid 6s. for watching Merrick's house. Between 22 February and 7 March 1611 one Robert Fludd was paid a wage and victuals costing £2 14s. 11d. were provided for 'the poore infected people'. In March it cost £5 4s. 8d. to care for the Beshell family. A further outbreak between 4 June and 10 August 1611 cost £6 19s. 1d., and was followed by another between 8 August and 8 October costing £5 3s. 0d. In June the Receiver noted that the money was spent before being received from the churchwardens and overseers of the poor. During this last outbreak seven graves were dug.

35 Remains of a 16th-century doorway in Silver Street. The premises are a glazier's shop and the 'window' in the door is a mirror.

In 1625 plague re-occurred and William Sealy loaned four guineas 'for the sick folke' which was not repaid until October 1626. A house in North Street was designated the Pest House in 1626, and was thought to belong to one William Hill who received 40s. per annum 'for the ground whereon the pest house standeth'. The Corporation managed to let the garden whilst patients occupied the house, which caused problems in 1626, John Baker receiving £1 2s. 0d. compensation for losses in 'cabbages and other herbs'. Next year he got £5 'for that he was hindred by the pest folkes in his Garden'. The compensation seems high for a domestic concern, and perhaps Baker ran a market garden. North Street was on the edge of the town so the Pest House was considered to be at a safe distance from the centre. Its site cannot be identified but must have been on the west side of the street.

The First Workhouse 1619-27

Bridgwater opened a workhouse in 1619, probably in unusual circumstances. The information comes from Receiver's Accounts but only a fragmentary picture can be obtained thanks to the paucity of records. Nothing is known about its organisation, discipline, or the role churchwardens and overseers played and it is not mentioned after 1639.

The town's immediate concern was to house six poor boys, presumably boarding them out as apprenticeship was unavailable. The officers rented a vacant house belonging to John Bond of Chedzoy for 16s. per quarter rent but in the first year the cost was offset by £1 10s. 0d. paid by Robert Lockier for use of the stable. This usage may have ended in 1627 because, although John Bond still received 16s. 8d. every quarter, it was 'for the house where Mr Clarke dwelleth', but a shoemaker, Alexander Neale, was still making shoes 'for the Worke house Boyes'.

In 1619 the town borrowed £10 from a wealthy townsman, George Gray, 'which was lent to Marmaduke Corme of the Worke husse uppon boncdes wch is in the chest'. Since Corme's name remained associated with the scheme until 1623, he was possibly entrusted with the £10 in order to establish it. He and his wife – who collected his wages on one occasion in 1623 – lived in the workhouse. He was called 'the workman' when paid 2s. 'for things Nedfull to his use', which was helping to rebuild the pound. In 1620-1 he was given 10s. on one occasion and £1 on another 'by Mr Mayor's order', a phrase which could mean anything but often meant the granting of relief, as it did for 'Robart peck of the worke house 10s.', whose entry indicates that not all inmates were boys. Other payments to Corme that year are wages: 15s. at Christmas and £1 8s. 0d. for the Midsummer quarter. On one occasion Corme sold the town four yards of canvas for bolsters for 2s. 6d., which suggests a link with administration, as does another entry: 'to Marmaduke Corme in p(ar)t of moneys for the boyes of the worke hose and Ive paid him the said is ... 9s. 8d.'

If Corme supervised the workhouse it is odd he was given no title and was sometimes absent doing other work. When Nicholas Box was sent to London to collect £44 for the Receiver he carried £12 to fulfil some other commission and Marmaduke Corme accompanied him. Doubtless this was for security and suggests Corme was a trusted servant of the community. He rode a horse lent by William Farmer for a fee of 11s. and was given 15s. for his expenses.

An incident in 1621 sounds like a man trying to escape: 'the belle man for whippinge of Thomas Chamber and returned to the worke hose is 4d.' The bellman whipped several vagrants that year and Chamber was possibly caught begging. The quality of the clothes provided varied and the higher cost of better materials could possibly be covered by a small endowment applying to a particular boy. There was also concern about personal cleanliness: 'to Dominicke Eddy to paye for washinge of his clothes before he was setled in the workehosse 3d.'

It is not known if the workhouse was furnished but since furniture is not mentioned it is reasonable to assume it already existed. Early entries do not mention bedsteads. 'Beds' were sacks 'filled with oaten dust for the boys to ly ther one.' This might imply they slept on the floor, but two had 'chambers'. A 1621 entry 'for towe Bedsteds sett up in the out workehouse 11s. 9d.' suggests that not everybody was expected to sleep on the floor, and these two bedsteads, set up in an outhouse, could mean that newcomers had arrived.

Bedding for the original six involved the purchase of:
16 yards of cloth	£1 0s. 0d.
2 coverlets	6s. 2d.
16 yards of canvas for two beds (supplied by Richard Tuthill)	9s. 0d.
4 yards of canvas for two bolsters	2s. 6d.
To J. Harris for making 2 pairs of blankets, one bed sank and two bolsters	1s. 4d.
2 beds filled with oaten dust	3s. 4d.

Although rough and ready it cost £2 2s. 4d. The poor were destined to sleep on bed-sacks filled with oaten dust for at least another two centuries. Clothes provided were made from the coarsest wool with grey cloth and grey stockings; together with shoes, they cost £4 18s. 0d.

The only household equipment mentioned is the old hand mill acquired in 1600 and kept in the Town Hall. The bills noted by the Receiver are:

Jefere Nele for a mylle set up at the Halle	30s. 0d.
Steven Slade for seting here upe	6s. 4d.
Corkey a daye and halfe to helpe him	12d.

It was brought to the workhouse to save the cost of milling flour. The mill must have been dilapidated as it was repaired at considerable expense, the work taking at least a week. The total cost was £2 1s. 3d. but whether it ever gave satisfactory service is doubtful since before long some of the framework was coming apart:

for Timbar and yron worke wth Carpintars wadges for Reparinge the hand mill of the worke hose 6s. 6d.

The workhouse policy towards industry considered only the cloth trade. The town acquired half a dozen spinning wheels, known as 'spinning turns', with stools, and two old looms were patched up for 15s. The authorities were anxious to encourage local manufacture of cloth but were inconsistent, buying cloth in Minehead for the not inconsiderable sum of £14 2s. 6d.:

> 1620 'Richard Crosseman of minhid for vj peces ½ of sade gray kerseye conteninge 38 yeardes wch is 18d. pr yearde and 2s. and the holle is £10 9s. 0d.
> John Eston of the sayd place One pece of kersey contes 22 yeardes and cost 18s. 0d.'

The Clergy

The church still operated under Elizabethan arrangements and for several years the same clergy remained: Mr Swanking as preacher, with a £20 stipend, and Mr Devenish holding a 'curateship' with a stipend of £13 6s. 8d. However, in 1626 George Worton is called 'Minister', with a stipend of £24 13s. 4d., and John Devenish 'Preacher', whose stipend is £20.

National sources show James I tried to crush the Puritans but the Bridgwater Archives provide no evidence of this. Visiting preachers were occasionally entertained: Mr Bayley in 1603 (10s.), Mr Maryshe in 1606 (20s.) and Mr Robinson in 1611 (£1 10s. 0d.). Some came under the aegis of the church and one, invited by the vicar in 1608, only cost 19d. Another visiting in 1616 was officially recognised, the entry recording: 'a pottell of wine to the preacher of Wellow at Mr Ware's house … 1s. 4d.' Three other preachers came that year and each cost 6s. 8d. One, a Mr Harding, returned in 1621 and received a bottle of wine costing 1s. 6d. when he preached at St John's, possibly the buildings on the medieval hospital site which were still recognisable then. There were also two visits from Mr Warre and one from Mr Allen. In 1623 preachers who spoke on four Sundays received 'diet and wine' costing 16s.

Wells Consistory Court records prove that all these visitors were Puritans, Devenish giving weekly lectures from 1607 to stimulate Puritan ideas. The bishop's warnings and admonitions went unheeded and the churchwardens failed to execute their official duties. When a parishioner was excommunicated by the bishop at his visitation the wardens never presented him at the Church Court. Two habitually attended conventicles held in Devenish's house. The Litany was not read out on Sundays and two weekdays as had been ordered and in the 1630s, contrary to the king's instructions, Devenish was still preaching on Sunday afternoons. He was suspended briefly in 1636 and one warden excommunicated but only two specific complaints were made to show he was a Puritan: singing psalms in his conventicle and spending half an hour in church explaining the catechism.

The town authorities used a spy in 1621 when 3d. was given to 'Thomas Glasse to spend and learne what company ther was at Thomas Caryes and James Burlandes ho[u]se'. They were probably looking for recusants, or persons, particularly Catholics, who declined attending their parish church. In 1616

Thomas Glasse was paid 8d. 'for the lent of 2 horses to huntspill for the Aprihending of papishes [papists]'.

Secular Matters

Archery was still being practised as the butts were repaired in 1612 but its popularity may have been waning. Fives was played against the wall of the parish church to the danger of the chancel windows. The only reference to fives is very late and records stopping a game in 1678: 'Wm. Duncome pro poynting the Chancell windowes & digging up the fives place per the Chancell ... 1s. 6d.' Those who suffered from the loss of this makeshift court were probably boys from the Free School.

Bull baiting continued to flourish. In 1619 8s. was spent on a collar with a buckle, and another 8d. on a swivel 'for the said rope collar'. An entry for 1616 has: 'Peter Taylor for a ring about the bullring & for prangs for the same ... 1s. 8d.' Bull baiting was still as popular at the end of the century.

A new prison costing £6 1s. 9d. was built following James I's accession. Most of the cost was for timber, particularly oak and elm boards. It was located in, or next to, the Common Hall. Sessions were still held in the open in the Cornhill with the benches set up near the High Cross.

Money was also spent maintaining pounds. An entry in 1619-20 illustrates the difficulties affecting building tasks. Timber posts were needed so a tree at Goathurst was purchased from Mr Poulett for £2 2s. 0d. Giles Warner and his partner earned 18s. for seven days' work at sawing and then two days squaring and thorn cutting. Thomas Torry, a husbandman, was employed to make a sawpit costing 1s. 6d. Having prepared the timber and sawn the boards, Goodman Dobill of Goathurst was paid 12s. for 'bryngin hom of the sayd Tembar'. On its arrival in Bridgwater, William Ellery and his man were paid 12s. 11d. for making the pounds and 2s. was paid to Marmaduke Corme for his work and 12s. 6d. to Peter Taylor for spikes, nails, twists and locks. It is difficult to know exactly what the expenditure obtained. Use of the plural suggests both the great and lesser pounds, but that year Goodman Gawland was paid 9d. for gravel for a pig pound and Goodman Celly 9d. for its haulage, so the pig pound was probably new. In the same account, Ralph Dyment was paid for 'pitching the pig pound', and later another 2s. 9d. was spent on pitching (spreading gravel), John Martin being paid 2s. for the work which included 2d. given to a man to return surplus stones to the workhouse.

A new door for the great pound cost 1s., 'the oulde Borde beinge Rente in peces', and Peter Taylor, locksmith, charged 1s. 6d. for a stock lock, 'the oulde one beinge brokin in peces'. The final bill was £5 5s. 5d., a substantial sum, but the work done lasted for many years. References to the pound suggest that it was approached from the western end of the High Street, and the 1806 town map shows it between Clare Street and the North Gate. The second pound had disappeared.

Property Kept for Public Use

An Inventory of the Town Armour was maintained because the traditional defence system had never been superseded, but other 'needful necessaries' were also included. The inventory for 1623 contained: 9 Millstones, 30 Grinding Stones, 24 Leather Buckets, 3 Corselets, 3 Pikes, 3 Ladders, 11 Black Bills, 1 Wheelbarrow, 1 Bull Rope and Collar, 3 Town Crucks, 1 Treble Millstone (at the Quay). A note stated that Jacob Andrews owed 28s. for one Treble Millstone sent to Mr Leslow at Chard, and 20 old boards of the crane were with Mr John Stradling. Military stores also included 16 lb. of match, 6 lb. being in Mr Bult's care, 5 lbs in Richard Speare's and 3 lb. in the chest. There was also a half barrel, 46½ lb., of gunpowder with Hugh Bult. Perhaps the authorities thought the powder was safer in private hands than in the Powder House!

The minimum amount of armour ever cleaned was constant: five corselets and three pikes, probably kept for the Watch. The next surviving inventory (1627) included five corselets, one being in Stacey's care and another in Edmund Dawes'. That year a barrel of gunpowder was broken and 10 lb. of powder lost. Two drums were recorded although the 1624 inventory listed two drums but one was punctured. The full quota of military bills was also 12, not eleven. Only two ladders were recorded and no buckets, which may be due to careless recording. Many houses were thatched so ladders, buckets and crucks were essential fire-fighting equipment, the latter being an iron hook on a long handle used to drag straw off a burning roof. A hinged metal arm below the hook closed on the bundle as it was being dragged down.

The Inventory often included tile-stones (slates) kept to repair the Hall roof. Numbers varied from one year to another: in 1620 there were 3,500 but only 200 in 1627.

Foreign Affairs

Trade was slow to recover in the early 17th century due to James I's attempt to stop unfinished cloth being exported so that cloth finishing would be carried out in England. It ruined traditional trade with the Low Countries and in 1621 the only traffic coming into Bridgwater were ships carrying coal.

In 1622 the town was asked to contribute towards recovering the king's children's patrimony in Germany. His daughter, Elizabeth, had married the Elector Frederick, who was driven out of both Bohemia and the Rhenish Palatinate in 1618, which event started the Thirty Years' War. A letter to the Privy Council signed by the mayor, John Spark, Humphrey Blake, father of Admiral Blake, and William Hill said that trade was stagnant, the only vessels working were in the coal trade, and most inhabitants lived in poverty. It ended, 'We shall be ready to collect such sums as are offered.' Frederick never recovered his lost lands but his two sons, Prince Rupert and Prince Maurice, both professional soldiers, became famous figures after coming to England to fight for the King in the Civil War.

Charles I

The earliest Receiver's account in Charles I's reign is for 1626-7, the next for 1639-40, then there is a partial account for 1644 and a full account for 1646, by when the Civil War was over. Without these, details of everyday life are lacking.

In 1626 Goodwife Daniells paid 10s. towards a £1 fine for brewing without a licence. She could brew for her household but not sell the ale. Selling ale from a private house was called 'tippling'. John Popham was fined 3s. 4d. for 'beinge found in an ale house at unlawful howre', presumably during the time of a church service. Another common offence was selling short weight bread. In 1626 Nathaniel Pie was fined 1s. 'for that his bread was not wayt'. Some good news arrived on 18 October 1626 when a messenger was paid 2s. 6d. to read a proclamation announcing that the king had 'dismissed the Benevolence [i.e. tax] which should have been gathered'.

In July 1627 John Robins, another messenger, was paid 2s. 6d. for reading a proclamation announcing that grain and all kinds of food could be sent to 'the Isle of Ree or Rochelle', but next year a Puritan fanatic murdered the Duke of Buckingham and Rochelle was never relieved. Buckingham's policies were costly, inconsistent and unsuccessful, and his unpopularity was so great that opposition to the Crown was already serious.

15

THE SIEGE OF BRIDGWATER

Bridgwater was represented in Charles I's third Parliament of 1628-9 and was thus aware of the political struggle for the Petition of Right. During the King's personal rule from 1629 to 1640 close contacts would be made between leading townsmen such as Robert Blake and the local gentry. Both Edward Popham of Huntworth and Sir Thomas Wroth of Petherton Park had been Bridgwater's Members of Parliament but the Pynes of Curry Mallet, the Rogers of Cannington, the Bulls of Shapwick and John Pym of Brymore were all Presbyterians. The one adviser closely tied to the Court was Edmund Wyndham, who was no friend to the Puritans.

In 1639 the town gave Wyndham sugar loaves costing £1 16s. 0d., and later a salmon worth 7s. 6d. These small presents were followed by silver plate costing £43 15s. 10d. The payments can probably be linked with £21 'fees for our mortmain business'. Since the King was employing various devices, including reviving old laws, to raise money without summoning Parliament, this probably explains the gifts. They cost over £88 but apparently the town avoided the mortmain penalty, which may explain why Wyndham was chosen as Bridgwater's M.P. for the Long Parliament in 1640, the only member in Somerset who was a courtier. All the others wanted reforms and Wyndham held monopolies, one of the abuses being attacked, and this led to his expulsion and replacement by Thomas Smyth.

In 1640 there was a high degree of unity amongst the Commons, but once the basic reforms had been achieved and the Prerogative Courts abolished, the most active reformers embarked on a more extreme policy and in 1641 the Commons divided in a way which foreshadowed the sides in the Civil War. Sir Thomas Wroth described the attempt to arrest five Members as an attack on British liberties and supporters of his declaration vowed themselves willing to defend Parliament with arms if necessary.

Both sides prepared for war, usually said to have started when the King raised his standard at Nottingham on 22 August 1642. But fighting had already begun in Somerset on 2 August at Marshall's Elm when John Pyne, advancing from Somerton towards Glastonbury, encountered Royalists commanded by Lunsford, a professional soldier. News of Pyne's defeat must have been disheartening for Bridgwater only a few miles away.

But the countryside was strongly Puritan and Hertford and the Royalists had to abandon the Mendips leaving the Roundheads in command of Somerset. The position was reversed next year when Hopton, having secured Cornwall, invaded the county in June 1643. He was joined by Hertford who took command. As Hopton moved north the opposition abandoned both Bridgwater and Taunton. The parliamentary forces concentrated at Bath under Waller but on 5 July 1643 were defeated at Lansdown, outside the city. By the month's end Rupert had captured Bristol and it seemed that the King was winning the war.

Bridgwater must have felt proud to hear that Robert Blake, who was born in the town (Fig. 36), had defended Lyme Regis against Prince Maurice. But, except for Gloucester, still being besieged by the King, the west of England was in Royalist hands. Prince Maurice superseded Hertford as royal commander in the west and concentrated his garrison troops in Bridgwater, leaving only 80 men in Taunton Castle. Parliament sent Blake from Lyme to seize Taunton, which he did and then defended against all odds.

The Royalists defeat at Marston Moor in July 1644 was followed by the Self Denying Ordinance by which all members of either House surrendered their commands in order to make way for the New Model Army commanded by Fairfax. Fairfax met the King's forces at Naseby in Northamptonshire on 14 June 1645 and inflicted a crushing defeat which virtually sealed his fate.

On 4 July 1645, as the New Model Army approached the Somerset border at Beaminster, the King still had a field army commanded by Goring in Somerset.

36 The Blake Museum in Blake Street, the house where Robert Blake was born. Originally a 15th-century hall house, it has been much altered over the years. At the end of Blake Street is an open stretch of Durleigh Brook and an old mill with some remains of machinery. This was being restored in the 1990s but was badly damaged by vandals.

Goring abandoned the siege of Taunton and sought to check the Roundhead advance. He had only about 7,000 men, whereas Fairfax commanded double that number. Chiefly through Goring's incompetence, Fairfax advanced to Langport without serious challenge. The battle of Langport on 10 July was fought at Pibsbury, east of the town. It was a short fight and the Royalists conceded victory early in the afternoon. The garrison made no attempt to hold Langport and the same day Fairfax directed his army towards Bridgwater. Some 2,000 Royalist infantry surrendered on the moors.

Fairfax simply by-passed the strong point at Boroughbridge, leaving a detachment under Colonel Okey to keep watch. The 140 men there surrendered three days later. Other Royalist troops must have been present between Bridgwater and Dunwear but they apparently offered no resistance. Fairfax placed his headquarters at Middlezoy on 10 July, moving it to Chedzoy next day. On Sedgemoor the soldiers camped near Penzoy Pound, occupying a site near the Bussex Rhine almost identical with that occupied by King James II's army in 1683.

By 13 July Colonel Holbourne had taken Sydenham House close to Bridgwater whilst Colonel Weldon detoured via Burrow Bridge to cross the river and occupy the rising ground at Hamp just beyond the town. To capture Bridgwater was a military necessity. Its defences appeared strong and theoretically might have held out for months but the Royalists were isolated. Roundhead forces were encircling the town and Roundhead ships patrolled Bridgwater Bay, and after the easy victory at Langport their morale must have been low. But the defences were formidable, the central arch of the bridge having been replaced with a drawbridge. During a wet summer the ditches round the town would be full and these were the principal defence, Bridgwater not being walled.

The inner defences comprised the castle moat backed by walls 12 to 16 feet thick but neglected from the time of Henry VIII; their condition in 1645 is unknown. Wyndham had 40 cannon and had had over two years to make preparations, nor was he without military experience. He had been accepting treasures, which the local gentry brought to the castle for security. The moat was about 30 feet wide 'which for a great part about the town, was every Tyde filled up to the brim with water' according to 'Josiah Sprigge', a description true of much of the moat during a period of spring tides. On the south Durleigh Brook was well supplied with water and the Town Ditch alongside Mount Street was fed by a stream.

Country folk, especially farmers, had had enough of warfare and formed a rudimentary organisation, the clubmen, whose object was to neutralise both armies. But their attitude in any situation was unpredictable. The townsmen were generally hostile towards Wyndham as they mostly supported the Puritan cause, but both Oldmixon and Sprigge thought the clubmen a danger to Fairfax.

They had recently met at Triscombe Stone in the Quantocks and at Penzoy Pound on Sedgemoor. On the morning of the Battle of Langport one of their leaders, called Willis, visited Fairfax, and used threatening speech. He was taken into custody but escaped. On the eve of the siege of Bridgwater Willis collected many clubmen carrying banners made of white sheets on Knowle Hill. Though he was busy, Fairfax rode over to meet them and said 'he came to protect them from the violence of war and to further peace by scattering the enemies of it'. Professor Underwood has identified Willis (named Hollis by Sprigge) as a Woolavington man. Willis was now disposed towards Parliament so the meeting passed off amicably and, as they rode back to Chedzoy, Fairfax's escort was startled by a volley fired as a salute by clubmen.

On Monday 14 July the Roundhead leaders had not finally decided on a siege, though preparations for it were advanced. Some troops 'cheerfully made their faggots', and, under Colonel Hammond's direction, constructed eight portable bridges 'betwixt 30 and 40 foot length, which … were of very great use to the Souldier in the storm'. Fairfax narrowly escaped drowning on 14 July. He and Cromwell were using a boat to inspect the dispositions between Hamp and Dunwear when they were almost capsized by the bore.

Massey was in command of Roundhead troops on the west bank, watching the area between the south and west gates in particular. He had six regiments with headquarters at Hamp. There were seven regiments on the east river bank, including Fairfax's own (the General's), Cromwell's (the Lieutenant General's) and those of two other famous commanders present, Sir Hardress Waller and Colonel Pride.

Several thousand horse must have been quartered in the Sedgemoor villages; the infantry numbered between 6,000 and 7,000. Fairfax also had many small calibre guns which would be distributed amongst the infantry. In describing the assembly of troops on 11 July Sprigge says, 'The whole army, horse and foot, with the Train, were drawn up in Weston-moor, otherwise called Pensy Pound.' Fairfax did not have a full siege train. For use in the field he would have had demi-culverins (9 lb. shot) and sakers (3½ lb. shot), with several guns of smaller calibre. He probably had a few heavier guns but nothing bigger than a culverin (18 lb. shot). For battering really solid defences very heavy cannon would be needed and moving such artillery over non-metalled roads was difficult normally but impossible after wet weather.

The defenders numbered about 2,000 men, enough for the task. Goring arrived after the Battle of Langport and went on to Barnstaple with 3,000 horse and for a time the Royalists deluded themselves into thinking that he might revive their flagging fortunes.

By Wednesday 16 July Fairfax had decided that the town must be stormed and on 18 July he held a council of war which decided to attack just before dawn on Monday 21 July. Sunday 20 July was a day of prayer. In the morning the men's resolution was strengthened by an address given by the famous preacher Hugh Peters and further inspiration came that afternoon from another chaplain called Bowles. At dusk all the troops quietly took up their stations.

Protocol demanded that the Governor be summoned to surrender the town before any attack and this was probably done on 20 July. Legend says that Lady

Wyndham fired a cannon shot in reply, narrowly missing Cromwell but killing a cornet by his side, but the story is too good to be true and similar tales were told of other places. The signal for the attack to begin was three shots fired from the east bank around two o'clock in the morning of Monday 21 July. Massey heard it on the west bank and immediately began a successful diversionary attack. The real attack developed on the north side of Eastover, where the portable bridges thrown over the ditch worked well, and troops rapidly entered the town. They seized the East Gate, lowered the drawbridge, and a squadron of horse cleared Eastover up to the main bridge, taking 600 prisoners.

The Royalists firing over the river poured 'grenades and slugs of hot shot' into Eastover and the whole area 'of goodly buildings' went up in flames. A summons to surrender was rejected and Roundhead batteries on the south bombarded the town, starting fires in Friarn Street and the neighbouring area as far as Pig Cross. A night of horror followed.

The next day the garrison was kept in a state of anxiety by a series of feint attacks and abandoned most of the defences. At 2 p.m. Fairfax declared a truce to allow women and children to leave, including Lady Wyndham. When the truce ended at four o'clock in the afternoon the Roundhead batteries opened fire using grenades and hot shot and starting a fresh conflagration. The situation was desperate and Wyndham sent a messenger, Tom Elliot, to ask what terms might be offered. At first Fairfax seemed inclined to demand unconditional surrender but Elliot, after some discussion, asked that further attack be withheld until he had seen the Governor again. He returned with a promise of submission on the condition that all should have their lives and freedom from plunder. Six hostages were sent out by the garrison and the town surrendered at eight o'clock the following morning.

At least 1,000 prisoners marched out. The victors also captured 44 barrels of gunpowder, 1,300 weapons, 44 guns, and four cwt. of match from the castle. Valuables deposited for safe-keeping by the Royalist gentry of Somerset, mainly silver plate, furniture and rich hangings, were sent to London to be sold. The sale resulted in 5s. each for the common soldiers, not a large reward for their efforts but, as pay was always weeks in arrears, probably welcome. The leaders were well rewarded by Parliament. Fairfax, who planned the campaign, benefited considerably. His second-in-command, Cromwell, was granted an estate. Their rewards were paid for from property sequestrated from Royalists.

John Tarleton, vicar of Ilminster, was amongst the prisoners taken, having come to minister to the defenders as a non-combatant. He was taken to London by boat and gaoled. Most of the other prisoners would have been allowed to disperse and some joined the Roundhead army.

A Receiver's Account for 1646-7 indicates what happened at the East Gate. The first entry notes that £2 13s. 0d. was spent 'on the Bridge at the east Gate'. Two further entries describe two quantities of 'chesle stones' (gravel) carried from the quay to the East Bridge at a cost of 5s. and 7s. 2d., the larger sum paying for 14 tons. The final entry is very clear: 'For taking up of the East Bridge

& filling of the Gap … £1 8s. 8d.' There is only one reference to destroying the defences: 'Three men for a dayes worke towardes the dismantleing of the Garrison … 3s. 0d.' The porters were paid 3s. 2d. for removing guns from the quay.

'Josiah Sprigge' was a pseudonym and his identity never determined with certainty, but it is believed he was a chaplain in the New Model Army. As an eye witness to the siege, his first remark on entering the town was, 'God be thanked, we found much more of it standing than we expected.'

The lord of the manor, Henry Harvey, had leased the castle and his property to Edmund Wyndham when he became Governor, and the Harveys recorded their losses which were published by Collinson in 1791. The list begins with 20 dwelling houses and 30 gardens 'pulled down and laid waste'. The most important

37 A 'tongue-in-cheek' drawing by Jack Lawrence illustrating scenes from the Civil War siege of Bridgwater.

comment comes from Fairfax, who was a humane and compassionate man. On 2 December 1647 he wrote to the Commission for Monthly Assessments pointing out that Bridgwater was assessed as one-third of the total value of the Hundred of North Petherton when its true proportion should be one-eighth. 'The said Towne,' he added, 'hath susteyned exceeding great losses by fire, almost one third part there of being burnt down to the ground in the late seidge.'

No source mentions the medieval hospital, which still stood close to the East Gate and was probably intact at the end of the siege. In 1697 it was sold to Thomas Dyke of Kingston, Doctor of Physic. The conveyance recites a description made in 1643: 'the site, circute and precinct of late dissolved House at Hospitall of St John's in Eastover, Bridgwater, Mansion House of said Hospitall and of church and chapell belonging to said Hospitall.'

Henry Mills, mayor in 1636, thought 120 dwelling houses had been destroyed. He referred to two piles of stone 'as yet left undisposed of', one near the bridge in a small sconce and the other against a wall near the Castle, 'about 50 feet in length and 5 or 6 foot in height'.

Although no records have survived it seems likely that the law courts functioned during the war, but economic life must have been seriously disrupted. There were food shortages whenever an army was in the neighbourhood, and the difficulty of running farms when men were being compelled to take up arms was obvious. The West Country cloth trade needed free access to London, where the cloth was sold, and this had become impossible to maintain.

Troops were paid for by Contribution Money levied by the party which happened to be in the ascendant. In Bridgwater, a Puritan town, levies were made by Royalists. Everyone now had to pay arbitrary taxes and risked being pressed into military service. Each party called the other side 'malignants'. Royalist rule was, for a time, tempered by local affiliation: Edmund Wyndham was a Somerset man, and above him was Lord Hertford, in command of the King's forces in the West, who came from Wiltshire but knew Somerset well.

Gone were the days when civilities were exchanged by opposing leaders. In June 1643 the Roundhead General Waller, rejecting a proposal to meet his opposite number, Hopton, used the phrase 'this war without an enemy' and assured him that 'hostility itself cannot violate my friendship to your person. But I must be true to the cause wherein I serve.' These were not merely polite phrases; they expressed Waller's true feelings.

Jack Lawrence made a light-hearted sketch illustrating scenes from the siege, which is shown in Fig. 37.

16

THE COMMONWEALTH

When the fighting ended in December 1646 most ordinary business continued. Twelve men were admitted as burgesses, each paying 3s. 4d. Two others without local qualification paid £5 each. The judges still came round, Judge Rolls staying at Shapwick, doubtless with the Bulls, and the town sent four sugar loaves plus a gallon of sack at a total cost of 8s. 4d. Fourteen loads of grinding stones arrived from Bristol.

Extensive repairs to the school cost £3 16s. 0d. The schoolmaster, Knowles, evidently a Puritan, was paid 16s. 8d. for preaching on two occasions. He and other lay preachers probably conducted services in the church. The vicar, John Devenish, retired in 1645 and was succeeded by the curate, George Wotton, who was never allowed to perform his pastoral duties. He eventually moved to Williton with his wife and six children to teach. On 1 January 1647 the Corporation took independent action and appointed their own minister, John Norman, whose wife was Humphrey Blake's daughter. The note concerning his appointment, signed by Humphrey Blake as mayor, ignores Wotton's existence and says that John Norman is appointed in succession to John Devenish. On his appointment 7s. 0d. was spent entertaining Norman with wine, sugar and biscuit in the Burgess Hall.

Several roads were repaired as were the stocks and 'the well in the street'. The arch of the North Gate was also repaired for £4 17s. 0d. The Bellman was given a new bell costing 8s. 0d. A new item appeared: associated with the garrison 'Candles for the Guard'. Allowing for 2 lb. per night, they cost £5 18s. 0d. from 13 December 1646 to 6 April 1647. The army guard also required food, coal, and turf. In November 1648, 30 bushels of coal cost £1 2s. 6d., carriage being 2s. 6d., turf was 2s. 0d. and two willies (baskets) 1s. 2d. A payment overdue since 1643 was settled: '31 lb. of candles delivered to John Lambert the Constable … at Mr Wyndham's first coming … to be Governor 10s. 4d.' The largest single payment for the army recorded in Bridgwater was for 400 pairs of hose and 400 pairs of shoes sent to Wells in 1644 (for the King) which cost £92 3s. 6d. plus 18s. 6d. carriage.

The Monthly Assessment or Contribution Money, started in 1643, continued as a regular levy for the army throughout the Commonwealth. The food alone for the soldiers cost £3 3s. 4d. in March 1648. A small celebration when the dragoons left in 1647 involved buying a gallon of wine for 2s. 8d. and spending 10d. on bread. The end of the garrison in 1651 is not even recorded. Many people must have gone hungry after the war and the poor were given 30 bushels of peas in 1648 at a cost of £2 5s. 0d.

More wandering preachers than ever seemed to visit, despite the town having its own minister. John Norman received £120 per annum until 1653 when it was reduced to £100. Visiting preachers were given dinner; Mr Haddridge and Mr Collier stayed at the castle during October 1650, and six dinners cost 13s. A single dinner usually cost at least 5s., and frequently more. In 1651 Mr Flanner was given a quart of sack (1s. 4d.), hay and provender for his horse (2s. 4d.), another quart of sack (1s. 6d.), and then £1 'for preaching here'. Often these sermons were preached at the castle. On 15 November 1650 Mr Collier's dinner when he preached there cost 5s., with a further 1s. 2d. for a quart of sack. He was paid £1 for preaching. Forms were sometimes carried between the castle and the Town Hall.

Augmentation Money was occasionally levied to help poor clergy: in 1648 it was noted as a grant of £15 and, in 1654, 15 townsmen contributed £11 'to give to the ministers'. The leading burgesses, Scaly, Andrews, Tuthill, Lyny, Haviland, Powe and Bickham, were included but Bere refused to donate, provoking the Receiver, John Lyney, to note: 'Recd of Mr Tho. Bere though voluntaryly subscribed 000.' Tithes were still being levied and in September 1650 the borough prosecuted for non-payment.

The borough's traditional privileges were jealously maintained. In 1648 the town paid £1 3s. 4d. to obtain an order from the Clerk of the Assizes discharging the townsmen from serving on any jury outside the borough. In 1650 a messenger was sent to the Sheriff 'to prevent the Towne from serving at quarter sessions'. The same year Judge Poole was given sweetmeats costing 12s. 6d. for his banquet, together with wine for 11s. 6d. and 2s. 6d. to ring the bells. During 1657-8 there was 'a man to Rake the streets a day before the Cessions 1s. 2d.', and in 1659-60 a trumpet fanfare which cost 10s. Although there is no word of explanation this could only have been to celebrate the Restoration of Charles II.

More mundane tasks undertaken during the Commonwealth included 'tidying up'. In 1649 this involved the porters 'heaving guns out of the street' for which they were paid only 6d. Seven years later they were paid 4s. for weighing 'the old guns which lay upon the Kay' and Mr Newborough then bought them for £4 16s. 0d., 24 cwt. at 4s. per cwt. In 1658 much old iron was sold including gates once used to cover the gutter at the West Gate.

Men were paid 17s. 6d. in 1657 for digging gravel and also making the ditch deeper in order to draw the water out of West Street. In 1658 digging round the West Gate Mount cost £1 3s. 10d. and C. Player, a builder, completed the alterations for £3 plus 9s. 6d. for four planks to lay over the ditch. Three men 'that cleaned the Castle Ditch' were paid 5s. 6d. in money, and beer.

One consequence of the Puritan laws was that travelling actors no longer came. Bear-baiting and cock-fighting were also suppressed. Yet in 1653 Achilles

Player, an iron worker, was paid 8s. 2d. for a bull ring weighing 24½ lb., 2s. 8d. for installing it, with 1s. 6d. for a 'piece of timber for the same' and 4s. 0d. for a bull rope. In 1658 somebody charged 4d. for splicing the bull rope – unsuccessfully – and a new rope cost 7s. 9d. Presumably both ring and rope were needed for market use, sometimes being the object called 'a bull collar'.

Swearing was illegal and enforced with a tariff of fines. This law must have survived the Restoration because fines for swearing were frequently imposed in Bridgwater during the 18th century. Most travel was forbidden on Sundays. In 1649 a man, Exon of Petherton, was fined 3s. 0d. 'for travelling into town with a horse on a saboth day'. In 1650 Robert Holcomb was fined 1s. 4d., and charged 10d. for horsemeat 'for stoping of a horse on a saboth day'.

The Civil War gave birth to British journalism and Bridgwater had its own correspondent, Mark Bell, who in 1650 was paid 'for a gratuity for sending of letters of newes for the Towne 11s. 0d.'. Dunster had been held by Francis Wyndham, younger brother of Edmund, until Blake took it in 1646, after which it was held by a Roundhead garrison that mutinied against Colonel Raymond in January 1648 because of lack of pay. The Receiver noted the 5s. spent sending Edward Deere to Dunster.

This kind of disaffection helped cause the Second Civil War which led to the King's execution. The Royalist defeat at Colchester in 1648 was celebrated in Bridgwater, where the ringers earned 10s. 0d., and later that year £1 was spent on 'Capt. Haviland & Capt. Ebsburyes souldiers upon a thanksgiving Day'. After the final victory Fairfax retired and Cromwell concentrated on the conquest of Ireland. As we have seen, Bridgwater records show much casual relief given to soldiers travelling to or from Ireland. In September 1649 the bell ringers received 6s. 0d. 'for ringing for a thanksgiving Day for a victory in Ireland'.

In July 1650 the Recorder was given a quart of sack when he brought the news that Cromwell had been made Lord General.

Puritan Rule

'The Rule of the Saints' came early in Bridgwater, with the vicar's exclusion in 1645. Although Bridgwater is considered a Puritan town its Puritan inhabitants were a minority, strong and sufficiently powerful to enforce their policy. The Puritans closed many alehouses but Bridgwater records provide no evidence of this. They were not against drinking and tended to be lavish with gifts of wine. In 1648 Sir Thomas Wroth was given two runlettes (two small casks) at a cost of £2 5s. 4d. plus 1s. carriage. The merchant who supplied it was Mr Goodridge. Much wine went to travelling preachers and official guests. In April 1651 eight quarts of sack were given to Lord Rule who had come to hold the Assizes. At the same time four quarts were given to General Blake and another seven to various ministers who had come here to preach. The total cost was £1 5s. 4d.

The Blake family became prosperous after they came to Bridgwater in the late 16th century but little is known of their dealings. Robert dropped an academic career in Oxford to manage the family business when his father died in 1625. For the next 15 years his activities remain a mystery but the Blakes were merchants and merchants often owned ships.

All men over the age of 18 were required to promise to be 'true and faithful to the Commonwealth of England, as it is now established, without a King or House of Lords', a promise known as 'the Engagement'. The Mayor of Bridgwater refused to make it in 1650 so was excluded from office and replaced by 'George Badon'. George Baden ('gent.') gave 20s. in 1661 as a freewill offering to Charles II.

'The Saints' sometimes quarrelled among themselves. John Norman got into serious trouble for not having 'taken the Engagement'. Parliament received a petition signed by the mayor, Recorder and others in Bridgwater, reporting his disobedience, and Parliament ordered him to comply on 1 July 1649 or face expulsion: 'if he will not sign, he must leave the town within ten days and stay ten miles away.' He would also have to give £500 in his own recognisance and find two sureties of £250 each. Norman was thus bullied into acceptance in 1649 but in 1651 was in trouble again when the town spent £8 to send Mr John Gilbert to London 'about Mr Norman'. However he survived until the Restoration.

Two important things happened to Bridgwater during the final years of the Commonwealth. John Desborough was the general commanding the West Country when the constitutional experiment broke down. He had visited Bridgwater and £3 6s. 4d. was spent entertaining him with wine and food in 1656. That year, the mayor wrote to him pointing out that during the siege of 1645 'an almshouse was uttorly demolished' and asked for modest help (permission to use some loose stones) in rebuilding it. For this help 'the soules of many poore shall bless you,' he wrote. Desborough sent the letter to London and received a favourable reply within a week. In 1657 the £100 legacy left to the town by Robert Blake was used to purchase 'Jacobs Land', a piece of ground measuring three acres and two half burgages on the north side of Eastover. It is the area near St John's Church.

In 1647 it cost 2s. 6d. to repair the mace of Stephen Harris, one of the town sergeants. A few years later there was a move to enhance civic dignity by obtaining new silver-gilt maces which resulted in the three maces kept at the Town Hall. The largest was ordered somewhat casually from a famous London goldsmith, Thomas Maundy, at the Sign of the Grasshopper in Foster Lane. He charged £25 6s. 3d. for a mace containing 56½oz. of silver, and 5s. 6d. for its case. The mace had to be made 'better than ordinary'. Maundy had to wait so long for payment that he was afraid of making a loss on the deal and in October 1653 wrote to Humphrey Blake saying, 'I thought I should abin payd when I had don my worke.' He was paid, eventually, in December. Somebody must have been clumsy since this new mace needed repair before it had been paid for: 'Oct 23 Mr Foote for mending the New Mace 5s. 3d.'

On 18 April 1654 the old mace was sent to Taunton at a cost of 9d. Its sale price is unrecorded but on 25 August two new maces were purchased for £25

16s. 0d. The town also bought a silver tankard costing £5 14s. 0d., then paid 5s. 0d. to have the town arms engraved on it. Carriage was 1s. 0d., implying that the work was not done in Bridgwater even though two goldsmiths were working here in 1661.

In 1660 spurs for hanging up the maces cost 4s. 8d. and were presumably placed in the Town Hall. That year Christopher Roberts, one of the Bridgwater smiths, was paid 1s. 0d. 'for righting the mace'. 'New making' was necessary in 1660 after the Restoration, when Commonwealth symbols would be erased and a crown formed by small triangular pieces of silver added to the Maundy mace around its top edge; it is called 'the Warwick Mace' for reasons unknown.

In 1674 there were two further items of expenditure on the maces:

> Mr Roberts for changing the maces 5s. 0d.
> Mr Ferdinando Anderson for Righting the maces in Mr Pettit's yeare 4s. 0d.

Edmund Pettit was mayor in 1674-5; he issued farthing tokens in 1654 but they do not name his business. He did not contribute to the freewill offering of 1661. The second goldsmith's name was probably Anderton because a goldsmith called John Anderton was able to contribute £2 to the freewill offering of 1661, when Christopher Roberts only gave 2s.

17

Town Life under Charles II

The Restoration led to the Receiver making two payments: £2 'for a hogshead of Beer given Captain Harvey souldiers on the Rejoicing day for the King', and £3 to Edward Sealy 'for his charges when the King was proclamed'. Soldiers were still here in 1678 when Horsey paid a contribution towards 'disbanding the army'; Haygrove and Hamp made similar payments in 1681-2. It cost £424 to run the town in 1661-2 and £446 in 1674-5, about the same as during the Commonwealth.

Members of Parliament selected to represent Bridgwater were drawn from members of the gild merchant, some of whom formed the Common Council. The right to vote was disputed after the Restoration and the report following an election petition in 1669 said that the franchise belonged to the Corporation, i.e. the Mayor, Aldermen and Capital Burgesses, a total of 24. The petition had been made by Peregrine Palmer and did not involve bribery. He claimed that some of the 24 who had voted were disqualified by the Corporation Act because they had held Conventicles in their homes. As a result of this action Sir Francis Rolle was unseated and Palmer was returned.

An unusual document concerns offerings made 'In pursuance of an Act for a free and voluntary present to his Majesty', a collection made in 1661 with 172 names on a list which included 11 gentlemen, 14 widows, one spinster, 60 husbandmen, 13 yeomen and 11 men of unstated occupation. The remainder worked at various trades. The large number engaged in agriculture suggests a rural township but most lived outside Bridgwater in the hamlets of Dunwear, East Bower, Haygrove, Chilton, Horsey and Hamp. Only 14 farmworkers lived in the town. The remaining 64 were engaged in a variety of occupations: innholders (8), cordwainers (7), woollen drapers (5), mariners (5), mercers (5), butchers (4), carpenters (3), blacksmiths (2), goldsmiths (2), grocers (2), tailors (2), cooper (1), courier (1), cutler (1), fuller (1), glazier (1), barber (1), haberdasher (1), helyar (1), joiner (1), maltster (1), mason (1), merchant (1), scrivener (1), soap boiler (1) and tanner (1).

Four of these tradesmen issued tokens ('brass farthings'), suggesting that that they were busy and needed small change for their customers. Another, James Safford had tokens struck in 1658 and is described as a mercer in 1661. He gave 10s. to the loyal fund. A leading townsman, he was Receiver in 1659,

1660 and 1661. John Palmer, a woollen draper, had tokens struck in 1664 with 'The Draper's Arms' on the obverse. His free gift in 1661 was 2s. Christopher Roberts had tokens struck in 1664 with the device of a covered cup and the date. A second goldsmith, John Anderson, who gave £2, was a Quaker who eventually died in prison in 1685.

A total of £40 6s. 3d. was collected for the 'free gift' to Charles II. The largest single donation, £3, came from Edward Sealy, a mercer. One innholder, John Lyney, Receiver from 1653-5, gave £2 13s. 0d. and Benjamin Blake, 'gentleman', gave 20s., as did George Bawden. He, like Blake, had served as mayor during the Commonwealth. Only one member of the cloth trade is listed, Edward Watts, a fuller, who gave 1s. Others on the list include E. Petit, G. Crane, grocer, T. Turner, haberdasher, T. Bickham, surgeon, and R. Turner, woollen draper, all members of the Common Council in 1672. George Crane was elected an M.P. for Bridgwater in 1698. The most touching gifts are 'widow's mites'. Mrs Ellis and Mrs Grady, described as widows, each gave 2d.

The Prelude to Rebellion

Receivers' Accounts during Charles II's reign record diverse activities including street cleaning, repairing the whipping post and stocks, and major repairs to the Town Hall in 1669. In 1682 the new Cheese Market established in the middle of St Mary Street generated rent of £5 per annum. Superficially such activities suggest that all was quiet and peaceful but this was far from being the case.

The 1661 Corporation Act decreed that only persons who received communion according to Church of England rites could become councillors. The 1662 Act of Uniformity introduced the new Prayer Book and led to the expulsion of 2,000 Puritan clergy. The Conventicle Act of 1664 authorised severe penalties for persons who attended religious meetings using rites other than those of the Church of England. The Five Mile Act of 1665 forbade any clergyman or schoolmaster from coming within five miles of any corporate town unless he swore a declaration that he would never try to make any alteration in Church or State. All completely violated promises issued by the king at Breda on the eve of his return. The Church, sensing victory following its suppression during the Commonwealth, was too strong for the king to hold back the tide. His sole attempt, the Declaration of Indulgence in 1672, allowed freedom of worship but only lasted 12 months.

The four penal Acts made an enormous difference to Puritan towns such as Bridgwater and Taunton, whose ministers were sent to Ilchester gaol to freeze in winter and be stifled in summer. When John Norman was freed he defied the law and continued to preach. Richard Whiting, a Quaker of Nailsea, summed up the causes of the Monmouth rebellion in one sentence: 'Had liberty of conscience been granted sooner ... there might have been no rebellion in the west.'

During the last years of Charles II's reign Bridgwater and Taunton suffered badly. In Taunton Stephen Timewell, a shopkeeper who was mayor in 1682-3, was mainly responsible for destroying the great centre of Puritan gatherings known as Paul's Meeting, together with the Baptist Meeting, and making a great bonfire of the woodwork in July 1683. A similar attack was made on the Puritans in Bridgwater, the evidence coming from State Papers where it is noteworthy that Puritans are called not 'Dissenters' but 'Fanatics'. It was made by Lord Stawell, who rode over the Quantocks from Cothelstone. He searched for arms and found a few which he locked in HM Customs warehouse. He also found 'the Fanatics' house of worship', which he described as being 'round like a cockpit' with seats for 400. Stawell had the place smashed up and piled the timber 14 feet high on the Cornhill and then placed pulpit and cushion on top. On 7 July 1683, with much drinking of royal toasts, there was a great bonfire.

Other evidence of Dissenters being pressurised comes from John Oldmixon. Writing about Robert Blake, whom he always calls 'the General', he says, 'His brother Humphrey, with whom I lived when I was a boy, suffered so many hardships for Nonconformity in the latter end of the reign of King Charles II that he was forced to sell the little estate left him by the General, scarce £200 a year, and transport himself to Carolina.'

The year 1683 was one of party violence and religious intolerance provoked by the Whigs. Their object was to prevent James, Duke of York, a Roman Catholic, from becoming king on the death of his brother. If Charles had had a legitimate heir, the situation would not have arisen, so unscrupulous Whig politicians tried to foment a belief that Charles had secretly married and that James, Duke of Monmouth, was legal heir to the throne. When Louis XIV decided to provide Charles with the revenue no longer available to him from the English Parliament, some extremists began to plot rebellion. Government agents kept a close watch on Bridgwater.

On Fair Day early in 1683, presumably at the Lent Fair, scandalous ballads abusing the Duke of York were distributed. Two members of the Common Council reported this to the mayor who only laughed and the incident was reported to London. On 19 June Lord Stawell wrote to the Secretary of State saying Bridgwater was as bad as Taunton 'and they have forfeited their Charter'. On 14 July, a week after Stawell's destructive raid, the Bishop of Bath and Wells, no friend to the Dissenters, mischieviously wrote to say he had met the Corporation of Bridgwater, who 'are resolved to lay their charter at the King's feet'. The Recorder, Sir John Malet, petitioned the Crown and asked that the ancient rights and privileges of the borough be preserved. It was already too late and on 30 July four members of the Common Council went to London at a cost of £30, plus £1 to hire a horse for the mayor, John Gilbert. A Dissenter, he was outweighed by the other three, Massey, Francis and Baker. Massey had received a letter from the Secretary of State telling him he could send the charter with a covering letter. On 22 September receipt of the charter was acknowledged and a note made that the borough seal would soon be brought by 'Captain Massey'. Before the end of September a new charter had been drafted. There is no complete copy of the text but it obviously contained a clause making all members of the Common Council removable at the king's pleasure.

On 3 October another delegation of three councillors went to London 'about the charter' at a cost of £41 1s. 6d. Massey, who became mayor at Michaelmas, was accompanied by Francis and Knight. Far into the next century the Whigs maintained that the charter's surrender had been completely illegal.

The stage for the 1685 rebellion

Depression in the cloth industry – 500 men in the Taunton area were said to be out of work – may have predisposed the nonconformist weavers to violent action, but nothing entirely explains why the Puritans came to accept Monmouth as the champion of Protestantism.

18

THE MONMOUTH REBELLION, 1685

In 1680 the Duke of Monmouth openly defied the king by holding a pseudo-royal progress through part of Somerset but not Bridgwater. Anthony Ashley Cooper, 1st Earl of Shaftesbury, had drawn Monmouth into a web of intrigue and may have visited Bridgwater because he owned Pawlett Manor. Monmouth first visited Bridgwater on 21 June 1685 when his rebellion was ten days old; he only stayed long enough to hear himself proclaimed king from the High Cross. His star seemed to be in the ascendant.

In reality the struggle to make him king had started in 1678 and failed in 1681 when French gold enabled Charles II to govern without Parliament. Shaftesbury had fled to Holland where he died. Monmouth remained in England planning rebellion with the Whig Council of Six. In 1684, losing his nerve, he fled to Holland where he was surrounded by a group of desperate men who, after Charles II died, urged him to invade England. According to Oldmixon, 'The Duke of Monmouth himself, and Mr Fletcher, thought they were in no condition to make such an attempt, but he heard arguments such as 'all the West of England would be for him', and 'there would be no fighting … the Guards, and others who adhered to the King, would melt to nothing before him'. Finally, it was probably Ferguson 'the Plotter' who talked him into taking the most dangerous gamble of all with little preparation and totally inadequate resources.

Landing at Lyme Regis on 11 June 1685, he advanced towards Bristol gathering many thousands of followers, but he turned aside, first from Bristol, then Bath, and returned to Bridgwater on 1 July. His men had deserted in droves but between 3,000 and 4,000 remained and were now trapped. The king's forces under Lord Feversham had reached Somerton on 3 July and on 5 July advanced to Westonzoyland.

That day Monmouth received information concerning the royal dispositions from a man who knew the moor. He was sent back to make closer observations and the duke climbed St Mary's church tower, from which he could just discern Dumbarton's regiment. Learning that royal troops were stationed behind the Bussex rhine, he decided to attempt a night attack.

'About seven o'clock,' says Oldmixon, 'the drums beat in Bridgwater for a rendezvous in Castle Field, and several meetings were privately held, where the officers went to prayers for a blessing on their undertaking; some of them praying in red coats and Jack boots, a sight that had not been seen in England before, since the Restoration …'. Then, at 'About eleven o'clock at night, I saw the Duke of Monmouth ride out, attended by his Life-Guard of Horse, and though then but a boy, observed an alteration in his look which I did not like; for not being able to judge of the goodness or badness of his cause, I ran down with the stream, and was one of its well-wishers.' Oldmixon was only 13 years old in 1685. These comments were written in 1730. His *History* shows that he believed there was a real Popish Plot but never accepted the story of Monmouth's birth being legitimised by a secret marriage of Charles II. By 1680, however, the Duke of York 'continued to shew by all his conduct, abroad and at home, that he was the most obstinate and inveterate enemy of liberty and religion'. Oldmixon's account of the battle of Sedgemoor is tolerably accurate.

The Hoare's Bank narrative, written by Andrew Paschall, vicar of Chedzoy, says that Oglethorp's patrol, riding over the moor towards the Poldens, just missed the head of the column of rebels, who left the road and took a track into the moor. Their route was obliterated by construction of the M5 motorway, which included removing the mound of a post-mill that only worked between 1400 and 1420 but was a landmark at the track entrance at the time. Marsh Lane, still an unmetalled track, was detoured to avoid passing a royalist house.

The rebel march towards the Bussex rhine continued silently until their guide missed the point for them to cross the Langmoor rhine, and before half the column had crossed a pistol shot gave the alarm. The royalist outpost fell back to the Upper Plungeon, the crossing over the Bussex rhine, everything depending on their ability to hold it. Oldmixon, who noted that Somerset people hated Feversham, wrote 'The alarm reached Weston, where Feversham was safe a-bed, and made not so much haste into the field as to forget setting his cravat-string at a little paltry looking-glass in one of the cottages.' The rebels' failure to seize the crossing meant that the foot were thrown into confusion and met their own horse riding off instead of lining the rhine along the front of the royal camp. Most of the fighting occurred towards the section held by Dumbarton's regiment near the Upper Plungeon, troops Monmouth had seen through his 'perspective glass' from St Mary's church tower the previous day. According to Oldmixon, he had been colonel of that regiment, and remarked: 'I know those men will fight and if I had them, I would not doubt of success.' Many casualties were inflicted on the king's troops by the rebel guns.

Feversham's artillery, 17 guns, were sited on the left flank but needed on the right. Oldmixon describes how they were moved: 'Mews, Bishop of Winchester, who was fitter for a Bombadier than a Bishop … very officiously put his coach horses to the artillery that was planted in the direct road from Weston to Bridgwater causing those guns to be drawn down against the Duke's Foot.' Mews had fought in the Royalist army throughout the Civil War. At this point in the battle, according to Oldmixon, the foot stood their ground crying out, 'Ammunition, Ammunition, for the Lord's Sake Ammunition, which not coming and the Duke and Grey being one with the Horse, the Foot fled after them, and the King's Horse pursuing them, kills twice as many as were slain in the fight.' Oldmixon add,: 'I was upon the spot before the dead were buried and, young as I was, observed the slain to be more on the King's part than on the Duke's, as they were distinguished to the person who carry'd me thither, by one of the King's soldiers.' Again as an eye witness, he notes: 'About 4 o'-clock Monday morning, the Run-aways began to come into Bridgwater and I saw many of them so wounded, that I wondered how they could reach so far: one fellow, particularly, had scarce lain himself down on a bulk, when he died away of his wounds.'

Monmouth made his escape whilst his Foot were still fighting. The slaughter continued long after the battle was over. At 7 a.m. Captain Dummer wrote, 'Our men are still killing them in the corne and hedges and ditches whither they are crept.' Louis Duras, Earl of Feversham, a French Protestant and continental soldier who had no compunction about killing prisoners, soon set about hanging them. 'Captain Adlam,' says Oldmixon, 'had about 100 broad pieces quilted in his buff-coat. He was so mortally wounded that he could have survived it, but Feversham would not trust to that, so he ordered him to be hanged the next day, and he was the first whom he hung up in chains on the Moor between Weston and Bridgwater where was a range of gibbets so decorated to a good length.' This continued until Bishop Mews intervened, saying, 'This is murder in the law and your lordship may be called to account for it ... [They] must be tried before they can be put to death.' The incident is not recorded by Oldmixon.

The church register at Westonzoyland records that 500 prisoners were brought into the church, of whom five died of their wounds, but only 238 were noted by Adam Wheeler of the Wiltshire Militia as he sat in the churchyard using his drum as a desk. The other 262 were either brought in when he had gone off duty or the church register records a poor estimate.

The Bloody Assize which followed was a travesty of justice. The judges were simply commissioners carrying out the king's orders. 'The country for 60 miles together,' says Oldmixon, 'from Bristol to Exeter, had a new and terrible sort of sign-posts and signs, gibbets and heads and quarters of its slaughtered inhabitants'. Nearly 4,000 rebels were presented for trial, and 890 were sentenced to transportation, of whom 612 are known to have sailed. Another 304 were executed. The nine men hanged at Bridgwater were Davis, a woolcomber of Bampton, Francis, Guppy, Harman, Harris of Huntspill, Ingram of Thurloxton, Moggridge of Chard, and Stodgell and Trott, both of North Petherton.

Seventeen rebels came from Bridgwater and at least six were imprisoned there but in only four instances is the man's occupation known: joiner, tailor, mercer and yeoman. Three were hanged, George Condick, William Cooper and William Meade, and nine sentenced to transportation to Barbados: George Carrow, Thomas Dennis, William Drew, Henry Meyer, Robert Teape, William Tiverton, Joseph Vinicot, John Wall and George Mihill, who died at sea. Transportation meant ten years (instead of the normal five) of slavery on a sugar plantation.

38 The Marycourt before alterations were made towards the end of the 19th century.

39 The Marycourt after the initial alterations. In the early 20th century the bay was removed, the doorway widened and the windows were replaced with shop-fronts. For some years it was a small shopping mall, but recently it has been converted to a restaurant.

The transported men were sold for between £10 and £15 each to plantation owners, whose names are known. At court there was a scramble to obtain prisoners, the queen being granted 100, and six other prominent personages acquiring between 50 and 200 each. As it happened, all were pardoned in 1690 after the Glorious Revolution.

Pardons at the time were rather a different matter. Oldmixon says Jeffreys 'glutted his avarice as well as his cruelty, taking between 14 and 15,000 pounds of Edmund Prideaux Esquire', the only instance in which Jeffreys is known to have done this. The normal price for a pardon was about £60 but in many cases several hundred pounds were extracted from a rebel's family. Five Bridgwater men were pardoned: William Coleman, Roger Hoare, John Palmer, John Webber and Edward Whitehead. Oldmixon points out that John Webber was excepted from the general pardon but alive in 1730 and Bridgwater's Town Clerk. Palmer deserved his pardon because the rebels had forced him to show them the way at some point on their march after capturuing him. Roger Hoare, who had pleaded guilty, and Edward Whitehead were reprieved under the gallows, according to Locke. 'The Duke's quarters were in the Castle,' says Oldmixon. 'Here he raised more voluntary contributions than in any other place, by the management of Mr Roger Hoare, Mr William Coleman and other inhabitants.' Their pardons came through in 1686. Next year James dismissed seven members of the Common Council in Bridgwater, nominating seven replacements, one of whom was Roger Hoare, a mercer by trade. He was a Dissenter, as were three others appointed, J. Gilbert, R. Balch and W. Bicknell, who was also made Town Clerk. James II was evidently preparing the ground for his Declaration of Indulgence.

Only faint echoes of the Rebellion appear in the Bridgwater Archives. On Oak Apple Day, 29 May, the trumpeters were paid 7s. 6d., which sounds loyal enough. An undated entry reads: 'John Boone for Beere for the Towne being opon duty night and day when Monmouth was coming ... 10s. 0d.', and: 'To the Executioner & takeing the Ropes of the Galows ... 1s. 0d.'

In 1686 the king visited the site of the battle in person and then visited Bridgwater. The streets were specially cleaned for the occasion:

> Sep 2 To Samuell Goos for 2 dayes worke about the streats when the King came to town ... 2s. 0d.
>
> To Will Stone ... 6d.
>
> To the Porters for removing tember wh lay in the street ... 2d.

On 29 September, following the king's visit, the town decided 'to drawe a petition in ordr to move the dragoons then quartered in towne ... 10d.' Apparently the dragoons had been quartered in the Common Hall: 'for Irron barrs for the Gratte at the Burges Hall for the soldiers ... 11s. 3d.' They also purchased a weight of coals for the Guard House together with turf, candles, three candlesticks, a lantern and an hour glass.

Modern historians would probably agree with Oldmixon on two matters: firstly, it was an error of judgement to proclaim Monmouth king, and, secondly,

Ferguson 'the Plotter' was probably a double agent. The 17 Bridgwater men 'presented' as rebels. seems insignificant compared with the 400 Taunton men who were indicted. Perhaps many rebels from Bridgwater and its immediate area managed to reach their homes without being caught.

Several myths have grown out of the battle. One, started in 1685, claimed that a rebel called Hucker, a Taunton man, fired the pistol which gave the alarm. The story was put about by the losing side, anxious to explain their defeat by treachery. Modern scholars are convinced the shot was fired by a soldier who was part of the large outpost stationed around Chedzoy and seem to have buried the original legend. Judge Jeffreys is firmly embedded in Bridgwater folklore although there is no evidence that he ever came here. The building where he is said to have stayed is of doubtful age (Figs 38 & 39) and he could not have seen the Cornhill from it. Anyone who wanted to watch men hanged there would, like Colonel Kirke, have stayed at the *Swan*. There is a story about a local athlete called Jan Swayne who was held by a group of soldiers on the Poldens. At night, by the camp fire, they invited him to demonstrate his prowess. He did so with a huge hop, step and jump, and vanished into the darkness. 'Jan Swayne's Leaps' are marked by stones near the edge of Loxley Woods adjacent to what is now the main road to Bath.

The story that the royal troops hanged the vicar of Westonzoyland from his own church tower is a modern invention. The Reverend Thomas Perrott held that living for a record length of time and was still there in 1700.

19

TOWN LIFE 1685-1774

After the Rebellion many things remained unchanged – stocks and whipping post were kept in repair, arms-racks were still provided in the Town Hall and bills carried by the Watch. The chain remained across the bridge but a turnpike was installed in 1688. Old tombstones were still used to bridge the stream at the West Gate. That year stones were cleared from the river for £2 14s. 0d., 27 men being paid 2s. each and 12s. given them for brandy and beer. The Bowling Green is mentioned frequently and in 1692 a new frame for the roller cost 9s. After many years without any entertainment being recorded, in 1695 rope dancers at the Town Hall were paid 1s.

Town running costs appear to be decreasing, from £273 in 1681 to £212 in 1694, but the Receiver's accounts die out before 1700 so this decline may be a change in accounting practice. Borough dignity was being maintained, for in 1692 a new staff and bell for the Bellman were provided for 4s.

The Town Hall's appearance was also improved. In 1692-3, 'for painting the wainscott railes etc in the Town Hall' the cost was £1 and in 1691-2:

> for colouring 72 yeardes of wainscot 3 times over in Oyl ... £3. 10s. 0d.
> for casting and gilding the 3 maces on the chimny ... 10s. 0d.
> for writing the names of the maiors and Recorders ... 16s. 0d.
> for painting 22 coats of arms and some empty sheildes ... £1 16s. 0d.

These panels are still on the Charter Hall walls but are covered by modern panels. The shields of arms have become unrecognisable.

Decorating constables' staves is a very old tradition. In 1683 nine were painted at a cost of £1 7s. 0d. Presumably they were only used on ceremonial occasions. A collection of 19th-century staves is displayed in the town's museum.

Repairs to the Bridge and Quay, 1697-1711

Trade revival in the late 17th century inspired an Act of 1693 (Fig. 40) designed to improve port facilities by re-building both the east and west quays. They were to be enlarged but 'not exceeding in length on each side 150 yards'. A detailed survey was made and solid foundations were laid using lias. Some came out of the river but much was quarried at Pibsbury. Oak was the main timber, used especially for posts and vertical supports, and shides (timber split into thin planks) for horizontal facing. John Trott made all the rope required and 16,000 bricks were supplied by Christophers for 10s. per thousand. 'The little house on the bridge' was also repaired. By 1701 £2,057 had been spent, much of it borrowed from leading townsmen such as Dr Morgan who lent £230. A new scale of dues was authorised to pay for all the work.

The trade revival continued for several years so that Defoe described Bridgwater as 'a very considerable town and port'. He summarised the local imports: coal from Swansea, heavy goods and merchandise from Bristol and 'Iron, lead, oil, wine, hemp, flax, pitch, tar, grocery and dye stuffs.' Later writers added that twenty sail, at least, were employed in the coal trade.

Thomas Cox's *Magna Britannia* (1727) mentions that 'ships of 100 tons may, and often do' ride about the bridge at Bridgwater and says that 40 ships were registered there. Compulsory registration came in 1786 when 33 ships were on the register, the same number that the Musgrave Papers quote in 1701. Spencer, in *The Compleat English Traveller* (1771), noted that Bridgwater's foreign trade was chiefly with Portugal and Newfoundland, adding that there were also contacts with the Straits, Virginia and the West Indies. He also commented on the large quantity of wool imported from Ireland.

Control of berthing must have been difficult, especially since there was only one crane. Strachie's map, c.1730, suggests the presence of a loading bay on the west quay near the bridge. In 1772 the Water Bailiff ordered one vessel belonging to Samuel Glover, a brickyard owner, to be moved. The master refused to obey so the Water Bailiff cut the cable and confiscated the few yards left hanging. This was flagrantly illegal and the borough had to pay costs plus £15 compensation to Glover.

Householders living on the waterfront apparently owned the quay in front of their property. A list from 1714 ends: 'Doeing the top course of Dr Morgan's', and quotes £9 4s. 11d. as the cost he was charged. This was not unfair as in 1706 he had been paid £100 'for the use of the quay'. The Roman Catholic church is on the site of his house in what is now Chapel Street.

40 Front page of the Act to repair the bridge and quay.

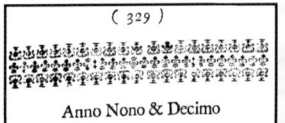

41 Preamble to the Act to repair the bridge and quay.

The New Almshouse

A new almshouse was built on the site of the South Gate in 1685, now three terraced houses, Nos 1, 3 and 5 Taunton Road (Fig. 42). Perhaps these houses contain bricks salvaged from the almshouse because their colour is yellowish

42 Three terraced houses at the start of Taunton Road which may have been built from bricks reclaimed when the South Gate almshouse was demolished. Detail of part of the wall can be seen inset.

and not the typical red Bridgwater brick. Clay taken from the Parrett's banks contains sand and slime and fires to a pale yellow ochre colour. The new building could hold many people and must reflect a change in policy. Hitherto poor relief, comprising money, food and clothing, was given to people living in their own homes and called 'outdoor relief'. This building meant that indoor relief was now to play a part in administering the Poor Law. Unfortunately the rules governing the lives and diet of inmates are unknown but the new building cost £345, about £50 less than the annual cost of governing the town. Obviously it was an important enterprise.

Four leading townsmen paid for almost everything; Mr Balch gave £200 and timber worth £4 13s. 0d. which came from the *Globe Inn*; Mr Roberts £61 4s. 6d., Mr Hoare £36, and Mr Parson £35 18s. 11d. Other gifts of materials included 48 feet of rafters, 125 bricks and 4,700 old tiles. An important development was extensive use of bricks made in Bridgwater. George Balch supplied 23,000 at a cost of £11. Hitherto the Castle Street houses have usually been considered the earliest use of local brick but the almshouse was erected 25 years earlier. The tiles were also made in Bridgwater, as were the old tiles which were re-used.

Limestone was burned to make lime. Robert Percy and his men were paid 'for repairing the Lyme Kill and digging the foundation of the hous ... £1 12s. 0d.' Further work on the kiln was done by 'a Welshman' (one day) and Thomas Baston (eight days). All workmen seem to have been paid at a flat rate of 1s. a day, though beer was probably provided too, but only mentioned in the case of Francis Witch, who got 6s. 4d. and some other payments, and Vincent Bolding, who got 6d. Two weighs of coal were purchased from John Venicot for £2 14s. 0d. for lime-burning, which was done by 'Bennet the Lime Burner'. He was paid £12 9s. 0d. – at 1s. a day this represents ten months' continuous work but perhaps lime burning involved night work too.

Some 23 workmen were named, a fairly large labour force. The title 'Mr' is reserved for town merchants, Mr Smith for instance being paid £25 18s. 3d., and Mr Ovars (or Evars) £5 18s. 6d. Mr Trot, who provided the scaffold ropes, was paid 9s. Amongst them was somebody who provided glass costing £12 19s. 6d. Shides (split wood) were provided by Mr Gilbert. Mr Alway lent balks without charge. Taylor and Dingley dug the cellars for £1 10s. 0d. as well as a ditch around the yard.

The only implements purchased were two wheelbarrows, supplied by Joseph Crocks for 11s., two willow baskets costing 1s. 6d., and 3s. 4d. for two iron clamps weighing 10lb. When the building was complete the window frames were painted: 'for colouring the windows twice over ... £1 15s. 0d.' Mr Venicot, who supplied the coal, was paid £1 to cut lettering on the stone at the building's entrance.

References to the almshouse in the minutes of the Common Council are sparse but show it was a workhouse as well as a refuge for the elderly. On 9 February 1723 'great irregularities' were reported; a committee appointed by the parishioners was to consult churchwardens and overseers and 'to inspect the Almshouse and to redresse and rectify all abuses and consider and direct on proper ways and means how to keep the poor at worke that the house may be serviceable according to the true intent and purposes of the benefactors of the same house'.

Trustees for lands given to the almshouse included John Balch as a leading member. On 8 March 1726 the Council authorised the trustees to place Rachel Taylor and Sarah Taylor in 'a Roome wherein Samuel Gause now lives', and each to have 15d. a week maintenance. They were permitted to have a third person join them and on 30 March the person was named as Hannah Scortch. On 15 April 1751 at 9 p.m. Frances Harding went from her room to empty her chamber pot into the brook at the bottom of the garden and accidentally fell in. The inquest verdict was accidental drowning. The banks of Durleigh Brook were steep and possibly slippery, and Frances Harding seems to have enjoyed considerable freedom in being allowed into the garden after dark. Three years earlier William Long 'in the afternoon was walking alone in the garden belonging to the Almshouse by the side of the brook when he accidentally fell in'. The verdict was 'drowned in the Almshouse Garden'.

Start of the Brick and Tile Industry

Before the Receiver's Accounts cease in 1696 there are distinct signs of change, the most significant being the start of brick and tile manufacture. From 1683 these building materials were ordered, often in large quantities, to build or repair public property – the new almshouse affords an example. Francis Warre, a builder working at Hestercombe, recorded in his account book on 7 June 1699: 'Pd at Bridgewater ... For two thousand of tyle ... £1 6s. 0d.' These tiles were probably made at Hamp. The estate book of the Tynte family of Halswell in 1708-9 mentions 'Brick Kiln Close' at Hamp.

Pantiles became the typical Bridgwater roofing material and cost 4s. per 100 in 1772-3; large Cornish slates at 1s. per 100 were cheaper then, which is probably why they were still being used. The Assize Court roof was part tiled and part covered with slate shipped from Padstow. Barnstaple 'creases' (ridge tiles) costing 3½d. each were used on the slate roofs.

Documents in the Carmarthenshire Record Office show that Bridgwater supplied thousands of bricks to South Wales. Thomas Kymer used many for buildings at his coal mines near Kidwelly. From 1768-73 bricks were supplied chiefly by Samuel Glover, whose bill-heads illustrate his brickyard at Hamp. Glover owned ships which returned from Wales carrying culm, anthracite coal dust used to fire bricks. In 1769 he sold bricks at 16s. per 1,000, pantiles at 40s. and creases at 18d. per dozen. Early bricks were solid but Glover also made bricks nine inches square and pierced by several holes for the floors of malt kilns; he sold malt as well as bricks.

Whigs and Tories

After the Restoration the town was dominated by several wealthy nonconformist merchants and tradesmen despite Anglican legislation designed to exclude dissenters from office. George Balch and his brother, both leading members of the Presbyterian church, were prominent. This domination abruptly ended with the 1710 Occasional Conformity Act, its repeal in 1718 not restoring the situation politically. Before the Act, however, so many Presbyterians were members of the Common Council that they filled a special pew in the balcony of their church, Defoe noticing but making no comment.

In the early 18th century the Whigs depended on occasional visits to Holy Communion to keep control of the Council but the Occasional Conformity Act removed one of their props and eventually the Tories were more or less in control. But, provided they did nothing worse than order the playing of 'The King shall enjoy his own again' at *The Swan*, it is difficult to believe the Whigs were seriously disaffected. Then, the 1715 rebellion gave the government a severe shock and the government's instructions apparently turned the army into agents provocateurs. This led to two unpleasant incidents in Bridgwater.

The first occurred in 1717 when a detachment of troops marching from Bristol to Exeter stopped for two days in Bridgwater. A group of officers, Ensign Dowsett, Lieutenant Timson and Cornet Freeman, and one non-commissioned officer, Quartermaster Cockram, who should all have been at *The Fountain,* spent Sunday afternoon and night drinking in *The Swan*. On Monday morning Dowsett noticed Thomas Martin, landlord of *The George,* sitting a few yards away in a passage behind the door opening to the Cornhill. Dowsett ordered Martin to drink damnation to Dr Sacheverell, a Tory hero impeached by the Whigs in 1710, but Martin refused and Dowsett, who was carrying a loaded weapon, 'cocked his Fusee and Swore if the said Martin did not drink damnation to Dr Sacheverell, he would shoot him in the eye'. He then fired at Martin 'but by good providence the shott missed his head about halfe an Inch and went into the wall behind his head.' The mayor summoned Dowsett before him but the two bailiffs carrying the message received an insulting reply so he issued a warrant for Dowsett's arrest. The two Constables also met with open defiance so a drummer beat the Assembly and 30 to 40 armed dragoons gathered outside *The Swan*.

The Constables read the Riot Act and then went to *The Swan*'s carriage entrance in St Mary Street where a real fracas developed, dragoons on horseback slashing at people. One levelled his firearm only to have it struck from his grasp by a blow from a staff. Eventually Dowsett was wounded, taken to *The Swan* for treatment, and then arrested. After an abortive attempt to hold an inquiry indictments were prepared and legal actions heard at the Assizes in 1718. Dowsett, Freeman, Cockram and a corporal named Thomas were all fined £20 each and Dowsett a further £50 for shooting at Martin.

The second affair occurred on 10 June 1721, the Pretender's birthday. Again troops were in the town and again trouble was triggered by the mayor displaying a Jacobite symbol, white roses. Soldiers armed with sticks went through the Shambles removing them and scuffles and fights ensued. Next morning a riot followed the posting of a special guard, who was pelted with stones, and a drummer was jostled as he passed through the Shambles. When Colonel Hamilton arrived the butchers swarmed around him and made blood-curdling threats whilst wielding knives and cleavers. Somebody contrived to place white roses on the Colonel's quarters and the mayor's wife displayed them prominently. Soldiers lost their tempers and one or two townsmen were beaten up. Later that day the army staged extremely crude anti-Jacobite insults but the townsmen refused to retaliate.

In 1755 a recruiting sergeant, drummer and corporal of the 19th Foot in the Pig Market offered two farm workers, James and Samuel Burston, beer, but refused cider in return and tried to trick the two farm workers into believing they had enlisted. When Samuel Burston told his brother to come away the drummer thrust a drumstick into his face, injuring his lower lip, and the sergeant threatened him with the point of his halberd and struck him on the head. There were no political overtones, in contrast to the tension which had existed in 1717-21.

A strong vein of cruelty ran through the 18th century. Few of the Examination Books have survived, but recorded examples include, in 1750, Moses Elworthy being whipped from the Gaol to the High Cross, and in 1752 Jane Bres sentenced to be whipped privately, 'on account of her being big with child.'

The New Assize Hall, 1720

No official record or balance sheet exists concerning the building of the new Assize Hall, only several pages of rough notes. Its roof needed 49,000 tiles costing 10s. per thousand; they were imported, and 'Landing & loading the tyle' cost 12s. 0d. They were probably Cornish, i.e. slate. Timber for the rafters cost £8 18s. 0d. The men who worked on the construction were paid either 16d. or 18d. a day. Since the workmen's ale cost £12 13s. 1½d. the total labour bill must have been high. Gifts of money towards building costs amounted to £247; the total needed was at least £382.

An entry in John Cannon's diary states: 'At this time was built a most magnificent large & capacious hall for the Assizes which was to be held in this Town for the County.' It was begun and finished in six weeks, and modelled on Westminster Hall. 'The Lady Tynt, Sir Tho. Wroth and Wm. Pitt Esqr. were great benefactors, and one John Pain, a shipwright, was the projector and undertaker.' Cannon also wrote: 'One old John Wells, a painter, was employed to depict the Arms of this Burrough in Front over the Entrance to the Hall lately Errected for the Assizes and instead of their own Arms, he drew the arms of Bridgnorth in Com. Salop wch I interupted him In & he grew in a passion but being convinced, he was obliged to take it down & work the right, wch was a great charge to him but owed me a corrosy' – i.e. earned me a cursing.

The old Assize Hall was a timber building and sale of recovered materials raised nearly £8. Volunteers raised money for the project by selling ale and stones for 10s. and 4s. respectively. Incidental costs included 3s. 2½d. for a broom and a servant's washing stool whilst 1lb. candles, six candlesticks, one glass and two pots cost 3s. 11d. Enough money was spent on seams of clay to prompt the question, whether the new building had cob walls?

The Chandos Enterprises

In 1721 the Duke of Chandos, one of the richest men in England, purchased the manor of Bridgwater from the Harveys. In 1734 he sold it to his friend Watts, because he had made little profit from the town and none

43 The Glass Cone a few years before its demolition in 1943.

44 Remains of the Glass Cone which were excavated in 1976 and are now preserved.

45 The north side of Castle Street as seen from the top looking towards the river.

of his enterprises had succeeded. He had had far-reaching schemes to develop new industries making Bridgwater rival Bristol. His distillery never reached full production and soap manufacture failed because the product was so caustic it blistered the user's skin. Chandos' glass manufacture changed the town's appearance as a huge brick cone was erected which dominated the northern part for 200 years (Figs 43 & 44), but production failed commercially, producing little more than a few wine bottles for the duke's own use. Chandos withdrew in 1729 but manufacture persisted until 1734. In 1736 the Distil House was let on a 50-year lease at a rent of £32 to Walter Ferguson & Co. who also rented the Counting House for £3 per annum. The thousands of bricks needed to build the Glass House and Chandos' other building schemes probably encouraged the incipient brick industry, although Chandos seems to have used his own brick makers.

Contrary to popular belief, Chandos visited Bridgwater twice. One of his ambitions was to turn the town into a pocket borough which he could use to acquire political power, but management of the borough was controlled by a tight ring that refused to move. Castle Street, 'the finest Georgian street outside Bath', was his sole achievement (Fig. 45), yet it was left unfinished. The duke had not decided where the street should end and consequently only the houses and outbuildings on the north side were finished, plus a street of small houses behind. The main street was named Chandos Street and the other Little Chandos Street. The shells of three or four houses on the south side were only finished much later, although the row was never completed.

46 The Castle Street doorway with the Gibbs surround. James Gibbs, 1682-1734, was an influential London church architect whose masterpiece was St Martin-in-the-Fields, which contains many examples of his surround; that in Bridgwater is one of the earliest.

Building was supervised by the shipwright Payne, who also suggested straightening the course of the Parrett. His scheme was seriously considered and a printed sheet including a map made to illustrate the plan, but Chandos declined to fund it. He dismissed Payne for dishonesty, appointing John Oldmixon, the Whig pamphleteer made Collector of Customs in 1716, to supervise the scheme and Benjamin Holloway to complete the buildings. Oldmixon proved as inefficient as Payne. Holloway obviously used professional designs supplied by

47 'The Lions', built around 1730 by Benjamin Holloway. Architecturally, The Lions stands in a class by itself. It is flanked by two small pavilions which need some restoration and the balustrades are deteriorating. The house is brick-built but the façade also has Ham stone mouldings, quoins and a roof balustrade. By the 1970s the building was in a poor state and only saved through its purchase by Messrs Brewer, Smith and Brewer. The roof-ridge line originally bore several ornamental features, mainly urns; these were removed several years ago, presumably for safety reasons.

48 This cottage was probably built to house one of the estate workers in the early 18th century. King Square was privately owned and under the jurisdiction of the manor court, namely the Manor of the Castle with Haygrove. In 1720 there were other similar houses as the court heard complaints about muck heaps before these houses 'on the way to the church'.

Chandos for the beautiful doorways (Fig. 46) and also built the house called 'The Lions' (Fig. 47) for himself. According to W. Dodd, writing to John Strachie in 1736, Holloway was also dishonest, building himself a large house at Brushford using materials stolen from Castle Street. Strachie wrote in his notebook that Chandos, 'having purchased the Castle of Harvey, demolished the greatest part & built a street between yt & the River'. Any buildings destroyed were probably cottages erected from time to time for estate workers. Fortuitously one, No. 24 King Square, complete with its garden, has survived (Fig. 48).

Minor thefts were common. In 1725 John Oliver was convicted of stealing deal taken from houses being built for John Gilbert, and also from Dr Allen, to make picture-frames and a shelf. Building work attracted one or two strangers, who were sent packing, and in 1729 ten people named as 'glassmen' were given orders on 24 October to get discharges by Christmas, certificates from their parish of origin freeing Bridgwater of liability for their keep, otherwise they had to leave. Nothing more was heard of them.

The Glass House provided warm shelter at night and attracted prostitutes, at least six being named during the enquiries. On 28 January 1725 '4 of the glassmen gave 6d. a piece to lye with Mary Ingram'. Some of these women were employed at the Glass House, one being described as 'finisher of glass'. The Glass House also attracted thieves: in January 1726 'there was lately stolen from the Glasshouse, two leaden halfe hundred weightes'. In 1736 it was let to Thomas Penny & Co. for £84 per annum.

Corrupt Electoral Practices

There is little evidence of corruption before George Bubb Dodington's diary of 1749. Dodington's uncle, George Dodington, was Bridgwater's M.P. in 1708, 1710 and 1714. The Dodingtons were an ancient but impoverished family until George Dodington (1638-1720) made a fortune as an army clothing contractor. His nephew was elected in 1722, 1727, 1734, 1741 and 1747; he was a wealthy man who spent £3,400 on the 1754 election, including three days 'in an infamous and disagreeable compliance with the low habits of venal wretches'. In the words of Horace Walpole, 'There never was such established bribery and so profuse.' Bubb Dodington believed he lost the election through the 'injustice of the Returning Officer ... of my good votes 15 were rejected. Eight bad votes for Lord Egmont were received.' He also thought the Custom House officers' hostility had much to do with it; presumably they were not 'properly taken care of'.

During the campaign Robert Balch 'canvassed near half the town. The people did not chuse to speak out, though very few declared they were engaged to Lord Egmont.' The result was Egmont 119; Balch 114; Dodington 105. Balch, who lived at Nether Stowey, was one of Bridgwater's wealthy Presbyterian merchant families and used the same methods as Dodington. His grandfather, Robert Balch, represented Bridgwater in 1692-5 and there is evidence he provided free drinks in 1692, so corruption in Bridgwater elections was deep-rooted.

John Cannon

John Cannon, born in 1684, was a schoolmaster at Meare who came to Bridgwater in 1720 as an Excise Officer. He noted 'above 120 houses that sold ale & cyder'. His stay was brief as in 1721 he happened on two hogsheads of wine and about ten gallons of brandy 'locked in a room'. Unfortunately it belonged to the mayor. During the subsequent investigation the mayor, John Oldmixon, and their friends held drinking sessions charged as expenses (according to Cannon) who only made £2 7s. 2d. Moreover, he had made enemies and lost his job. He attempted to make a living as a maltster but abandoned this and left the town.

His diary gives glimpses of Bridgwater between 1720 and 1722. The North Gate 'against the fields' was already dilapidated (Fig. 39). There were markets on Tuesdays and Thursdays, 'the best in the county for corn, cheese and cattle', and four fairs – Lent, Midsummer, St Matthew's and 28 December – plus 'a Fair only for scythes and hard ware viz. the Monday after Ascension day. There is also a great Beast Market viz. Ascension day yearly.' Writing of the Friary he says: 'There are no buildings left, only the cemetery & churchyard.'

Wages in the Town

Bridgwater Quarter Sessions could regulate wages but only two lists have survived, for 1727 and 1728. The 1727 list names 40 occupations, seven of which were agricultural: ditching, faggot-making, harvesting, hedging, mowing, ploughing and reaping. The remainder included baker, blacksmith, bricklayer, brick maker, butcher, carpenter, cooper, currier, cutler, grazier, glover, hatter, joiner, labourer, lime burner, mason, milner (i.e. miller), plasterer, pewterer, plumber, railing-maker, sadler, sawyer, servant, shoemaker, shipwright, tanner, tailor, thatcher, tile-maker, tiler, tucker and turner. In 1696 Gregory King thought 'all labouring people' could earn £15 a year, an over-generous estimate.

Craftsmen were called artificers and it was ruled that their apprentices should receive 10d. a day in summer and 8d. in winter. In Bridgwater, if meals were provided, pay was 5d. in summer and 4d. in winter. Often the master paid his men yearly. The workman earning most was the Tanner's Market Man who received £5 10s. 0d. per annum; the Glover's Waterman was next with £5, then the Baker's Man (Setter, Seasoner or Fournier) with £4 10s. 0d. A large group earned £4 a year: blacksmith, butcher, cooper, lime-burner, milner, pewterer's foreman, the sadler's best servant and the wood turner. The next group, including currier, cutler's foreman, shoemaker and tailor, earned £3 10s. 0d. Only the hatters and tuckers (i.e. fullers) paid their best workmen less, £3. Workers of inferior status in other trades were also paid £3, except for the shoemakers who only got £2 10s. 0d.

In other trades pay was by piece work. Brickmakers earned 3s. 6d. per 1,000, and tile-makers 1s. 4d. per 1,000, except for ridge tiles where the rate was 2s. per 1,000 tiles. Men working for a shipwright called the Master Hewer received 1s. 6d. a day; the Cleniker (perhaps equivalent to a riveter) and the

Caulker earned 1s. 2d. a day, but if meals were provided rates were reduced to 9d. and 7d. respectively. Carpenters', glaziers', joiners', masons', plasterers' and plumbers' pay was fixed at 1s. 4d. a day but 1s. 2d. in winter.

The best manservant could earn £5 per annum, the second best £3, and 'other sorts' £2. The best woman servant was rated at £2 10s. 0d., the 'second sort' at £2, and 'others' at £1 10s. 0d. Servants' wages, revealed in law suits, varied enormously, as did their working conditions. There are many instances of servants or apprentices absconding and occasionally being bound over for attacking the master. There were six complaints in 1724 of masters withholding wages. The magistrates appear to have supported the servants.

The regulations excluded many occupations, presumably because few were involved. Those appearing in court records include: whip-maker, pipe-maker, chapman, glass-maker, clock-maker and goldsmith.

Inns

Counsel's opinion in 1710 said the number of ale houses should be reduced to 30 — something never achieved. Numbers can be obtained from records of Special Sessions held for inn-holders to find sureties and to collect licences. A £5 guarantee was required in 1728, but £10 after then. Many lists have survived, some only naming inn-holders but others naming the inns. In 1726 34 were licensed but numbers usually exceeded 40 and often reached 50. The recognisance was set out in Latin and followed by an explanatory note saying that the landlord could keep a common ale and victualling house provided he kept the Assize of Bread and of Ale and did not permit unlawful games or allow any drunkenness or disorder.

The oldest inn was *The George*, mentioned in borough archives in 1411 when it was kept by Philip Clopton. *The Swan* and *Saracen's Head* are probably as old. A manorial document of 1533 in the Bodleian Library gives the rent in each case as 4d.: 'the price of 4 iron horseshoes and 38 iron keys as free rent of John Buckeland for his hostelry called the Swanne at Michaelmas' and 'the price of 100 pairs of spurs, free rent of the abbot of Athelney for an inn called the Sarosenshed, not paid because the monastery dissolved'. These rents are obviously medieval. The 1539-50 Ledger of John Smythe, a Bristol merchant, shows that at that time his firm kept a man in Bridgwater to organise the sale and distribution of Gascon wines in West Somerset, who stayed at the *Saracen's Head*.

In 1789 *The George* passed briefly into the hands of John Acland of Fairfield. The landlord, William Caine, was bankrupt but told Acland 'a well varnished tale', and sold him the inn. Two local creditors, one Amory and John Chubb, were owed £900 and £400 respectively, and both were re-paid. The notebook of the solicitor handling this transaction contains a plan of *The George* which shows a wide carriage entrance in St Mary Street, a yard leading to stables, and a back entrance in George Street; these are still visible. *The George* continued as an inn until 1841 and then around 1900 re-opened as a temperance hotel.

The Swan's site is now a building society office, Nos 6-7 Cornhill. It too had a carriage entrance and stables round the corner in St Mary Street. Its official standing was high for it was the government Leather Office, which collected Land and Window Tax, and was also used as a court handling bankruptcy cases. Its balcony on which musicians frequently played and spectators watched important events faced the Cornhill. *The Swan* ceased to be an inn at the end of the 18th century, becoming a mercer's shop with living quarters above in 1820.

The White Hart is first mentioned in 1597 when its owner, Richard Stradling, a prominent townsman and Receiver from 1591 to 1596, owed the town £111 13s. 5d. It was agreed that the town should hold the inn for nine years for £12 a year rent. The first landlord, Morlon, paid six months' rent, but there must have been a more detailed contract covering the high cost of repairs. Other charges were to be met: Chief Rent 12d., Queensilver 12d. and £1 6s. 8d. payable annually to Honor Gibbs, widow of Philip Gibbs, as part of her dowry.

Initial repairs cost 13s. 6d. but in 1601 almost £9 was needed for glazing several windows, mending beds, repairing the backstairs, benches, and curtain rods, and supplying locks and keys. A new 'house of office' (privy) was built and thatched. A new bedstead cost 8s. and repairing the stable 7s. 10d. The 'tallat' (loft) was also repaired which, with repairs to the roof, totalled £4 7s. 10d.

A 1603 repair bill included a cupboard in the hall, Stradling being charged 10s.; eight feet of new glass cost 4s., 20 new quarrels (diamond-shaped leaded glass) 12d., mending the hall hearth cost 2s., and 8s. 6d. was for making a new penthouse (a small roof) over the well. The penthouse was fitted with an oak rainwater gutter for 18d.

In 1679 an inn at the bottom of West Street, on the south side, was called the *Three Mariners* but by 1715 it had become *The Bell* and was ultimately named the *Cardiff Arms* until West Street's demolition in the 1950s. Many of the inns were simple beerhouses occupying little more than one room. One such, the *Sheep Fair*, was located across the street in Moat Lane behind Bowering's Bakery, the end house in Friarn Street. Between these two buildings was a drang (passage) measuring three by 100 feet, the town moat site. Thomas Bowering purchased *Sheep Fair* for his bakery in 1775 and built over it. Some unusual inn names appeared in the 17th century – the *Sergeant's Head* (1649), the *Black Boy* (1683) and the *Unicorn* (1686) – but none lasted very long.

An extraordinary experiment involved using the town gaol, *The Cock Moile*, as a beerhouse. Two incidents occurring in its kitchen were reported to the justices; both involved Robert Harding, butcher. On 1 January 1744 Harding was assaulted by William Neale and other members of that family, but on 5 January Harding attacked Elizabeth Sopham; 'he also threw a pint of ale in her face'. The experiment was short-lived but, according to the survey of 1836, it had been known as the *Cross Keys Inn*.

A glimpse of the *Noah's Ark*'s interior was provided when the landlord, J. Mounsher, died in 1729. The inn's entrance was from the passage now called Mansion House Lane. It had a linear plan, extending for several yards to the west and inter-locking with the Town Hall. The entrance room contained 24 pewter dishes, six dozen plates, four patty pans, one pewter pint, two half-pints, two noggins, and two punch ladles. The assessors then named four utility rooms, the Fore Room, the Cider Cellar, the Brewhouse and the Beer Cellar, followed by five bedrooms, the Back Chamber, the Inner Chamber, and Chambers Over Sergeant Hall, Over Burgess Hall and Over Common Gaol. The only furniture mentioned is beds and bedsteads. There was a withdrawing room called the Puppy Parlour, named presumably after a painting on the wall. The inn lacked a malt-house but had a brewing vat and a beer cellar with hogsheads. The total value was assessed at £29 19s. 4d. An inn with 11 rooms was evidently of some importance.

Several malt-houses in the town were owned by maltsters but some inns had their own. Evidence for their existence comes chiefly from the law courts, where they were mentioned in bastardy cases as the rendezvous of illicit lovers. Drinking during church services was evidently treated severely but stopping the ale-taster tasting the ale in 1724 only attracted a fine of 2d. In 1726 the *Three Swans* was reported by the constables for being 'a very lewd and disorderly house' but such cases were rare. In 1728 the Justices heard that Catherine Davies had been seen in bed with three men at the *Prince Eugene* where she lodged, so she was returned to Swansea where she belonged. Thirteen persons including two women were forbidden from keeping any inn within the borough. Although neither signed nor dated, the list naming them must have had legal authority.

The Dam

In Elizabethan times the river-bank dam was let as pasture, but the town paid to repair its gates and the railings which enclosed it. A 1559 lease says that it contained eight burgages covering three-and-a-half acres of land, including an acre of orchard. A dock and dock-yard were on the river bank. A narrow strip of land extended to Eastover where, in 1575, an inn, the *Three Crowns*, was located. Another lease of 1600 mentions a 'new built house' here which was used for meetings, and at least once (in 1616 'when the soldiers were here') by the Justices as a law court. It was demolished in 1653 but rebuilt in 1672.

20

The Age of Improvement

During the late 18th century Bridgwater shed many medieval characteristics and reduced much of its street clutter. A councillor, John Chubb (mayor 1787-8), was a skilled artist who sketched many of the buildings before they were demolished.

In October 1778 the Common Council called a public meeting 'to consider what improvements can be made to the town'. The meeting suggested building a Market House on the Cornhill's west side, all markets hitherto having been held in the streets. The Market House Act was passed in 1779 and the scheme went ahead. The Council opened a subscription list, granted £500, and suggested that the turnpikes levy an additional toll on Sundays. If this proved insufficient they offered to raise a rate not exceeding 3½d. in the pound. The Market was to be administered by a separate Market House Trust. The Act forbade street stalls selling fish, meat and poultry within 1,000 yards of the new market, apart from the butchers who could continue using the Flesh Shambles on High Street's north side. Bakers who had always sold bread in their houses could also continue to do so. Another clause aimed at getting the streets paved, lighted and watched, although an inserted note indicated that Chandos Street (now Castle Street) and Horn Alley (now Chandos Street) were excluded because they were private streets and part of the Castle Manor.

Seven properties were demolished on the site where the Market House now stands. Chubb's drawing (Fig. 49) shows two dilapidated timber-framed houses there. Some 25 houses were listed for demolition, including 'all those which adjoin the eastern end of the churchyard', a decision not fully implemented. There is no record of which houses were demolished. The four-centuries-old High Cross was removed although not on the list. It was present in 1791 when Collinson mentioned 'A spacious and most convenient market-house of brick lately erected, near the church'. Early local historians thought it remained well into the 19th century but it is not on the 1806 tithe map. William Baker thought it was taken down *c*.1800, which is probably right. The tithe map shows a row of buildings down the middle of the High Street as far as the Cornhill. The Act listed none for demolition but Chubb's view of High Street from the Cornhill suggests some were demolished as far as the *Old Oak Inn* (Fig. 50). His picture shows that an important clause in the Act was ignored: 'that

49 The Cornhill, drawn by John Chubb, showing the buildings that were pulled down in order to build the new Market House.

a good street ... be made to extend from St Mary Street to the south part of the High Street', which was intended to preserve the old line of High Street where it turned to run along the churchyard's east wall. It was easy to build here and close the gap on High Street's south side. Chubb drew the corner of this street (closed by 1806) showing a substantial building which was probably part of the Market House. The *Old Oak Inn* is on the right of the picture and has a passage alongside.

The Market House Act gave trustees control over the town's streets and told the corporation to remove two columns, a spout and two stops. The Council replied that only the stops and spout would be removed. On 2 June 1780 it resolved that 'the pillars at the front door of the Town Hall, projecting against the street, being unsatisfactory, the same to be pulled down'. The Act also stated that every householder must 'scrape, wash and cleanse the pavements along the front of his house between the hours of 7 a.m. and 9 a.m...' and insisted that street cleaning was only to be done by official scavengers.

Amongst the buildings to be demolished was the wholesale cheese market, a permanent stall standing in the middle of St Mary Street between the bottom of Friarn Street and the south-east corner of the churchyard. It measured 94 feet by 11 feet, and posts in the street protected it from damage by passing

50 The buildings forming 'the island' in High Street. Chubb thought their demolition was imminent but it didn't happen until many years later.

carts. Despite serious difficulties caused by this obstruction it was still present in 1821 when the County Surveyor considered improvements to the turnpike road. As insufficient space was available in the Market House a new Cheese Market was constructed in 1822 at the south-east corner of Friarn Street. The Market House trustees gave 200 guineas towards its cost.

The 1779 scheme was inadequate for the town's needs and, following new proposals in 1825, another Act was passed in 1826. No documents exist apart from a rough draft of 1825 concerning an agreement between the trustees and two men to re-build the north and south sides of the Market House, and 'to erect a new front with centrepiece and wings to face the parade'. The partners were Thomas Hutchings, a well-known Bridgwater builder, and John Snook, a druggist of Wiveliscombe, whose interest was presumably financial. The work would cost £1,423. Since this draft precedes the Act the scheme was presumably adopted.

In 1790 the corporation purchased the archway over the entrance to the Langport or Back Quay, which supported a room belonging to the *Castle Inn*, for £15 10s. 0d., and the materials were used to make a slipway. In 1792 it bought the section of quay next to the inn for £115 10s. 0d. The cellar was leased to the innkeeper, James Witherell, an original Market trustee, for 10s. a year. John Chubb drew the scene before and after the arch was removed (Figs 51 & 52).

Opposite the *Castle Inn* was a dilapidated building in Fore Street which was offered free to one John Jeffery, provided that he built a new house and paid 5s. 4d. rent a year in perpetuity. His building, erected in 1795, is the *Punchbowl Inn*, which was built on a curve and surmounted by a solid roof parapet (Fig. 53). It is no longer an inn, and the anachronistic rent, although notionally not terminating until A.D. 3879, was stopped in 1978.

In 1798 the Council decided to remove the North Gate and use the materials to repair the road. Chubb's sketch (Fig. 16) shows that the gate was virtually collapsing anyway.

The New Bridge

As trade improved the medieval bridge became increasingly inadequate. In 1792 a solicitor was appointed to organise the legal work involved in its replacement, and an Act of Parliament authorising this was passed in 1794. Financial estimates were made in 1793 and the bridge was to be paid for by new tolls levied on roads leading into the town.

51 John Chubb's picture of *c*.1790 of the arch above the entrance to the Langport or Back Quay (now Binford Place). The arch supported a room belonging to the *Castle Inn*.

52 A later picture by John Chubb of the scene in Fig. 51 after the Corporation had bought the arch and demolished it.

Thomas Pyke was in charge of negotiations for the new bridge but it was probably Robert Anstice, whose sister had married a Shropshire ironmaster, who persuaded Bridgwater to turn to Abraham Darby's company at Coalbrookdale, makers of the first iron bridge. Pyke himself was an experienced metal worker, capable of casting church bells and of making anything in brass from watch parts to a cannon. He persuaded the Common Council to accept the revolutionary idea of a single span metal bridge.

Negotiations with Coalbrookdale proved difficult but on 4 March 1795 'the plan provided and drawn by Messrs Gregory and Parry for an Iron Bridge to be erected' was adopted by the Common Council. Gregory was the Coalbrookdale company representative who came to Bridgwater to supervise construction of the bridge from pre-cast parts shipped down the Severn. Parry, a Cardiff architect, undertook to deal with the stonework. The original estimates were £1,370 for the ironwork and £500 to erect it. The stonework cost another £1,300 bringing the total to £3,170. Other costs including legal charges brought it to £4,000.

It was difficult to remove the old bridge and on 1 October 1798 the piers were still standing. The ship builder on East Quay used them to moor boats undergoing repair. The new bridge's completion date is unrecorded but an account in *The Western Flying Post or Sherborne and Yeovil Mercury* reads: '1 October 1798 Bridgwater Bridge, which is principally composed of cast iron, brought

53 The chimneys on No. 2 Fore Street, formerly *The Punchbowl* inn, which show interesting examples of kiln-fired clay.

in pieces from Colebrook-Dale, Shropshire, by water carriage, is now pretty well completed. It consists of one arch, the span of which is 75 feet, the road way is 25 feet in the clear, including two foot paveways: and is lighted with six lamps. The expence of erecting the bridge is about £4,000 which was collected by an additional toll on all the turnpikes leading to the town of Bridgwater. The former bridge, which was very difficult to demolish, had stood 500 years, and was built by an ancient lord of Bridgwater: the piers of this bridge are not yet quite taken away. The iron bridge is a very great ornament to the part of the town in which it is situated, and is one of the handsomest in England.'

The Port

The heavy stakes securing the salmon butts menaced shipping and there were so many in 1785 that the Common Council decided to remove them: 'Robert Biffen is ordered to remove salmon butts which he has erected and obstruct the navigation of the river.' But this had unfortunate consequences as, on 30 April 1789, 'The destruction of Salmon Butts has caused a shortage of salmon and a great advance in prices.' The policy was abandoned but the mayor and two councillors were to ensure that salmon butts did not interfere with navigation.

Between 1786 and 1827, 149 vessels were registered here, most being single-masted sloops. Although three full-rigged ships were registered it is unlikely that they ever came up to the quay. They were used in the Canadian timber trade and unloaded at Combwich; the timber then floated to Bridgwater in the form of rafts.

Some of the Bridgwater-registered boats were built in the town either at Crowpill or on the opposite bank near the East Quay. Between 1800 and 1880 some 167 ships were built in Bridgwater. John Gough's shipyard at Crowpill flourished in the 1830s, producing about one ship a year: in 1834 the *Elizabeth*; in 1835 the *Sarah* (a schooner of 120 tons); in 1837 the *Admiral Blake*, a brig of 190 tons, and the *Charles* (130 tons); and in 1838 the *Fanny Jane*.

The dock on the east bank was eventually lined with masonry and Carver's shipyard was located here. An earlier document relating to the area is David

Williams' day book. He went bankrupt in 1786 when his yard contained timber worth £40 in deal and oak planks. There were also two vessels being built: a brigantine valued at £480, and a sloop worth £100. Much of his timber came from Fairfield Woods, where he left oak worth £17. Williams lived in a well-furnished house as his household effects were valued at £115, a substantial sum. His Fore Room had 12 pictures, 11 chairs, two corner cupboards and three round tables, together with much glass, china, delft ware, plates and bowls. He was back in business before 1808.

In the 18th century multiple ownership of vessels was common but by the 19th century fleets were formed and owned by a few families who created a virtual monopoly. Two Langport families, Stuckey and Bagehot, formed a partnership in 1704 and operated the equivalent of a parcels delivery service; they also owned the *British Empire* (1,347 tons), the largest vessel ever registered in Bridgwater. The Havilands owned vessels carrying coal and culm. The Axfords acquired the London and Bridgwater Shipping Company fleet in 1815 but, defeated by steam, ceased trading in 1846.

Thomas Sully first appears in 1796 as master of the *Speedwell*. In 1807 he purchased a French prize, a brigantine which he re-named *The Brothers*. Later he acquired an interest in the Forest of Dean coal mines. Following construction of the floating dock in 1841, the Sullys acquired a coal yard into which they could unload coal from ships moored in the outer basin of this dock.

In 1811 a grandiose scheme for constructing a canal from Bristol to Taunton was sanctioned by Parliament. By 1824 this proposal had been considerably reduced in scope, the intention now being to build a canal from Bridgwater to Taunton. This project was completed in 1827. Its Bridgwater terminal was a basin and a lock to the Parrett at Somerset Bridge.

54 St Mary's church from Mansion House Lane. The *Mansion House* is on the left and its stone wall is medieval. The scene has scarcely changed since the *Mansion House* was the Church House except that the external stair was removed in the mid-19th century. There was also a well in High Street outside the *Noah's Ark* which stood on the right.

New Municipal Buildings

In 1801 the Council decided to sell the Mansion House and use the money

55 The *Royal Clarence Hotel* built in 1825. This shows the building before its closure in 1984 and conversion to shops and offices called Clarence House. An iron plaque is fixed above the entrance porch which displays the town's arms and the date 1795. This is one of two plaques removed from the cast-iron bridge when it was replaced by the present town bridge; the second plaque is in the Blake Museum.

raised towards improving the Assize Hall and building a Grand Jury Room. It was sold to John Hawkins for £334 plus an annual rent of one guinea. He erected a new front which, with its roof parapet, still exists (Fig. 30). The stone side wall (Fig. 54) and external stair (removed in 1868) were retained, both having existed since the early 16th century. Hawkins converted the *Mansion House* into an inn, which it still is.

In April 1808 Edward Sealy was requested 'to take immediate measures for securing the Guildhall from falling down'. Next year it was proposed to sell it and in 1810 the officers were instructed to prepare a Parliamentary Bill to grant authority for its sale. In 1811 the Attorney General was asked if the Common Council could move into the Assize Hall, 'the Burgess Hall being in a ruinous state'. In 1812 the Council was still attempting to buy land adjacent to the Assize Hall and a year later the costs of moving into the Assize Hall were still being debated. In 1819 a group of wealthy men from the Grand Jury formed an 'Improvement Committee'. Sir Thomas Buckler Lethbridge M.P. of Sandhill Park, Sir Alexander Hood of Butleigh, William Dickenson M.P. of Kingweston, William Astell M.P. of London, Charles Kemys Tynte of Halswell House, William Gore Langton of Newton Park and Jeffreys Allen of Bridgwater undertook to build, at their own cost, a new Guildhall, Grand Jury Room, and appurtenances, together with a house to accommodate the Assize judges. In 1821 they bought out a man called Phelps who received £5 per annum for life for his cellar under the Town Hall. Next year the Council met in the new building. In May 1824 the judges' house was nearly complete and the Improvement Committee granted the reversion of the *Crown Inn*, provided a new hotel was built there. The *Royal Hotel*, later re-named the *Royal Clarence Hotel*, opened in 1825 (Fig. 55). It was subject to £2 annual ground rent which was bought out in 1873 for £50. The street alongside was also widened as part of the scheme.

Pigott's Directory of 1830 says the new municipal buildings cost £8,000. A clause in the deeds made the Council the legal owner and entitled it to any fees paid to use the buildings. The contract stipulated that Richard Carver, the county surveyor, was to draw the plans. His deposited drawings are undated but show a grim-looking building, with a prison block in the western part containing 40 cells on two levels. In 1831 it was decided to construct a gallery in the Assize Hall for the Common Council and this was built by public subscription.

King Square

The Duke of Chandos never decided what to do with the castle's outer bailey. He thought of extending Castle Street to the west but sold the manor leaving the bailey untouched. His successors were also hesitant and undated drawings made c.1790 show tentative ideas for King Square, a kind of double crescent linked to North Gate by a short street to be called North Street; this was a bad choice as the present North Street already existed and the north side of the High Street was usually called 'North Street' for short.

Eventually the south side was sold in 1806 and houses were built in 1807. Building on the east side began in 1813 when No. 10 was built. The north side was left vacant until 1850, when Thomas Hutchings erected the large building at the north-west corner. The design of the building followed established principles adopted in the Regency period and was in keeping with the south and east sides of the square. Had customers been forthcoming the north side of the square would have been completed in a similar fashion and, in anticipation, Hutchings left a jagged line of bricks waiting to be bonded into the next house. They are still waiting (Fig. 56).

The South Gate was probably dismantled soon after the old cheese market was removed. The new Taunton road was then constructed but was of relatively short length and there was no canal to cross then. The toll house still stands at its southern limit (Fig. 57).

Construction of the Bristol road was planned in 1821 and involved cutting a road from a point on the northern side of the town near Bull Baiting Acre to Dunball. The old Bath Road route went to the foot of Puriton Hill and then forked left to Dunball. An 1830 press report suggests that it was almost complete by that date. The toll house (Fig. 58) is by the roundabout at the junction of the A38 and A39.

56 The building on the north-west corner of King Square erected by Thomas Hutchings in 1850. Anticipating building next to it, Hutchings left a line of alternate protruding bricks, as shown in the inset, which could be bonded into the wall of the next house.

Other road improvements were made following the turnpike route survey. Five small cottages narrowing the street inside the East Gate were demolished in 1824, and access was improved to Monmouth Street. Near the town bridge two houses, four stables, out-buildings and a yard were removed in 1826; this should have been done when the bridge was replaced. The West Gate had long since vanished but the narrow street entrance left behind was widened by cutting a curve through the property at the north corner.

57 The tollhouse on Taunton Road. This relic of the Bridgwater Turnpike Trust was built in the 1830s and appears not to have been altered. It ceased to be used when the trust was dissolved, and it became a private house.

58 The tollhouse at the Bristol Road end of Monmouth Street. Built in the 1820s, it is an elaborate Gothic building with prominent drip-stone mouldings over the windows. Its porch has been removed.

The Workhouse

In 1771 materials 'for Carring on the Woolen manufactury in the Alms house' cost £4 3s. 4d. Occasionally small items were renewed, such as turn strings for 4½d. in 1773, and spills and wherrows in 1774, which indicates that something was being done but on a small scale since returns were meagre. In 1774 the quarterly returns were £1 2s. 8½d., 15s. 9½d., 10s. 0d. and 3s. 0½d. In 1778 there were two entries: 'received for spining …6d.' and 'To Paupers' labour & Gains … 16s. 7d.'

The rapid growth of the population was accompanied by soaring costs for maintaining the poor. Calculation suggests that poor rates in Somerset increased by 158 per cent between 1750 and 1785, 91 per cent between 1785 and 1805, and 55 per cent after 1805.

In Bridgwater the average poor rate around 1776 was £902 per annum but this had increased to £1,023 by 1783-5. It was £2,846 in 1801 and by 1817 had risen to £3,465. The town's population rose from 3,654 in 1801 to 4,911 in 1811, and 6,155 in 1821. The number of houses in the Rate Lists increased from 353 in 1769 to over 400 in 1784, and 529 in 1828.

The Bridgwater poor rate cost £4,505 in 1824 but then declined. Nationally, however, numbers receiving relief rose from 1,040,000 in 1801 to 1,850,000 in 1827. In 1834 the government proposed drastic cuts in public expenditure by passing the Poor Law Amendment Act. One development blamed for the high costs before 1834 was the Speenhamland system, a table of payments of outdoor relief linked to age and sex of the claimant and the price of bread. The system was never adopted in Bridgwater but discretionary cash grants to supplement low wages were given, so the principle was recognised. John Bowen the pamphleteer thought the system worked well.

A Year of Despair

In 1801 Stogursey labourers went on a hunger march. Their route took them through Nether Stowey on 30 March, where they collected recruits, and then to North Petherton, where they met with no response to their initiative. They continued to Bridgwater intending to meet county magistrates and persuade them to pressurise the farmers into setting lower food prices. They achieved some success although few, if any, of those approached signed their petition. Although reputed to be 500 strong, only three or four of their number went to Castle Street to find the Reverend Wollen, the vicar and a magistrate, who was living there. Information about the meeting is contained in a letter to Mr J. Acland which says the deputation handed their petition to Mr Wollen, who then refused to return it: 'Mr Woolen took 3 of them into his house, one of witch was Sam Symons he Broke one of their coats pulling him in But he was obliddge to Give tow of them a shilling a piece and Give the man a new coat.' A letter from another source says it was 'the Justice's Coat [which] was rent from top to Bottom', and that during the altercation 'he collared Symons … and gave him a black eye'. The soldiers were called out and 'the sailors placed their little swivel Guns in such Direction as to command Castle Street'.

The magistrates met at the *Globe Inn*, Nether Stowey on 22 April 1801 and ordered certain quantities of wheat or bread to be sold at prices which they fixed, the quantity varying according to the number in the family. The order, which was to apply to parish overseers, concluded with this instruction: 'A stock of Rice, Beans and Herrings to be also provided which the Poor may purchase at a price not exceeding the first cost.' The order was signed by Jeffreys Allen of Bridgwater and by John Evered of Otterhampton.

The end of the war with France in 1815 did not bring peace and plenty. The same social problems persisted and the same policy guided those administering poor relief. The sole new development before 1830 involved purchasing stone, which was broken up and sold at a profit. In 1828 the total was worth £26 17s. 3d. and the profit £10 19s. 5d. In 1829 the total was £33 1s. 8d. and profit £17 8s. 4d. By 1830 the scheme had almost tripled in size and the total value was £92 15s. 6d. It does not appear at all in the accounts after 1830.

The New Poor Law, 1834

From the late 18th century poor rates increased yearly to the great alarm of the middle classes and by 1830 it was considered that drastic cuts were needed. The 1834 Poor Law Amendment Act restructured the system so that parishes were no longer responsible for their poor. The Bridgwater Workhouse Union was created, covering 40 surrounding parishes. A new Workhouse serving the area would be administered by a Board of Guardians elected by the ratepayers. The Guardians first met on 12 May 1836 but the new Union Workhouse was not ready until December 1837. During that interval a major scandal occurred. Tenders for building the Workhouse came from Pollard & Son for £4,540, Thomas Hutchings for £4,393 and J.W. Wainwright for £4,200. The contract was given to Wainwright, a Taunton builder.

After 1834 it became increasingly difficult to obtain outdoor relief. The food in the dietary scales published by the Poor Law Commission for Boards of Guardians was intended to cost as little as possible. Parish poor houses – little more than rent-free cottages – were closed and people needing indoor relief concentrated in the old parish workhouses at Bridgwater and North Petherton. The new Union Workhouse would be able to house 300, possibly too large for immediate needs, but the two old workhouses were certainly too small. In August 1836 there were 73 paupers in the Bridgwater house and 51 children at North Petherton. The Guardians calculated that the Bridgwater house would hold 98, and that North Petherton, which was usually reckoned to take 30 or 40, might hold a hundred.

Bridgwater's Overseers paid a rent of £50 a year, and those at North Petherton £25 for their workhouse and £30 for the newly built governor's house. Numbers admitted at North Petherton were achieved by sleeping children five or six to a bed. These makeshift measures, plus a lavish desire to make the greatest economies, led to disaster. The diet contained no milk and the staple food was oatmeal gruel made with water which had a disagreeable taste and purgative effects. Milk was not restored until 12 May 1837 and a severe outbreak of dysentery erupted during the interval. According to the printed dietary, gruel should have been given once a day, at breakfast. There were three meals a day. Meat was to be provided twice a week and, on other days, seven ounces of bread and two ounces of cheese for men, less for women. Mr Poole, a medical officer, said in evidence that the inmates were given one pint of coarse oatmeal gruel 'which always tasted poor and disagreeable' three times a day.

Knowledge of what occurred comes from pamphlets published by John Bowen and evidence given to a House of Lords Select Committee in 1839.

The Board minutes are reticent and Visitors' Books and Medical Books no longer exist, so precise figures are unobtainable. Bowen was an overseer for four years who did not intend becoming a Guardian but was persuaded to put his name forward and then served for one year. He was a member of the Visiting Committee and was very critical of the general treatment of the Poor under the new system. One of his pamphlets, *The New Poor Law; the Bridgwater Case 1839*, has the following sentence printed in capital letters on the outer cover: IS KILLING IN AN UNION WORKHOUSE CRIMINAL IF SANCTIONED BY THE POOR LAW COMMISSIONERS? He reported 30 deaths in nine months from an average of 94 inmates, whereas the year ended 31 March 1836 saw only nine deaths from an average of 66 residents. On the cover of another pamphlet he printed: 'Deaths of convicts in Hulks ... 2.3% Deaths in the Bridgwater Workhouse ... 41.4%' The epidemic of dysentery was followed by an outbreak of typhus (also called gaol fever) causing six deaths within 20 days.

There was no guarantee that certain decisions, such as the doctor ordering tea and sugar for a patient, would be implemented. The Medical Officer recommended using rice rather than oatmeal and was told his business was caring for the sick, not experimenting with those who were well. Eventually, six months later, the Guardians agreed to implement his recommendation. The inmates' sufferings were awful. 'The sufferers,' says Bowen, 'however cleanly in their former habits, involuntarily voided their faeces ... The foetid stench was so intolerable that an active and humane member of the Visiting Committee ... declared himself utterly unable to inspect the wards.' Ordinary Board meetings were held at the Town Hall but their Minute Book takes very little note of these conditions. The Guardians knew what was happening but wanted to turn a blind eye. The Chairman's report of 26 March 1837 makes no mention of diarrhoea but pointed out that the cost of one year's operation was £8,544. He was duly congratulated by the Poor Law Commissioners. The Medical Officer of No. 1 District (Bridgwater) was granted £15 in consideration of the extra duties which he had performed. There were seven medical districts in the Union and the other medical officers all received a ten per cent bonus in their next quarter's salary. One alarming aspect of such scandal was that the workhouse was controlled by 'responsible people' including several clergy. Scandals which occurred elsewhere were also exposed by pamphlets, as at Morpeth in 1837, by R. Blakey, and in 1842 at Eastbourne, the Murder Den, by Charles Brooker.

The Hospital

In 1853 Jonathan Toogood, a surgeon who had settled in Bridgwater, recalled how he had been obliged on one occasion to operate 'on a ricketty table, hardly strong enough to support the weight of the patient, in a small room, admitting very little light', and how, in another case, 'It was necessary to remove the patient into the door-way of the cottage to obtain sufficient light by which to amputate.' 'The frequent occurrence of these difficulties,' he says, 'induced me in the year 1813, to invite my medical brethren to attempt the establishment of an infirmary in the town.' They rented a small house in Back Lane (Clare Street) which would accommodate eight in-patients. In 1820 the governors acquired a better house in Salmon Parade with accommodation for 30 in-patients.

Parliamentary Elections

The answer to a petition made in 1768 by Mr Anne Poulett (*see* p.184), a defeated parliamentary candidate, stated that the right to vote belonged to inhabitants living in the borough and paying scot and lot. This gave the vote to about 160 men. Lord Perceval had claimed that only capital burgesses could vote so had his election cancelled and the seat was given to Poulett. In practice any male householder who paid the Church Rate had the right to vote. Poulett continued to represent the town but in 1780 a petition for bribery brought by J. Acland, a defeated candidate, succeeded against Poulett's colleague, Benjamin Allen.

It has always been assumed, probably correctly, that elections took place on the Cornhill, but eye-witness accounts are lacking. One of the Clarke family who lived in Bridgwater described around 1820 a wooden platform next to the High Cross used for conducting judicial business, and the Cornhill had long been a centre for this. Parliamentary elections required a larger platform called the 'hustings', but no records of payments for erecting and removing the hustings exist. An entry in the index of Council minutes of 1710 (the minutes are missing) states: 'yt Ye Recorder do make a Convenient Passage to accomidate ye Electors for parliament men'.

There was no official register of electors so every man voting was examined by the Returning Officer. This could be a lengthy process and the election described by Clarke lasted for a fortnight, with several townspeople sitting on benches on the hustings. In 1720 legal action was taken on behalf of 30 householders who had been disfranchised by the ruling clique, who had simply omitted their names from the rate list.

The Brick and Tile Industry

Coles and Anstice bought Glover's brickyard in 1787 and continued to supply bricks to Kymer, as did Edward S`ealy from 1788 after he acquired the yard. Sealy already owned another yard in Hamp and was connected with 14 vessels trading with Wales between 1786 and 1819. Although documentary references to Bridgwater bricks and tiles are sparse, during the 18th century the industry contributed significantly to the local economy and became increasingly important as the Industrial Revolution gradually eroded the local cloth trade. Dublin historians believe that some of their 18th-century houses were built using Bridgwater bricks.

The Reverend William Holland of Over Stowey visited Sealy in 1810 and his diary says, 'He deals large in various ways, has many ships and is with his two sons in the Banking Way. Vain and Pompous and full of Money. He has many houses in the Brick Grounds and a whole company of people there seemingly in a comfortable way.'

This section of the brick industry operated on paternalistic lines and Enumerators' early 19th-century Census Lists show workers living in cottages in the brickyard. In 1815 Edward Sealy was paying 12s. 6d. Land Tax on Coles's brickyard and he still owned it in 1830, by when he had been supplying bricks to Bridgwater Corporation since 1772. His yard was eventually taken over by H.J. & C. Major and remained in production until 1939.

In 1784 bricks were taxed at 2s. 6d. per 1,000; this rate doubled after 1793. Brick makers evaded the impact by making larger bricks and this made brick laying slow and heavy work. In 1802 the tax on large bricks doubled so bricks reverted to their earlier size. From 1806 the tax was stable at 5s. 10d. until 1850, when it was abolished. The Excise Regulation of 1784, quoted in 1836 by the Commissioners of Inquiry, says, 'Every person before beginning to make bricks must make entry in writing with the Officer of Excise of his name and place of abode, and of the sheds, workhouses and other places used for preparing and finishing the same.' The number of bricks moulded was to be noted and duty charged accordingly but no survey book has survived. The only figures available in Parliamentary Papers are for Somerset and only quoted for certain years, but production increased enormously between 1829 and 1846.

Various rates of tax aplied to different types of tile, including paving tiles, but no separate figures for the county of Somerset were ever produced. The tax on tiles was removed in 1833.

The *Universal British Directory* of 1790-1 does not name a single Bridgwater brick maker, and the 1835 *British Almanac* describes Somerset industries without mentioning brick making.

21

Victorian Times

'The present Market House was completed about the year 1827', says Robson's *Somerset Directory* of 1839. Pigott, in 1850, described it as 'a very elegant market house' and added, 'Few provincial towns have exhibited so much public spirit for improvement as this little sea port.' He also noted that there was a reading room above the market house. The creation of the dome and peristyle was a stroke of genius, and gave Bridgwater the most pleasing Market Place (Fig. 59), but the new building had two defects: the Bath stone used was badly selected, so as a result re-surfacing of the walls became a perennial problem, and most of the area intended for use by traders was open to the sky.

The Trustees had originally borrowed £10,850 from the Corporation and were supposed to pay them an annuity of £50 per annum, but they were unable to pay this after 1833. When the Town Council took over the market in 1872 the price it paid was £4,071, but after essential repairs had been carried out the total had risen to £7,000. It sold 33 properties in order to meet the cost. In 1874 a plan to cover the main hall with a glass roof was to cost £4,871 and another £350 was spent in making suitable accommodation for the post office. This work was completed in 1875 and the post office moved from East Quay, where its former quarters are still recognisable. At the Market House the words 'Post Office' are still visible at roof level in the High Street.

In 1834 a private company built a gas works in Taunton Road and gas lighting was installed in the town's main streets. The High Street is not mentioned until 1826. The houses which Chubb drew there (Fig. 51) still existed on 21 December 1855 when the Town Council decided to buy them for demolition. In August 1836 a man called Wyvern threatened to re-build a house in front of the *Bristol Arms*, 'by which the difficulties of removing it, and others, commonly called the Island, would be greatly increased'. Wyvern was bought off with the grant of a lease on the *Old Oak*. The Borough Treasurer was then authorised to borrow £550 at three per cent to remove of the houses, and a committee was set up with power to take two houses down.

At that point the Council minutes fall silent on the subject, but many years later, on 5 February 1854, the Treasury was asked to consent to the demolition of two houses which were 'in hand'. A year later, on 4 May 1855, it was asked to give permission for the demolition of three houses. Consent was received and

59 The Cornhill provides an interesting town centre with its variety of buildings, many having architectural merit. The area is dominated by the façade of the Market House with its dome and peristyle built between 1826 and 1828. The statue in the foreground is Admiral Blake and was unveiled in 1901. The church with the spire is St Mary's.

duly minuted on 3 August 1855. On 30 November William Danger surrendered his lease on the last of these houses in exchange for £15 per annum for the remaining period.

If Chubb made his drawing around 1805 he obviously thought the 'island' was about to disappear. He could never have dreamed that the last three houses would still be there fifty years later. The Market House trustees were, perhaps, fortunate to get as far as they did in improving the approach to the market but their legal powers and funds had been inadequate. The last house came down on 24 January 1856 and on 1 February the Town Council gave thanks to John Hurman and J.R. Smith, 'for the activity they have used in arranging matters for the removal of the island of houses in High Street'. Hurman now turned his attention to St Mary Street where some slum cottages were still standing on the churchyard edge.

In commenting on the changes in the High Street the *Bridgwater Times* looked forward to 'when the fronts of the adjoining houses are brought out in uniform'. The editor evidently expected the building line to be moved forward but fortunately this was not done, and the wide pavement was retained. The turnpikes had outlived their useful role and were causing obstruction and inconvenience. On 8 January 1869 the Town Council decided that all the gates must go. In 1853 it petitioned the Queen to keep the Assizes here but this was a vain hope and Bridgwater ceased to be an Assize town, probably during the same year.

The County Court and New Town Hall

The County Court, built in 1859, was probably the last building in the 18th-century classical tradition. The county court for debt recovery was originally held at Ilchester but one court for the whole of Somerset became increasingly inconvenient and so others were created. One was operating at the *George Inn* in Bridgwater by 1848. In 1852 it was in the Assize Hall, but obviously a new building was needed. This (Fig. 60) gave its name to Court Street, and the old name, Coffee House Lane, vanished.

An extraordinary house stands almost opposite the Court. It was built of pre-fabricated concrete blocks in 1851 by the brick-making firm of John Board to advertise this new building technique. Its design is an imitation castle using architectural details of unknown style (Fig. 61). A statue of Napoleon I stands in a recess. John Board called the house 'Portland Castle' which is possibly a more appropriate name than its present one, Castle House.

In 1862 a public meeting gave voice to the demand for a new, larger and more convenient Town Hall. This was quickly made official policy but it was an expensive undertaking and much corporation property was sold to pay for it. The

60 The County Court, built in 1859, is the most important building in Queen Street, which also contains several old houses. Queen Street loops from the top to the bottom of Castle Street and is joined to Fore Street by Court Street, which was previously called Coffee House Lane.

61 Castle House in Queen Street. This extraordinary house was built of prefabricated concrete blocks in 1851 by the brick-making firm of John Board in order to advertise the new building technique. The design is an imitation castle using architectural details of unknown style. A statue of Napoleon I stands in a recess. John Board called the house 'Portland Castle', which seems more appropriate than its present name. It is the first building of this type but unfortunately fell into dereliction and was attacked by arsonists. Its restoration is in hand.

new building was designed by Charles Knowles, a Bridgwater man. There was considerable delay in starting building as the Taunton firm given the contract, Shewbrook's, dropped it. A Bridgwater firm, T. Searle and W. Cook, was called in but William Cook died, causing further delay. Eventually, on 4 August 1865, there was an official opening ceremony with a big parade of Rifle Volunteers and Friendly Societies. The main concern of the architect was to incorporate a large public hall with a stage and galleries into his scheme. It is still the largest public hall in the town and continues to fulfil a useful function.

Possibly parts of the old building were retained and refurbished. The two porches look very much like the old ones and the present Charter Hall is often called the 'old Assize Court' even though it does not correspond with either court shown on the 1824 plan. Beneath the modern light oak walls are old panels displaying the names of Recorders and other officials.

62 A typical Bath brick. Until over 50 years ago these were made by the million and sold for scouring purposes. Their demise followed the introduction of less coarse scouring powders packaged in canisters. This example is reasonably typical, measuring 6½ by 3 by 2 inches thick.

The Brick and Tile Industry

Hunt and Co.'s 1848 *Directory* says of Bridgwater: 'The manufactures here are chiefly bricks and tiles', but it emphasises Bath bricks. Similarly Bragg in 1840 only mentions 'a peculiar kind of scouring brick'. Bath brick (Fig. 62), so called as its colour resembles that of Bath stone, was made from clay from the banks of the Parrett in the immediate vicinity of Bridgwater, clay taken from more than a mile away being unsuitable. Consequently Bath brick manufacture was unique to the town. The makers worked in small family groups containing a high proportion of women. *Murray's Handbook (Wiltshire, Dorset and Somerset)* of 1856 states that 'the business gives employment to a great number of persons, 8,000,000 bricks valued from £12,000 to £13,000 being made every year'. In 1822 *Pigot's Directory* listed four brick makers: Axford, John Edwards, and Edward Sealy and Sons, all of Ham Yard, and Robert Ford of King Square (presumably his office). In 1840 William Bragg named three brick makers: Browne & Co., Charles Burnell and John Sealy.

Census Enumerators' Lists from 1841 show that 68 people were employed in brick making, 37 of whom lived in Roper's Lane (now Albert Street) but there were only 13 tile makers. However, the 1851 Lists show that brick and tile maker numbers had increased to several hundred and the workers no longer lived mainly in Roper's Lane but also in West Street and other parts of the town.

Brick making tended to be seasonal with low wages. In May 1896 the brickyard workers demanded pay increases to 3s. instead of 2s. 6d. for a ten-and-a-half hour day. On 29 May 800 men went on strike. One hundred additional policemen were billeted in the Town Hall as strikers overturned wagons attempting to remove bricks and, on 2 July, 108 soldiers were drafted into the town to join

63 Soldiers and police assembled in the Town Hall ready to deal with rioting during the brickyard workers strike in 1896.

the police in the Town Hall (Fig. 63). High Street was filled with a howling group of brick workers, who showered the Town Hall roof with stones, and the mayor read the Riot Act. The troops fell into line across the street fixing bayonets before advancing towards the Cornhill, but the decision to use them was a mistake; fortunately worse did not follow. The strike petered out despite stirring words from Ben Tillett and other early trade union leaders who came down from London. Sheer hunger and misery drove the men back to work on 15 July at the end of six weeks.

Poor Law

The Union Workhouse built in 1839 was a single-storey building in the Regency tradition, much of which was demolished in the latter quarter of the 20th century, only its hospital, a two-storey building at the rear, remaining (Fig. 64). The 1841 census shows that it had 197 inmates and a staff of six: Master, Matron, Schoolmaster, Schoolmistress, Nurse and Porter. The original Master, Gover, was dismissed when it was discovered he was illiterate. His successor was called Govier.

The history of the Workhouse is a long story of administration carried on within the narrow lines laid down in 1834, although from time to time changes

64 The Union Workhouse hospital. This is all that remains of the Workhouse built in 1839 and is marred by the modern single-storey extension along its front.

were made. The making of shoes in the House was discontinued in 1849 and soon afterwards baking was stopped. Occasionally one or two inmates would come into the town, where they were easily recognised from the dark grey clothes they wore. The even tenor of life was disturbed from time to time by problems such as somebody absconding with clothes, returning to the house in a state of intoxication, gaining admission by forging the signature of the Relieving Officer, or smashing windows, usually either in the Infirmary or in the Casual Ward.

In 1849 highly critical reports of the Workhouse administration appeared in the *Bridgwater Times*. One concerned the treatment of a vagrant, Ann Young, and came from two leading townsmen, Joseph Thompson JP and George Browne, both members of the Town Council. A second report, potentially much more damaging, bore the signature of J. Haviland, a doctor practising in the town who was now mayor. It dealt with ten separate subjects, over-crowding and bad ventilation being high on the list. The boys' bedroom contained 17 beds for 36 boys and the girls' six beds for 19 girls. In each bedroom a fireplace had been bricked up and in both rooms the walls were very dirty and some of the windows broken. The girls had a privy in a recess where the floor was covered with foul straw. The boys had a WC which had no water. All WCs were made of iron and were badly corroded. Washing troughs outside the bedrooms were left with dirty standing water and taps did not appear to be working. The casual ward was in a disgraceful state. The shortage of water was chronic, only one well being mentioned during the building operations in July 1836. It was already 35 feet deep but had to be excavated another 12 inches. Large water tanks were made but there was not enough manual power available to keep them full.

This attack was deeply resented and the Guardians said 'a great portion of the charges were unfounded'. Similar remarks had greeted Bowen's charges, although the Select Committee had found they were true. Haviland's visit of

65 *Bertha* (the only vessel with a smoke stack), the unique dredger built by Brunel to agitate silt which was then flushed out using the complicated sluicing system installed when the dock was built. This picture taken in 1907 also shows Ware's warehouse and workers using a crane to move timber.

10 February was followed by another a week later. A certain amount of cleaning and white-washing had been done but the beds were in a filthy state. The dispute became acrimonious and the situation was complicated by jealousy between the two bodies involved who were separately elected.

It is possible that the criticisms of February 1849 provoked improvements which helped when cholera broke out in August, for only the first seven victims were in the Workhouse. Parliament did not decide to bring administration of the Poor Law within the scope of local government until 1929. Boards of Guardians were abolished but the workhouse system continued to operate until 1948.

The Floating Harbour

Between 1811 and 1835 a proposal to create a floating dock in Bridgwater was being discussed. No fewer than eight plans were drawn up before agreement was reached, several of which were based on an idea proposed by the Easton family of Taunton to seal off a section of the river for use as the dock and drive a new cut through Eastover. An alternative plan put forward by the Canal Company in 1837 was finally adopted. This extended the canal from Somerset Bridge around the town on the west bank of the river to a point at Crowpill where it entered the new floating harbour to be built there.

The dock's designers realised that silting would be a problem so they incorporated an elaborate winch-operated sluicing system supplemented by a special dredger, the *Bertha* (Fig. 65), designed by Brunel. This worked by lowering a heavy

Victorian Times

pole from the vessel's rear whilst its on board steam engine dragged it from one side of the dock to the other by means of chains. The dredger worked for the entire lifetime of the docks and was taken to a maritime museum when they closed. Another interesting feature was the bascule bridge spanning the road to Chilton Trinity. It was operated by hand winches which could raise each span independently of the other. This too lasted for the life of the docks though not without certain repairs and strengthening.

From 1837 to 1841 town life was disturbed by hundreds of labourers pouring in to dig the basin for the docks and to take the canal round the town. The project cost £100,000. At the official opening in 1841 the tug *Endeavour* was used to carry a party of ladies and gentlemen plus a band to meet the first ship to enter the dock, a Bridgwater vessel called *Henry*. Tugs (Fig. 67) could reduce the sailing time from Burnham-on-Sea by as much as a day.

66 The former Custom House situated on the north side of Castle Street's junction with West Quay.

The docks brought prosperity to certain enterprises, such as flour mills, Spillers, timber yards, and ship's chandlers. HM Customs also benefited (Fig. 66) and products of local industry, particularly bricks and tiles, were handled. Shipping peaked between 1880 and 1885 when an average of 3,600 ships a year entered the Port of Bridgwater (Fig. 68).

In 1840 the canal carried almost 90,000 tons of freight, yielding a net income of £5,000. Its success continued for a short time after the new docks opened,

67 The paddle tug *Petrel* in the vicinity of Saltlands in 1865. Without the assistance of a tug, sailing ships might need three tides to reach Bridgwater from the Parrett's mouth.

68 The floating harbour (sometimes called the inner basin) in 1885 as seen from 'the Mump', the name given to the spoil heap created by excavating the docks. At this date well over 3,000 ships a year were entering Bridgwater.

net income rising to £8,200, but then canal trade dramatically decreased owing to competition from the railway. Its traffic peaked in 1847 when it carried 79,000 tons of freight. By the 1850s the canal was in the Receiver's hands and was eventually purchased in 1866 by the Bristol and Exeter Railway for £64,000.

At the same time the docks were being built another labour force was extending the Bristol to Exeter Railway to Bridgwater. The station still stands on what was then the town's edge, off the bottom of St John Street. It opened on 1 June 1841 when the first train arrived in the morning. The track was broad gauge. In 1845 a horse tramway was constructed to connect the railway station with East Quay. The corporation sold the tramway in 1863 to the Bristol and Exeter Railway Company who, in 1869, converted it for use by steam trains. The railway company also purchased the docks in 1866 and carried out major repairs and improvements in 1867. In 1870 both railway and docks were acquired by the Great Western Railway.

Until 1892 the track was broad gauge, a short length of which carried a steam crane on Sully's Wharf on the town side of the tidal basin for many years. It was replaced by another steam crane on standard gauge track in about 1950. In 1871 the telescopic bridge, locally called the Black Bridge (Fig. 69), was

69 The Telescopic Bridge, sometimes called the Black Bridge, a listed structure believed to be just one of two remaining examples of its type. Unfortunately the building on the east bank housing the steam engine to operate the bridge was inadvertently demolished.

built over the river to connect the railway with the docks; it cost £25,000. The bridge had a section on the east bank which could be moved to one side and a central sliding section then retracted to allow ships to pass. The mechanism was powered by a steam engine housed in a building on the river bank.

In addition, a huge timber wharf equipped with rails was constructed from East Quay to a point about a mile downstream (Fig. 70), which indicates how busy the port was whilst small craft remained commercially viable. Some remains of the timber wharf are still visible near the Black Bridge (Fig. 71) and in one or two other areas, but they are disappearing fast.

A public meeting in June 1880 considered the possibility of the Midland and London and South West Railway Companies extending their network to Bridgwater. Ten years later construction work commenced linking Edington with Bridgwater and was completed in July 1890 when the first train arrived.

70 Ice on the river near Saltlands in 1867, an unusually cold winter. A long length of the wooden staging enabling moored ships to unload their cargo is clearly visible. The relatively new St John's Church in Eastover is silhouetted on the left.

Unfortunately it was so wet that the civic reception on the platform had to be abandoned. The station was located on the site currently occupied by Sainsbury's supermarket and reached via a road just below the turning for the Drove. The water tower (Fig. 72) could easily be seen. The line closed in the early 1950s and the track, station and all other buildings were removed shortly after so that there is virtually no evidence of their former existence.

71 Fragments of the old wooden wharf near the Telescopic Bridge in 1999. Very little of the wharf remains.

Parliamentary Elections and Disfranchisement

The borough was represented by two Members of Parliament and each elector had two votes which were openly used before the Returning Officer until the Ballot Act of 1872. After an election local printers produced a list detailing who had voted and how; 18 lists have survived from 1754 to 1866. Between 1832 and 1870 Bridgwater held 13 elections; all were corrupt yet only four petitions were

72 The water tower and an engine alongside the Somerset and Dorset Railway line just outside Bridgwater North station in 1949. Virtually all traces of the railway within the town have vanished.

presented, of which two went to trial, in 1836 and 1839. Election petitions were rare in Bridgwater because each political party knew 'its own corruptions were quite equal to those of the adverse party', and an enquiry might result in disfranchisement. Action in 1838 under the existing laws revealed 'the detailed methods of the great organisations for bribery purposes in use at Bridgwater elections at all times and on both sides of politics'.

Although the agents were much to blame, many candidates were eager paymasters. In 1847 the managers of both parties came to a secret understanding in order to save the candidates from 'an expenditure already become ruinous'. In the 1835 election the opponent of Broadwood, a piano-maker, was said to provide 'piano fifties' against Broadwood's piano 'forties' (i.e. £40 bribes). The idea was to choose an agent and then persuade his employer to grant leave of absence 'for ill health'. The agent then listed electors known to accept bribes and opened an office, on one occasion in the house of John Murlis, the Conservative agent. On polling day it was crammed with electors each of whom received a ticket which he took to a darkened room where a stranger sat at a table. The ticket was exchanged for a packet containing ten sovereigns known as 'a cartridge', the stranger being 'one Croucher, a low fellow from London', who hired himself out as 'Man in the Moon' to any party requiring his services.

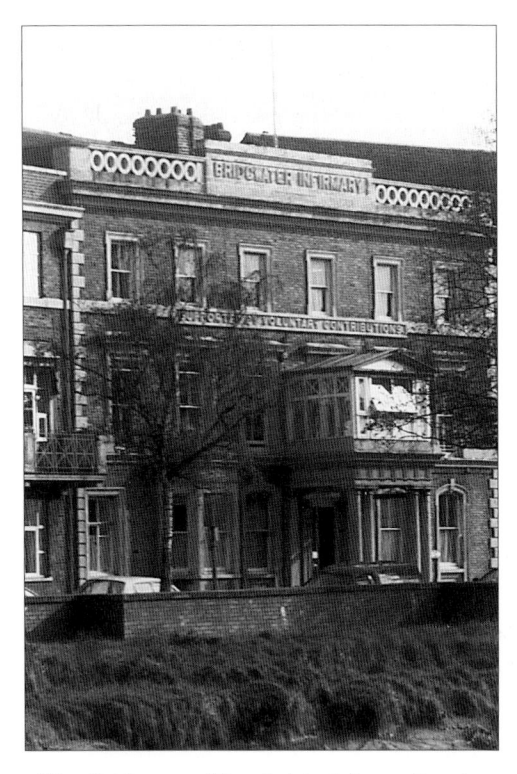

73 Bridgwater Hospital in Salmon Parade. Originally in Clare Street, it moved in 1820 and was extended in 1862 by purchasing an adjoining house. The classical front was added in 1876.

There was debauchery at all these elections, each party allowing £300 to cover free drinks to voters and consequently 'many voters were polled who did not know what they were about'. The malpractices sometimes 'led to street encounters between one set of bribery agents and another, which very strongly resembled riots'.

One of the most unprincipled men helping to operate the Liberal election machinery was James Bussell. His scandalous services were rewarded by his being made town gaoler in 1836, and then, in 1849, Superintendent of the Borough Police and Bailiff to the local County Court, with his son as Deputy. In 1859 Bussell received lucrative offers from the Conservatives, and changed sides. His son, Henry Chapman Bussell, who had helped the Conservatives, was landlord of the *Anchor* in 1857, which he placed in the service of the Liberals, and was instrumental in causing an unexpected result in the 1859 parliamentary election. John Murless had bribed men to vote Conservative a fortnight before polling day, but 'The Liberal bribe agents picked them up on the polling day and so they got paid on both sides'. The Liberals used chiefly the *Golden Ball* (Fig. 74) to dispense bribes to voters. Men who had votes were brought up to believe they had a right to be paid for using them.

In 1868 the Conservatives considered it safe to present a petition against the election of the Liberals Kinglake and Vanderbyl. The case was tried in 1869 and heard by Mr Justice Blackburn in Bridgwater Town Hall. Both Liberals were unseated but that was not the end of the matter, a Liberal petition having succeeded in unseating the Conservative, Westropp in 1865, and Parliament now appointed a commission to investigate corruption in Bridgwater elections, which sat in Bridgwater Town Hall from 23 August until 16 October. Its first report contains evidence from 46,500 questions put to 515 people and

74 The *Golden Ball* in High Street. This rather ordinary hostelry built about 1820 was frequently used in the mid-19th century by the local Liberals to dispense bribes during parliamentary elections. For some years it was known as the *Holts Arms* but very recently has reverted to its original name.

its second report offers its comments and advice. The commissioners who wrote the report of 1870 made no reference to any problems, but spoke of 'polling day' and quoted the 1837 Petition as having been signed by '156 out of 568 registered voters'. They commented that the gradually increasing size of the electorate had no effect on the scale of bribery and estimated that of the 600 electors in the 1868 election only about 50 took no part in bribery! Their evidence also showed that, of the large sums dispensed to the agents, a substantial proportion was never passed on.

The same commissioners decided to extend their inquiries back to 1832. They believed that the original class of small gentry in the borough had dwindled, and by 1847 management of parliamentary elections had somehow passed to certain local lawyers. In practice, though, the situation was similar to that of the early 18th century when the Duke of Chandos had been unable to penetrate local political affairs.

As a result Bridgwater was disfranchised in 1870. This was an obvious disgrace but it needs to be seen in perspective, for Bridgwater was not alone; other rotten boroughs disfranchised in 1870 were Beverly in Yorkshire, and Cassell and Sligo in Ireland.

The 1832 Reform Bill had eliminated some rotten boroughs but Bridgwater escaped. In boroughs the vote had been given to male householders with houses worth £10 a year but this would not have greatly influenced the size of Bridgwater's electorate. In 1867, however, the vote was given to all male householders, which raised numbers of Bridgwater voters from 700 to 1,500. The third Reform Bill (1885) restored politics to Bridgwater by abolishing the distinction between county and borough; it also gave the vote to all male householders and created single member constituencies. The Bridgwater County Division encompassed a large, traditionally Conservative, rural area.

The Cholera Epidemic

Whilst the town depended mainly on wells, the water supply was never adequate and was liable to pollution. The well shafts were not sunk through an impermeable layer and so surface water could always seep in. Many houses had cesspits and low-lying areas of ground were readily saturated. In 1877 the wells in Barclay and Devonshire Streets were badly polluted. 'Let us look to our drains and our cess pools', had said the editor of the *Bridgwater Times* in 1852; this was obviously a difficult problem to solve.

Cholera did not erupt before 1849, but then some 200 people died, the highest incidence in small insanitary cottages often crowded together in 'courts', particularly on both sides of West Street, in Albert Street, and on the west side of North Street. There were many tiny houses along the older streets. The 1887 Ordnance Survey map shows that West Bow Terrace contained eight cottages between Mount Street's entrance and the corner of Pig Cross, then the row continued with another eight cottages in Pig Cross and ten more round the corner of Mount Street. Many lacked a water supply and sanitary conveniences.

The first death in the 1849 cholera epidemic occurred in the Workhouse but was the only death there. Nobody suggested opening a special burial ground for cholera victims but the vicar refused to accept further burials at St Mary's, directing them instead to Chilton Trinity. Many were buried in the new cemetery at St John's. The most informative document concerning the outbreak is a letter by John Hurman published in the *Bridgwater Times* in 1853, quoting official figures and giving the incidence of cholera, street by street. Hurman stressed the need for cleanliness and pure water and in the ensuing public outcry sanitary improvements were demanded but were slow to arrive.

The medical officers appointed under the Poor Law were rewarded by the Board of Guardians, Mr Parker receiving £50 and Mr Symes £40. Their report shows that Mr Parker treated 254 cases of cholera and 475 cases of diarrhoea. Mr Symes treated 73 cases of cholera and 480 cases of diarrhoea. Nevertheless, Bridgwater was reputed to be a healthy place and many other towns had to cope with problems similar to those experienced here. Published national statistics concerning public health problems in the later 19th century show that Bridgwater figures were usually similar to the national average.

The Hospital

The hospital governors bought the adjoining house in Salmon Parade in 1862. In 1876 the entire front of the hospital was rebuilt and a classical portico (Fig. 73) added in honour of a generous benefactor, Mr G.S. Poole. By 1934 there were 72 beds. The hospital was maintained entirely by voluntary contributions until 1948 when it was taken over by the state. Since then the site has been extended, new buildings have been erected, and other property acquired. The development of the National Health Service has meant that services are largely based on Taunton but the strength of local feeling has ensured that the Bridgwater Hospital continues to play an important part in the life of the town.

Water Supply

The *Bridgwater Times* of 14 February 1850 reported that some houses in St Mary Street were without water and necessary conveniences: 'Nuisances are frequently to be seen in the street in consequence.' On 21 March the newspaper published further comments: 'On Monday morning the grating opposite Mr Dare's house was completely choked with filth and night soil thrown from the unwholesome dens adjoining St Mary's churchyard, and an ash pan had been made the convenience of the inhabitants of the back house adjoining the south gate of the churchyard, the pan standing at the end of the entry and close to the door through which the house is entered. These are pretty exhibitions for a corporate town of between 10 and 11,000 inhabitants, in a street where there is a constant thorough-fare, opposite one of the principal entrances of our parish church, and in the centre of the town.'

In 1870 there was a severe drought and in August the wells dried up and Durleigh Brook ceased to run. The *Bridgwater Mercury* asked the all-important question: 'Why is there no piped water?'

A public meeting in November 1866 discussed the medical profession's concerns. A committee of the Town Council authorised a report from an experienced engineer called Hawkesley, who advised a scheme very similar to that which was eventually adopted. Unfortunately, a second public meeting voted for a scheme by a private company and years passed without results. Eventually, in November 1876, the corporation applied for a Water Act to enable it to undertake the enterprise, which became law on 2 August 1877. The corporation acquired land at Ashford but, in order to take water at Blackmore, it had to compensate local landowners. The accounts were settled by arbitration.

The work involved the construction of reservoir, subsiding tank, filter beds, boiler house, engine house, coal store and two pumping engines at Ashford, and contracts for the waterworks were signed in 1878. A service reservoir holding 800,000 gallons of water was constructed at the top of Wembdon Hill, 90 feet above the Cornhill, and some 13 miles of piping were laid. The first man to turn a tap on in his house was the Town Clerk on 30 December 1879. The scheme cost about £40,000 and was capable of supplying water to some 20,000 inhabitants.

Housing Problems

In 1883 a special report was made on Honeysuckle Alley, which ran from Clare Street to Corporation Street, almost in line with Mansion House Lane. Technically it was not a 'Court' since it was open at both ends, a court being a confined space opening off a street, but it comprised 12 tiny cottages crammed along the west side, which could be described as half-houses for they had only one door and backed on to the wall of a candle factory; another ten cottages on the east side; and a further five in a separate group at the north end. Some lavatory accommodation existed at that end of the alley, consisting of three cubicles without doors served by a trough lavatory and a flush at one end. There were over a dozen of these in different parts of the town which were often reported as being defective. One survived at Eastover Infants' School until 1950.

Improvements tended to be on a small scale. Although the 1850 newspaper report was enough to condemn the hovels along the edge of the churchyard in St Mary Street, eliminating them was a Herculean task. In 1879 two, both lacking water and sanitation, could not be purchased for less than £75 and the corporation refused to pay more than £50, so eventually the churchwardens added £25. Even so, the 1887 Ordnance Survey map shows that four similar cottages remained.

The process of improving street surfaces is not well covered by documentary evidence. John Chubb's sketches c.1790 seem to show that the early method of pitching gravel had been stopped. Pavements had been reasonably laid with flagstones and gullies were constructed with masonry. Some road surfaces had cobbles, but most were small stones beaten flat.

In 1883 a crossing in Church Street was said to have been macadamised. The road surface must have been rough since it was necessary everywhere to provide pedestrians with crossings made of small rectangular granite sets. A surviving example is at St Mary Street's junction with Penel Orlieu.

The century ended with the statue to Robert Blake being unveiled on 5 October 1900. Blake was Bridgwater's most famous son, Cromwell's 'General at Sea' during the Commonwealth. Some authorities argue that he was at least Nelson's equal. Originally the statue stood before the Cornhill but it was recently moved to the Cornhill's junction with Fore Street.

22

BRIDGWATER IN THE TWENTIETH CENTURY

Queen Victoria died early in the new century and the mayor, standing on the Cornhill, proclaimed Edward VII king. The late queen was commemorated by opening the Mary Stanley County Training Home for Nurses in the Castle Street house with the Gibbs doorway (Fig. 47). The 1901 Census showed that the population, 7,800, had doubled since 1801 when it was 3,600. Various improvements to the town's amenities were made over the next few years.

Blake Gardens were opened in August 1902 by the mayoress, Mrs T.W. Manchip, the 2½-acre gardens covering the former grounds of Binford House which the town had bought in 1898. In 1904 electric lighting – agreed to in 1899 – was installed. Following a formal civic procession on 20 September 1906 the mayor, Mr H.W. Pollard, opened the town's public library on the site of Binford House, which was demolished in 1905. Designed by local architect E. Godfrey Page, its features, including a peristyle, dome and cupola, reflect those of the Market House. It cost £3,500, a proportion being given by the Carnegie Trust. Before the 1892 Public Libraries Act only boroughs with over 10,000 people could provide a library, as long as two-thirds of the rate payers agreed; book purchase was limited to 1d. per £1 rate but this restriction was removed in 1919. The library has been sympathetically extended in recent times and provides good facilities in a pleasant environment.

The town purchased Blake House in 1924 and made it into a museum, which opened on 16 April 1926. This late medieval building (Fig. 36) originally belonged to the Blake family and it is supposed that Robert Blake was born there. In an upper room several wall drawings of ships from Blake's period were uncovered in 1908. In 1946 the Arts Centre, the first of its kind in Britain, was opened in Castle Street by the Arts Council. Its purpose was to bring together all persons with an interest in music, drama and painting. The venture nearly never got started as the Council declined to purchase the building, but fortunately a philanthropic Wembdon resident stepped in. In 1965 the Corporation relented and bought the premises.

Parliamentary Elections

The first Liberal election win following restoration of the franchise in 1885 was the 1906 'landslide', but they lost the seat in 1910. They did not stand in

1918 and the Labour Party candidate was defeated by the Conservative, R.A. Sanders, who retained the seat following a three-cornered contest in 1922. Next year there was no Labour candidate and the Liberal, W.E. Morse, won. In 1924 the Conservatives won an overall majority against Liberal and Labour candidates and Bridgwater appeared to have become a safe Conservative seat.

In 1938 the sitting member, R. Croom-Johnson, was made a judge and the following by-election was contested by Vernon Bartlett, a well-known journalist and broadcaster who was very critical of the government's handling of foreign affairs. The issues were so important that Bridgwater became the focus of national interest. Some of the best speakers in the country visited to address meetings. Turnout was 82.4 per cent and Vernon Bartlett defeated the Conservative. The result 'gave the government an unwelcome surprise', said *The Times*.

In the post-war election of 1945 Vernon Bartlett successfully defended his seat against Labour and Conservative candidates; in 1950 he retired and since then Bridgwater has returned Conservative members. When Sir Gerald Wills (elected in 1950) died in 1970 the by-election attracted national attention because it was the first time that persons aged 18 could vote. This new factor did not change voting patterns and Bridgwater's new member was Tom King, who had a distinguished parliamentary career. He did not contest the 1997 election and shortly afterwards was elevated to the peerage, Ian Liddell-Grainger becoming the new member.

Public Health

The Medical Report for 1902 complained that many courts were choked with filth and decaying vegetable matter. In 1905 the Health Committee carried out a special inspection of courts: 'It took 8 long evenings,' said their Clerk. It visited 85 courts with 534 houses. The great obstacle to getting improvements was 'the extreme poverty of the owners'.

Conditions at the borough mortuary were clearly unsatisfactory in 1913 as a doctor complained that there was no soap, no hot water and no towels. The number of private slaughter houses also caused concern, the 14 in existence in 1900 almost invariably in unsuitable places. The Medical Officer of Health had always lobbied for the borough to build a public abattoir; the problem was only solved after the Second World War with a government-imposed scheme centred on Weston-super-Mare.

Another problem was the number of small dairies scattered about the town, some with cowsheds and many in very unsuitable places. Few were eliminated before new regulations were implemented after the Second World War. Of 48 premises making ice-cream, inspected in 1926, four were closed (one in a rag and bone yard, one in a pigeon house and two in over-crowded court houses) and another 15 were ordered to make improvements.

Dozens of wells must be concealed in the older parts of the town. Occasionally one is uncovered and then sealed but no record of them has ever been kept. One, uncovered *c.*1980 behind No. 16 Angel Crescent, was obviously a communal well serving the cottages at the Crescent's northern end. It was brick-lined, about five feet in diameter and almost full of water. In the western part of the town a well of a different type was discovered *c*.1940 in the kitchen of a house in Roman Road. This unlined well was rectangular, measuring about three feet by 4ft. 6in. and dry, but a lead pipe cut off at ground level had presumably served a pump.

A chlorination scheme for the water supply was adopted in 1923. Chlorination was first introduced in Lincoln in 1904-5 following a typhoid epidemic. By the 1930s there was an increasing need for water, particularly by industry, so a new reservoir linked with Ashford was opened at Durleigh in 1938. Two years later a new water treatment plant had been added. The modern water supply attracted new industry to Bridgwater, Courtaulds 'Cellophane' factory on the Bath Road being a particularly important example. In 1962 a new reservoir was constructed at Hawkridge in the Quantocks to provide a reserve supply for Ashford and Durleigh.

The provision of piped water soon led to the introduction of water closets and flush lavatories. The change was gradual but by 1910 the installation of water closets was more advanced than in many other towns. However, piped water was not used in the town swimming baths in Old Taunton Road until 1935, and they were filled with water from Durleigh Brook. The swimming baths, built in 1889, were originally a private venture but were purchased by the Corporation in 1893. Being open-air and unheated, they were demolished in the late 1950s to permit construction of Broadway, and Broadway Lido opened in 1960. More recently these baths and the adjacent rugby ground were sold to a supermarket chain and a new facility, the Sedgemoor Splash, was built in Northgate.

A proper sewerage system required stoneware pipes and manholes so changing to this system took time. The old drains were usually brick-built, and in theory a man could walk through them to dig out the silt. In practice there was insufficient height for a man to stand upright, and inadequate ventilation made it impossible for anyone to work there for any length of time. Stoneware pipes were laid in Wembdon Road and Provident Place in 1904, Mount Street in 1905, and Albert Street in 1906. Bath Road and Bristol Road were dealt with in a three-year programme which started in 1909. Many old brick sewers remain *in situ* and occasionally one is uncovered and townsfolk speculate about secret passages. Knowing the location of the old sewers is possibly not a recent problem as in 1873 the Health Committee asked Mr Knowles, the architect, to lend Dr Parsons, the M.O.H., his plan of the town drains. There were ten outfalls into the river and in 1915 the M.O.H. wrote, 'The town is fortunate in having a tidal river into which it can pour sewage and surface water without harm to the inhabitants.' It is only in recent years that a sewage treatment plant has been brought into operation.

In 1934 £11,000 was raised to build a new wing on the hospital and provide an X-ray department. The hospital was never taken over by the local authority but maintained entirely by voluntary contributions until 1948 when it was absorbed by the new National Health Service.

In 1921 the Health Committee noted that the town possessed a horse-drawn ambulance but only for infectious diseases. It was a large vehicle, painted black, and a horse had to be hired when it was needed. It remained until 1939 to carry bedding for fumigation. In 1925 a motor ambulance for accidents was presented to the local St John Ambulance Brigade. It was housed by Bridgwater Motor Company and driven by one of their staff. Calls within the borough cost 5s.; elsewhere the charge was 1s. per mile. In cases of urgency people were told to phone the motor company between 8 a.m. and 5.30 p.m. and at night to ring the borough police station.

The St John Ambulance Brigade was given another vehicle in 1931. This came at an appropriate time, for the M.O.H. said in his 1930 report, 'The frequency of deaths due to violence (13 males and three females) is noteworthy and may be largely attributed to the risks of motor traffic.'

The Two World Wars

The effects of the First World War were noted by the Health Committee. In 1915 a significant fall in the number of inhabitants was largely attributable to men being called up for the armed forces. Women were used on a previously unknown scale to make shirts and bandoliers for the army and mothers engaged in war work were blamed for the 1917 rise in infant mortality. The influenza epidemic of 1918 sent the total death rate up to 16.1 per thousand but the 1920 birth rate was the highest recorded for many years.

Bridgwater was presented with a tank following the town's success in 'Victory Loan Week' during July 1919, when £162,237 was raised instead of the £100,000 expected. The tank was placed on a plinth at the station end of St John Street where it remained for many years. The town's memorial to those killed in the war was erected in King Square and unveiled in 1924.

Fortunately Bridgwater only suffered one bombing raid during the Second World War when some bombs fell on 24 August 1940 causing damage and several casualties, including some deaths. Many evacuees were billeted throughout the town and the surrounding area for much of the war and a London school shared Dr Morgan's Grammar School facilities. The 200-year-old brick-built glass cone was demolished in 1943, the reason given being to prevent its providing a landmark for enemy bombers.

All towns needed new houses after 1918. Bridgwater rapidly identified land for new housing estates but the Ministry of Health was slow to sanction loans and further delay was caused by the procedure which had been used to fund road works and sewerage. In 1923 the M.O.H. was able to report that 'housing has begun in Newtown and Taunton Road'. The town's first council houses were in Kidsbury Road and Rhode Lane, an interesting feature being the use of Bath bricks laid dry to build the retaining wall of the front boundary of these houses. Sales of the bricks were declining and it is said that the Council bought a large quantity cheaply, although another story claims they were rejects that were too hard to use as intended. They have lasted remarkably well (Fig. 75). In 1930 four areas were scheduled for slum clearance under a new Housing Act and by 1934 considerable progress had been made.

The 1929 Local Government Act added 600 acres to the borough. In 1930 four areas were scheduled for slum clearance under a new Housing Act and by 1934 considerable progress had been made.

Shortage of housing was also a serious problem after the Second World War and led not only to further development in the Rhode Lane area but also the creation of large new estates in areas served by the Durleigh, Quantock, Bath and Westonzoyland Roads. Developments in Wembdon and Durleigh meant that the town had expanded in every direction.

75 A soil retaining wall built of dry-laid Bath bricks on the front boundary of one of Bridgwater's earliest council houses. These particular walls are in Kidsbury Road and Rhode Lane and date from the 1920s. Since Bath brick was never intended to be a construction material they have lasted well.

Demand for new housing persists and almost 1,000 homes are being built in Chilton Fields, a low-lying marshy area between Wembdon and Chilton Street.

Pressure for new and improved roads had existed for years. Quantock Road, which by-passed Wembdon Hill, the site of many accidents, was opened in 1922 but the idea for constructing that road had been proposed in 1893. The war delayed the implementation of various schemes for new roads and bridges, and the increase in motor traffic, especially in the post-war years, resulted in Bridgwater's unenviable reputation for traffic jams.

In the 1950s a new road, Broadway, was built from Monmouth Street to the Taunton Road via a new bridge, Blake Bridge; it was opened in 1958, and an extension to Penel Orlieu in 1964. Following closure of the docks and removal of the rail track between docks and station, the telescopic railway bridge was temporarily converted in 1973 for motor traffic whilst a new road bridge was built a few yards upstream. Unfortunately the new bridge obstructs sight of the listed telescopic bridge from the town.

In 2000 a road bridge built at Chilton was opened as part of the road improvement scheme intended to divert Minehead-bound traffic from the Bristol Road. It provides access to numerous new houses being built along its route. The scheme was vehemently opposed, as the Wembdon Road-Quantock Road section would encroach on Whitegate field. Whitegate not only provided a green belt, albeit narrow, between town and village, but was also said to have been purchased by the Town Council in the early 1950s to provide a recreational area. Relevant documents confirming this were apparently lost during the transition from Bridgwater Town Council to Sedgemoor District Council in 1974.

BRIDGWATER IN THE TWENTIETH CENTURY

The End of the Brick and Tile Industry

In the 1920s the London Brick Company started to monopolise brick production. They owned enormous sources of clay in Bedfordshire and their mass production methods gave a uniformity of product unknown in Bridgwater. Bath brick manufacture was also declining because the bricks were being superseded by ready prepared, packaged and move gentle abrasive powders. The failure to meet the challenge of cheap machine-made tiles imported from France for use on London County Council housing schemes in 1929 was a warning that the Bridgwater industry was out of date.

Curiously, hand-made tiles still succeeded because traditional pantiles, Roman and double-Roman tiles, were of a sound design and very efficient. Machine-made tiles were less attractive in appearance. The hand-made tile was also larger so the cost of covering a given roof area (a ten feet square being the standard for calculation) was no greater than using machine-made tiles.

After 1945 the demand for bricks and tiles seemed to open great prospects for the industry. All yards that closed during the war were re-opened, except for Colthurst, Symons at Crossways, and New Yard, but the virtual monopoly

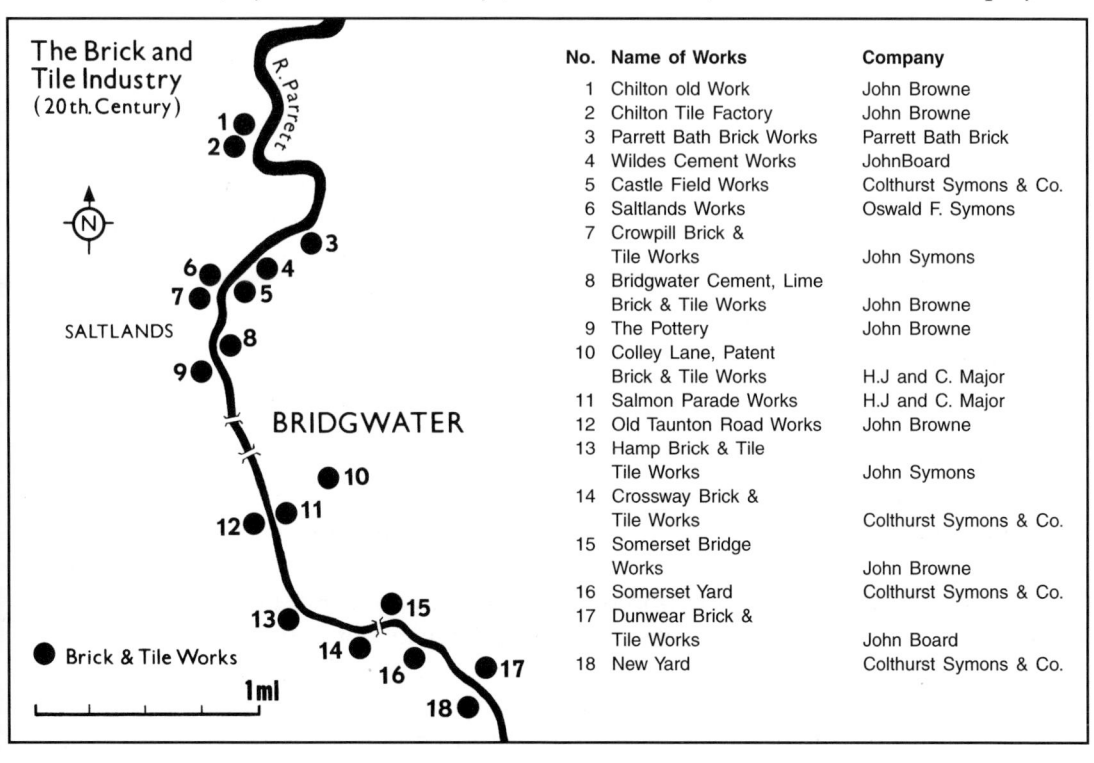

76   A typical Bridgwater brick. The holes provide two advantages: reduction in weight, making handling easier, and an excellent key for mortar. The brick measures 8½ by 4 inches and is 2⅝ inches thick.

The Brick and Tile Industry (20th. Century)

No.	Name of Works	Company
1	Chilton old Work	John Browne
2	Chilton Tile Factory	John Browne
3	Parrett Bath Brick Works	Parrett Bath Brick
4	Wildes Cement Works	JohnBoard
5	Castle Field Works	Colthurst Symons & Co.
6	Saltlands Works	Oswald F. Symons
7	Crowpill Brick & Tile Works	John Symons
8	Bridgwater Cement, Lime Brick & Tile Works	John Browne
9	The Pottery	John Browne
10	Colley Lane, Patent Brick & Tile Works	H.J and C. Major
11	Salmon Parade Works	H.J and C. Major
12	Old Taunton Road Works	John Browne
13	Hamp Brick & Tile Tile Works	John Symons
14	Crossway Brick & Tile Works	Colthurst Symons & Co.
15	Somerset Bridge Works	John Browne
16	Somerset Yard	Colthurst Symons & Co.
17	Dunwear Brick & Tile Works	John Board
18	New Yard	Colthurst Symons & Co.

77   Map showing the location of the brickyards.

of the London Brick Company, cheaper concrete blocks now being used, and the introduction of concrete tiles extinguished the industry and the hand-made Bridgwater product shown in Fig. 76.

Six firms operating after 1945 were Colthurst Symons, John Browne, H.J. and C. Major, John Board, Barham Bros. and the Parrett Brick & Tile Co. The most highly mechanised yard was John Browne's at Chilton Trinity, where mechanical diggers looking like an endless chain of buckets moving up a sloping bank extracted clay. If these firms had amalgamated, the industry might possibly have survived, though much of the best clay was exhausted. Barham's might have continued to make tiles if the clay from new ground off Bath Road had proved suitable. By 1957 only Colthurst Symons remained, having closed two of their seven yards, and by 1971 all had gone. Brick and tile-making firms, with their location and closure dates, are shown in the following table together with brick-making companies in the neighbourhood but outside the borough:

Company	Location	Closure date
Barham Bros.	East Quay*	1964
John Board & Co.	Bristol Road*	1958
	Dunwear	1958
John Browne & Co.	Chilton Trinity	1968
(formerly the Somerset	Dunwear*	1960
Trading Company).	Hamp	1963
Colthurst Symons & Co.	Dunball	1970
	Castle Fields*	1970
	Somerset Bridge*	1959*
	Huntworth	1939
	Combwich	1964
	Burnham-on-Sea	1966
	Saltlands	1966
H.J. & C. Major Ltd.	Colley Lane	1956
	Salmon Lane	1956
	Hamp*	1939
The Northgate Pottery	Northgate	1939
(operated by the Somerset Trading Co.)		
The Parrett Brick & Tile Co.	Bristol Road*	1954
Yards outside the borough:		
J. Pitts & Co.	Highbridge	1955
J. Cox & Co.	Highbridge	1955
Apex Brick & Tile Co.	Burnham-on-Sea	1944

*Asterisked locations also made bath brick.

These firms' main business was roofing tile manufacture but all produced building bricks, too, and most made land drainage pipes. The sudden and total decline of the industry after 1945 was a tremendous blow to the local economy.

The geographical location of the Bridgwater yards is shown in Fig. 77 and Fig. 78 illustrates a few of the products manufactured. A Brick and Tile Museum which includes preserved examples of kilns has been opened on East Quay.

The Port and River

In 1900 about 3,000 ships entered the port and consequently the harbour and quays were very busy (Figs. 79 & 80). In practice numbers were declining, the peak having been reached in 1880-5 when an average 3,600 vessels a year berthed. The decline coincided with the Severn railway tunnel's provision of ready rail access from Wales to the south-west of England. The last ship built at Bridgwater, a 99-ton ketch named *Irene*, was launched from Carver's yard on the East Quay in the spring of 1910. She was owned by Colthurst Symons & Company and used to transport bricks and tiles but is now in private hands on the south coast. Carver's yard continued to repair ships until 1940.

Despite the tidal basin's ingenious sluicing arrangements silting remained a problem, as a spring tide could contain over half a pound of solid matter per cubic foot of water. To counter this problem the docks were closed for two months in 1910 to install a culvert 3½ feet in diameter beneath the floor of the basin and the river. A chain and winch-operated slide valve covered the dock end of the culvert, and opening this at low water provided vigorous flushing since the head of water could be 16 feet. Next year Mr F. Wills' local engineering firm built a boat fitted with a powerful pressure hose to clear silt from the river's jetties and slipways. Called

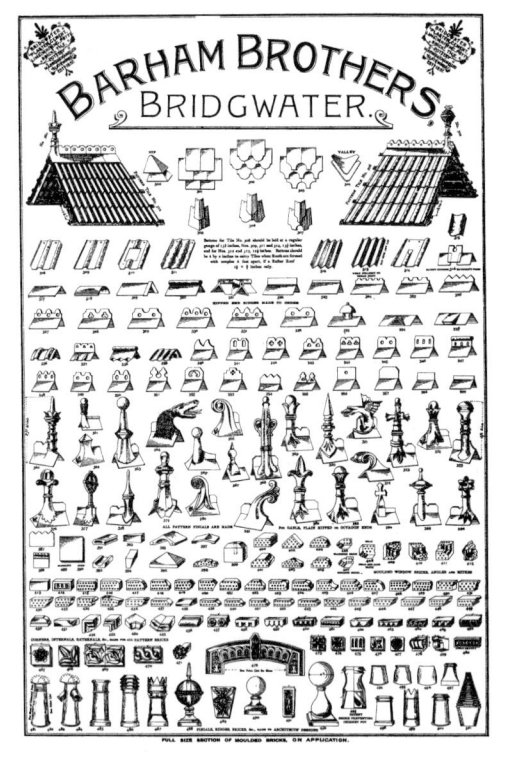

78 Barham Brothers catalogue of bricks, tiles and decorative mouldings. The page shows 200 designs.

79 Shipping seen from the Town Bridge in 1907. A boat in Carver's yard can be seen in the centre. There was a gridiron next to East Quay, the use of which attracted an extra charge.

80 A boat that has brought slate from Portugal is moored at East Quay early in the 20th century. Messrs Wilkinson & Leng imported slate for manufacturing fireplaces.

81 The canal looking from the towpath towards West Street bridge. The canal is in a deep cutting here which is lined with red sandstone and buttressed every 10-12 feet. Following the collapse of part of the wall in 1968 it was repaired with modern blocks. An adjacent portion appears to have been reinforced with massive timber baulks secured with enormous iron brackets and bolts, but this is a work of art and is a listed structure. Words are carved on 11 of the beams: (1) Navigators (2) Hard Graft (3) Sinew & Bone (4) Jolt of the Pick (5) Crack of the Hammer (6) Iron on Stone (7) Red Quantock (8) We Cam & Went (9) Our Legacy (10) A Boat (11) Through the Hill.

82 The *Crowpill*, one of Sully's colliers, leaving the tidal basin in 1962. A 'bee hive' kiln can be seen on the horizon to the left. Unloading coal was incredibly labour-intensive as a large steel cauldron was lowered into the hold and filled by hand. The steam crane then lifted it over the wall into Sully's yard to be unloaded.

the *Eroder*, she cost Bridgwater Corporation £3,280 and supplemented a similar vessel, the *Pioneer*, built in 1894. The *Pioneer* was withdrawn in 1917 but the *Eroder* lasted beyond the end of the Second World War.

Commercial traffic on the canal continued to decline after its acquisition by the railway company and the last commercial barge left for Taunton in 1907. However, the canal was maintained as its water was used to help flush silt from the docks. In 1947 it passed into public ownership and when the railways were nationalised in 1960 it came under British Waterways management. Part of the sandstone wall lining the cutting under West Street and Albert Street collapsed in 1968 and was shored up (Fig. 81). Somerset County Council and the relevant local authorities produced a scheme in 1970 to renovate the canal for recreational purposes, which over the following years was gradually implemented, and the canal became available for pleasure craft and the towpath for walkers.

One hundred years ago 2,971 vessels entered the port but during the 1920s the average was only 530 a year. Numbers then increased to reach 797 in 1939, but the dock could not take boats over 180 feet in length and consequently these relatively small boats became progressively less economical. Moreover, the coastal shipping trade declined because goods were increasingly being moved by road.

83 The *Tiny*, a Dutch ship registered at Groningen which more or less fitted the length of the tidal basin, had brought timber from Scandinavia *c.*1949. The photograph was taken from Sully's wharf, and Russell Place is in the background.

84 The *Sandholm* steaming up-river into Bridgwater, c.1950. The vessel was a suction dredger operated by the Holmes Sand & Gravel Co. that collected sand from the Bristol Channel which was then discharged into hoppers located at the west end of the floating harbour before being distributed to the building trade.

After 1945 the decline accelerated and was not helped by complete failure to attempt any modernisation, all locks and sluices being manually operated as they were in Victorian times. Nevertheless, small colliers still brought coal from South Wales (Fig. 82), timber came from Scandinavia (Fig. 83) and a suction dredger brought sand from the Bristol Channel (Fig. 84). Brunel's original dredger was still in use after the war, a tribute to his design and the workmanship of the period.

The riverside quays were last used commercially in 1947 and the telescopic bridge rarely withdrawn after that date. The docks were losing £7,000 a year and British Railways offered to sell them to the town, but the civil engineer's report to the borough mentioned that maintenance and running costs would be about £21,000 per annum exclusive of making improvements or interest charges on any loan. The town declined the offer in 1967 so the docks were closed on 31 July 1971 under powers granted by the 1969 British Railways Act. For a time it appeared that the docks would be filled in and perhaps used as a car park but, fortunately, Somerset County Council realised that they were possibly the last remaining example of an essentially unaltered early Victorian hand-operated dock and purchased them together with the surrounding land in 1974. The Secretary of State for the Environment recognised the docks as being of special architectural or historic interest and made the buildings and harbour facilities a conservation area. Unfortunately, the engine which used to open and close the transporter bridge was demolished by British Rail before anyone realised it had been listed and thus a unique example of industrial archaeology was lost.

Closure of the docks and cessation of brick manufacture obviously affected employment, but the town diversified and encouraged a variety of small industries to come to Bridgwater. The trend to more service industry has also helped and large warehouses and distribution depots have been constructed on both Bristol and Taunton Roads.

Towards the Century's End

Major historic sites have had some degree of protection since Victorian times but several Acts of Parliament since have gradually extended and strengthened local authority powers. The 1971 Town and Country Planning Act introduced the system of listing buildings but only Grade 1 listing provides permanent protection. A list of such buildings in Bridgwater was compiled in 1975. The

85 The Priory was originally an 18th-century private house, and then it became the offices and meeting place of the Bridgwater Rural District Council until the creation of Sedgemoor District Council in 1974. Left vacant for some years, it has recently been converted into flats, but how much of its original interior remains unscathed is uncertain. The photograph was taken before conversion.

Local Authority (Historic Buildings) Act of 1962 enabled councils to offer grants to maintain historic buildings irrespective of listing. Whether a council was prepared to make such grants was another matter.

Revolutionary changes in local government structure implemented on 1 April 1974 resulted in Bridgwater losing its mayor and corporation and the abolition of the Rural District Council to be replaced by a new administrative authority, Sedgemoor District Council. Bridgwater's former councillors became Charter Trustees with responsibility for the town's heritage. Until a new building, Bridgwater House in Northgate, was completed the Council continued to meet in the Priory (Fig. 85), home of the Bridgwater Rural District Council since its formation in 1895 and one of the most important houses in Bridgwater. It had been known as the 'Mansion house in St Mary Street' until 1892 when, with Victorian snobbery, it was incongruously re-named.

In the 18th century this was the home of the Allen family. Dr John Allen bought three properties on this site in 1702 and 1703, pulled them down and built the modest town house which is still recognisable between the two chimney stacks containing some yellow

86 The Venetian window in the Priory.

87 The George Williams Memorial Hall, built as the headquarters of the YMCA to commemorate its founder, who was apprenticed in Bridgwater, was demolished in 1965 and replaced by an extremely nondescript three-storey building.

88 Market Street (foreground), Penel Orlieu and West Street, which has the massive tower block that competes with the church spire for dominance of the town. The Odeon buildings to the right of Penel Orlieu were erected in 1936 on the site of the former cattle market. They were an excellent and pleasing example of Art Deco architecture but were spoilt in recent years by loss of the open roof and unsympathetic conversion of the shops to housing.

bricks. Dr Allen's son Benjamin probably added the large dining hall with bedrooms above. A plan in the County Record Office indicates that his son, Jeffreys Allen, seeking privacy, virtually turned the house back to front and built a high wall along the side of St Mary Street. A porch was built at the back of the house to create the main entrance and a beautiful Venetian window was inserted in the upper storey of the south wall (Fig. 86).

Had the whole house been planned and built in one operation it would surely have been listed as Grade 1. The interior fittings were very fine and the large addition to the ground floor, whether it was banqueting chamber or music room, made a very fine Council Chamber entered by two remarkable rosewood doors. The building was purchased by the Rural District Council in 1936 and ownership now transferred to Sedgemoor who, when their new premises were complete, left The Priory empty for several years. It seems a pity it did not keep the building as an asset to the community but sold it instead to a private developer who converted it for multiple occupancy as flats.

The Council for British Archaeology included Bridgwater as one of the 232 English towns 'the historic quality of which requires careful treatment in any planning or redevelopment proposal' in its 1965 report. Almost coincidentally the George Williams Memorial Hall (Fig. 87) was demolished. The hall was built in 1887 as the headquarters of the Young Men's Christian Association and commemorates the organisation's founder, a Bridgwater apprentice.

The re-development of West Street in the 1960s was long overdue as much of the housing was in a very poor state. Whether any could have been salvaged and renovated is doubtful but, unfortunately, the character of the medieval street was lost by alterations to the road and the construction of unimaginative buildings. The tower block (Fig. 88) was opened by the mayor in 1965 when

89 The shell porch above the entrance to No. 15 Friarn Street.

90 Buildings in Friarn Street with fine examples of mansard roofs. The town has several buildings with this type of roof.

91 The group of three Regency houses with an iron-work verandah comprising Friarn Lawn. There was a well between the houses and the street, given *c*.1800 by Jeffreys Allen M.P. for the townspeople to use 'for ever'; it must have been capped many years ago.

92 Some of the dock-side features that have been retained near the bascule bridge and the tidal basin. The new blocks of flats built on the site of the Mump can be clearly seen.

BRIDGWATER IN THE TWENTIETH CENTURY
181

93 The High Street entrance to Bridgwater's modern shopping centre, Angel Place. The alterations to the original High Street buildings are less intrusive than many expected but use of stone for the pillars would have considerably enhanced the appearance and also complemented other local buildings, particularly the Market House.

buildings of this nature were much in vogue, but this un-aesthetic structure dominates the town as much as the elegant 800-year-old church spire.

However, improvements to the town have been made following a 1972 report, a requirement of the 1971 Town and Country Planning Act, which seeks to identify 'areas of special architectural or historic interest, the character of which is desirable to preserve or enhance, and to designate such areas as conservation areas'. Consequently Castle Street (Fig. 46), one of the finest Georgian streets in the country, has Grade 1 listing; apart from Eastover, the whole of the area which was once the medieval borough is now in a Conservation Area. Church Street, Northfield and the docks are also included. The report suggested retaining the bollards and railings alongside the river as important reminders of the once busy port, but the need to improve flood defences against exceptionally high spring tides has resulted in the railings being replaced by walls which in many places obscure sight of the river.

Many Bridgwater buildings are worthy of preservation. For example, Friarn Street has several interesting houses: No. 15 is a Queen Anne-period house with a shell porch (Fig. 89) and towards Broadway are two tall buildings with mansard roofs, probably of the 18th century (Fig. 90). No. 41 is a small cottage which in the 1700s was an inn called the *Seven Stars*, a remarkable surviving example of vernacular architecture. Friarn Lawn, at right-angles to Friarn Street, comprises three Regency houses with an iron-work verandah (Fig. 91).

Whether the marina located in the old floating harbour will be successful remains to be seen. The canal can only be used by boats with a shallow draft and the lock gates to the river are heavily silted and need renovation. Moreover, the new bridge at Chilton and the now non-retractable telescopic bridge would seem to negate the use of masted vessels. But the dock area has been made into an interesting and attractive environment. Ware's warehouse alongside the floating harbour has a hostelry on its ground floor and offices above, and various dockside features have been retained and restored (Fig. 92) including the bascule bridge and all the sluicing winches together with other furniture. The Mump has been removed and blocks of flats erected but these are not intrusive.

Recently Fore Street has been pedestrianised and a replica of one of Bridgwater's former crosses placed at the Town Bridge end. It seems extraordinary that just over 40 years ago all traffic going through the town passed along this street. A new shopping centre, Angel Place, was built off High Street and its entrance (Fig. 93) blends well with existing buildings. It was opened by the Queen in 1988, the first visit by a reigning monarch since James II. The restoration of Angel Crescent has created an interesting street but the conversion of windows to shop fronts in the former *Royal Clarence Hotel* (Fig. 56) detracts markedly from its appearance; the upper floors have become offices.

Bridgwater suffers from problems that beset most British towns, such as ever-increasing traffic, lack of demand for retail shops leading to some being more-or-less permanently boarded up, a glut of charity shops, demands for more housing and limited resources to make necessary improvements. It seems that central government exerts more and more control and electors are powerless to influence local matters as much as they did in years gone by. In 2001 Bridgwater's population was 36,500, five times that of 1901 and ten times that of 1801. Its boundaries have also been extended several times during that time to encompass parts of some of the surrounding villages. These villages strongly and successfully resisted all attempts to include them in the borough but whether they can continue to survive as separate entities remains to be seen. The town is to get an elected mayor and Town Council but its powers will be limited and Sedgemoor will continue to administer the town and surrounding rural area. The councillors bear the heavy responsibility of maintaining and enhancing Bridgwater's numerous historical features whilst providing its inhabitants and businesses with an environment consistent with contemporary expectations.

Appendix

A – Re-building St Mary's Church

The church's battlements shown in Fig. 34 were replaced during Victorian 'renovations' started in 1851. The nave roof is now higher and the clerestory windows, originally not visible from the churchyard, are now large and easily seen. The projection on the right of the south porch has been removed and the external wall set back into line and there is now a Decorated window in place of the projection.

A competition to restore the fabric resulted in nine plans being submitted under pseudonyms and these were on view in the Town Hall. The winning design was that of by Messrs Dickson and Brakspeare of Manchester. The nave roof, the clerestory walls, the walls of the south aisle, and the south porch had been declared unsafe. Brakspeare gave Bridgwater much larger clerestory windows filled with 'Stansell's diapered glass'.

The 1851 New Year began with much argument but ended with Brakspeare's being asked to restore the tower arch, which had slipped. A serious note of dissent followed, first from the Somerset Archaeological Society and then from the Architectural Institute meeting in Bristol. The restoration was called 'a species of destruction'. In 1853 the

94 The picture above the altar of St Mary's Church given to the town in 1775 by Lord Poulett, a Bridgwater M.P. between 1769 and 1784. Fourth son of the 1st Earl Poulett, he had the misfortune to be christened with a girl's name in honour of Queen Anne. Tradition says he bought the picture, taken from a French privateer, at a Plymouth auction.

churchwardens requested an estimate to repair the tower and spire. Brakspeare proposed to pull both down and replace them with his own design. He said the cost would only be £110 10s. 0d. above the cost of repairs. Thomas Hutchings, the doyen of local builders, poured scorn on this statement, saying it would cost at least £2,300, and according to the *Bridgwater Times* the vestry was unanimous in rejecting the proposal. An anonymous comment noted: 'Break spire would be a more appropriate rendering of the gentleman's name, than Brakspeare.' In August everybody agreed that about £100 would rectify the tower arch and Hutchings was given the contract.

On 17 March 1853 the *Bridgwater Times* revealed that the architect, supported by the vicar, did not want the picture (Fig. 94) replaced above the altar as it would hide his new window. The editor predicted there would be no dispute since the churchwardens had decided to put back the picture, the corporation having made replacing it a condition of the £200 grant towards the chancel's repair. However an unseemly and scandalous brawl ensued. Late in November Haviland, one of the wardens, decided that he would be responsible for carrying out the parish's instructions. He, together with workmen and ladders, entered the church one evening to hang the picture. They must have previously cemented hooks into the stonework. All four wardens had been informed but one decided to stay away and the other two, Davies and Bussell, came with the express purpose of wrecking the attempt. They turned off the gas, plunging the church into darkness. Haviland produced candles and tried to carry on but Davies and Bussell threatened to throw the workmen off the ladders. Haviland wisely retreated so they tore down the iron frame, threw it into the churchyard, and knocked the metal hooks out from the wall. This unpleasant scene, accompanied by much shouting and brawling, took place close to the High Altar.

Consequently, on 1 December 1853 Archdeacon Denison travelled from Taunton to hold an inquiry. He persuade the two belligerent wardens to shake hands with their colleague and publicly apologise. After hearing the facts and arguments, Denison was satisfied that the painting had been given as an altarpiece and the donor had specified the site, and neither the vestry nor the corporation could place it elsewhere. Bussell argued that the picture had been given to the church and not the town, which the Town Clerk refuted by producing corporation books proving that the picture was presented to the town in 1775. The entry for 12 December says:

'It is ordered that Leave be given by this Corporation to put up in the Chancel of the Parish Church of Bridgwater a Picture which the Honble Ann Poulett has made a Present to the Town'.

The 'Honble Ann Poulett' was the fourth son of the 1st Earl Poulett, born in 1711, who had the misfortune to be christened with a girl's name in honour of Queen Anne. When he made the presentation he had been a Member of Parliament for Bridgwater in 1769, 1774, 1780 and 1784. Tradition says he bought the picture at a Plymouth auction but there is no record of this.

B – St Mary's Church Bells

The peal of eight bells does not include a medieval one. Only three bells were hung here in the Middle Ages.

1. 'Glory to God in the highest cast by T. Bayley 1745.' This inscription and all the others which follow are set in block capitals (6 cwt.). The bell was recast at Loughborough in 1899 (Taylor).

2. 'And on earth good will towards men cast by T. Bayley 1755.' Both bells were cast at Bayley's workplace in St Mary Street (7cwt.).

3. 'I.L. W.C. 1650' (by R. Austen) (8cwt.).

4. 'W.P.: G.P. ANNO DOMINI 1615' (10cwt.). The initials are those of William and George Purdue, famous bell-founders in Closworth. An 18th-century table-tomb in the churchyard there has a large bell sculpted on its eastern end.

5. 'Santae Marise Anno 1634' (11 cwt.). Re-cast by Taylor in 1899, this bell too was originally cast by one of the Purdues.

6. 'From lightning and tempest good Lord deliver us A.R. 1721' (11 cwt.). The inscription on this bell refers to the practice of ringing the bells during a thunderstorm.

7. 'William Methuen William Bryant church wardens A.R. 1721' (with a band of fleur de lys) (16 cwt.). Both these bells were cast by A. Rudhall in 1721.

8. 'John Taylor & Co. Founders Loughborough 1868 Recast by subscriptions obtained 1867 John B. Hammill Mayor' (together with the arms of the borough) (25 cwt.). The following is inscribed on the bell:

'I call the living mourn the dead
I tell how days and years are fled
For joys for grief for prayer and praise
My tuneful voice to heaven I raise'

From 'Somerset Church Bells' MS deposited in S.R.O. by H.A. Walker

C – Other Bridgwater Churches

Holy Trinity Church in Taunton Road was built in 1839 when St Mary's was operating above its capacity. It was demolished in 1958 when Broadway was constructed but its attendances had been falling.

In 1847 the Oxford Movement created a new church and parish, St John's in Eastover, to meet the population growth in St John Street and the surrounding area fostered by the railway's arrival in 1841.

In 1882 an Anglican mission church, All Saints, was opened at the entrance to Westonzoyland Road as an offshoot of St John's Church. It is now a Boys' Club.

New churches were built to meet the needs of new housing estates. The Church of the Good Shepherd started in 1953 from a large house in Hamp, close to the Rhode Lane estate, in anticipation of the closure of Holy Trinity.

The new Church of the Good Shepherd in Hamp Street was built in 1960 and consecrated in 1961.

The Church of St Francis on the Sydenham estate was built in 1960 but not completed until 1963. It is in the neighbourhood of Parkway.

The Presbyterians in Bridgwater became known as the Unitarian Church in 1815. Their early meetings were in a disused Dampiet Street barn but in 1656 they acquired a dwelling house and shop 'in Damyat'. In 1689 a licence was granted 'at Guildhall in Bridgwater' allowing Presbyterians to worship 'in a certain place comonly called Christ's Church' which indicates that a chapel had been built in 1688 before the licence was issued. Re-building took place in 1787-8 for £394 16s. 4d., much being spent on the façade (Fig. 95). A plaque records that Coleridge preached there on two occasions.

Baptists were in Bridgwater before 1656 and flourished – there were some 200 members in 1718. Before the Monmouth Rebellion militant Anglicans led by Stawell of Cothelstone entered the town and destroyed the chapel. The present chapel (Fig. 96) was designed by Edwin Down, a local architect, in 1837; it stands on the site of the earlier building.

The Independents in Bridgwater registered a house in St Mary Street for holding religious meetings in 1787. In 1792 they obtained a disused malt house in Friarn Street which is described in the lease as a malt house converted into a Meeting for divine worship of Protestant dissenters. In 1822 the old malt house was demolished and a new church, Sion Chapel, was built which stood until its demolition in 1971. In 1817 a separate group of eight had met at a malt house in Salmon Lane.

A community now called the Congregational Church left Friarn Street in 1864 and moved to Fore Street. A chapel and school rooms designed by Edwin Down and built by W. Shewbrooks of Taunton were erected for £4,000. They were demolished in 1966 when the Congregational Church, now the United Reformed Church, opened at Westfield. The Congregational Church buildings in Friarn Street were used by various commercial enterprises until 1881 when they became the Salvation Army Citadel. The Salvationists moved to Moorland Road in 1971.

The Mariners' Chapel in St John Street was built in 1837 and was intended to attract seamen although it

95   The Unitarian Chapel in Dampiet Street, a brick building of outstanding importance. Its site was originally a barn. A plaque on the wall records that Coleridge preached here on two occasions.

96 The Baptist Chapel with its massive pillars and pediment which stands on the site of an earlier building. This somewhat pretentious building with a Palladian façade was designed by Edwin Down, a local architect, in 1837.

was not near the river. It kept its own congregation for many years but its use as a chapel ceased in 1960.

The start date of the Methodist Church in Bridgwater is uncertain but John Wesley preached here six times between 1746 and 1769. The Wesleyans took the same course as the early Dissenters by holding meetings in private houses. The first house was licensed for Methodist worship by County Sessions in 1763. Soon after 1800 meetings were held in Eastover where a small chapel was erected. In 1816 a brick-built chapel was opened in King Street and for many years this was the chief Methodist church in Bridgwater. It was raised and enlarged in 1860. A splinter group, the Bible Christians, erected their own church in Polden Street in 1876. Their minister lived in Monmouth Street, the manse still easily recognised from its pseudo-medieval façade. Another group known as Free Methodists met in the dome above the Market House in 1851, and then in a room in Albert Street. By 1855 they had opened a chapel in St Mary Street. Traces of ecclesiastical windows can still be seen inside the building (No. 27). Yet another group, the Primitive Methodists, began to meet in 1852 in Angel Crescent. By 1861 they had their own minister and a meeting place in West Street. By 1880 they had moved to St John Street. The building of the United Methodist Church in Monmouth Street in 1911 brought some of these groups together. It caused immediate closure of the Polden Street church. The St Mary Street chapel closed in 1906 when the Bible Christians and United Methodist Free Church amalgamated nationally. In 1980 the King Street complex became redundant, leaving the Monmouth Street church as the Methodists' sole building.

A Roman Catholic chapel opened in 1846. For many years Catholics used a building in Gordon Terrace which is now a welding shop. In 1882 they built a church, St Joseph's, in Chapel Street. Although most church attendances have declined nationally, that of the Roman Catholic Church has improved. In Bridgwater the Catholics built a new primary school and, in 1981, extended their church.

Five unnamed and unidentified Protestant groups registered buildings with the Somerset Quarter Sessions in order to hold religious meetings. The owners

97 Part of St Matthew's Fair early in the 20th century. The carousel with the 'galloping horses' still features, as do 'cheap jacks'.

of these buildings were Mary Morse (1689), Thomas Hymans (1689), Thomas Millner (1700), Charles Payne (1711) and Joseph Ball (1719). In 1792 Protestant dissenters applied to the bishop for licence to use 'a certain low room in a house the property of Mr Reed – occupier Margaret Bond'.

Bridgwater was traditionally a Protestant town, typical of the West Country in having many different sects. In Tudor times Bridgwater traded with the Low Countries and traders' families and friends would have been aware of Protestant ideas in mainland Europe. From medieval times Bridgwater had a strong connection with Wales, too, and at a later date Wales became a stronghold of nonconformity, many preachers and teachers visiting Bridgwater from there. These influences helped to produce a society which was never strictly orthodox in its outlook, either in politics or religion.

D – Bridgwater Fair

In earlier times Bridgwater had several fairs: including one on the second Thursday in Lent (from 1468); another at Midsummer (dating from the original charter of 1200); the third on 28 December; and 'a Fair only for scythes and hardware viz., the Monday after Ascension Day', according to a comment written in 1720.

By the 20th century only St Matthew's Fair had survived, first mentioned in a court roll of 1379: 'From the fees of the Fair of St Matthew the apostle ... 7s. 4d.' It is no longer held on St Matthew's Day (21 September) but the last Wednesday in September and the two following days. On the first morning a sheep fair is held and hundreds of sheep are penned behind hurdles to be sold at auction, which preserves the purpose for which such fairs came into existence. For the rest of the time it is a normal fun fair, which is so popular that it is always extended to a fourth day (Saturday). Fig. 97 shows part of the fair early in the 20th century.

E – Bridgwater Carnival

Long before the Carnival began Bridgwater took a special interest in Guy Fawkes Night and many people paraded the streets in fancy dress. By 1830, when Guy Fawkes had become something of a folk hero, there were occasions when another 'Guy' was burnt as a demonstration of popular hatred: in 1850 it was the Pope; in 1854, during the Crimean War, it was the Tsar; and in 1857, the year of the Indian Mutiny, it was Nana Sahib.

During these years certain elements which fore-shadowed the Carnival had appeared: the processional route, the torchlight procession with brass band, and a bonfire on the Cornhill. In 1856, after peace was made with Russia, there was a memorable fire on the Cornhill when two old boats were burnt. In 1881 the first fully organised procession took place, and another was arranged to celebrate the opening of the new bridge in 1883. After that the Carnival became an annual event.

The scenes designed by the Carnival Clubs have become amazingly elaborate, expensive to produce and brilliantly lit. It is estimated that 100,000 visitors crowd into the town to watch the event, originally on the Thursday nearest to 5 November but on Friday since 2002. Some seventy tableaux are produced and silver cups and cash prizes awarded. There is an interval after the procession has ended when gangs of men march out like soldiers and line the High Street from end to end. Each man shoulders a long wooden handle to which is attached a Bridgwater Squib. These are lit from flares on the ground and held up high over the heads of the competitors and for several minutes fountains of fire spout as high as the roof tops. These fireworks are specially made for Bridgwater and measure 18 inches by 26 inches in diameter. Needless to say the shops are securely boarded up.

F – Bridgewater, Massachusetts

In 1654 Bridgewater, Massachusetts came into existence. Fifty-four settlers already living in New England were granted lands for a new township by an edict from New Plymouth. Probably the new town took its name in accordance with the wishes of its first Town Clerk, John Gary, who had emigrated from Somerset in 1659. There is an entry in the Register of Baptisms at St Mary's Church which may refer to this man: '2 July 1610 John the sonne of Thomas Carie and Anne his wife.' In New England he had lived first in Duxbury and then in Braintree; by 1654, he was married with four children and had eight more in the following years. As Town Clerk he had many tasks to perform. Besides clearing and farming his own land he was involved in solving and recording all the basic problems of the pioneer community, which included organising land grants and marking town boundaries. The boundary with Taunton for instance had to be agreed and marked with posts. In addition, wolf traps had to be constructed, fish weirs created and a bridge built, and soldiers maintained as protection against Red Indians. The colonists were Puritans and much concerned with maintaining a minister and keeping a Meeting House. John Gary had to keep records of all these activities as well as participate in them. He seems to have thrived and remained as Town Clerk until his death in 1681.

Since the celebration of 500 years of the mayoralty in 1969, when delegations were exchanged between the two towns, Bridgwater has had a link with the American town. Several other towns in different parts of the world are also named Bridgwater and many owe their origin to men from Somerset.

BIBLIOGRAPHY

The following abbreviations have been used:
D.N.B. – Dictionary of National Biography
P.R.O. – Public Record Office (now The National Archives)
S.A.N.H.S. – Somerset Archaeological and Natural History Society Proceedings
S.R.O. – Somerset County Record Office
S.R.S. – Somerset Record Society

Archbold, W.A.J., *Somerset Religious Houses* (1892)
Barnes, T.G., *Somerset Assize Orders*, 1629-1640, S.R.S. Vol. 65
Bassett, *et al*, *Registrum Omnium Brevium* (1687)
Beet, Toni, *Francis Frith's Around Bridgwater* (2001)
Bellchamber, J.K., *Somerset Clockmakers* (1968)
Chubb, M., 'A Forbear and His Hobby'
The Countryman, Vol. 61 No. 2 1963 p276
The Countryman, Vol. 62 No. 1 1964 p89
Census Returns (1801 onwards)
Census Enumerators' Lists 1851 etc. S.R.O. Microfilm
Collinson, J., *History of Somerset* (1792)
Cox, T., *Magna Britannia* (1727) (Part No. 60 Somerset)
D.N.B. contains brief lives of:
    Allen, John (1675-1741)
    Allen, Benjamin (1732-91) (MP 1768 &1774)
    Allen, Jefferys (1761-1844) (MP 1796 & 1802; Mayor 1805)
    Blake, Robert (1599-1657)
    Brydges, James, Duke of Chandos (1645-1744)
    Desborough, John (1608-80) (Major-General in Control of Bridgwater 1655-9)
    Haviland, John (1785-1851)
    Moore, John (1642-1717)
    Norman, John (1622-88)
    Oldmixon, John (1673-1742)
    Williams, Moses (1686-1742)

(Vicar of Bridgwater 1732-42)
Brief lives of all Bridgwater MPs are included in *History of Parliament*.
Dilks, T.B., *Bridgwater Borough Archives*, S.R.S. Vols. 48, 53
Dilks, T.B., *Bridgwater in Brief* (1927)
Dilks, T.B., 'Bridgwater Castle & Desmesne towards the end of the 14th Century', S.A.N.H.S. Vol. 86
Dilks, T.B., 'Bridgwater & the Insurrection of 1381', S.A.N.H.S. Vol. 73
Dilks, T.B., *Charles James Fox & the Borough of Bridgwater* (1937)
Dilks, T.B., *Pilgrims in Old Bridgwater* (1920)
Dunning, Robert, *Bridgwater: History and Guide* (1992)
Dunning, R.W., *Bridgwater Borough Archives*, S.R.S. Vol. 70
Farr, L.G., *Somerset Harbours* (1954)
Green, E., *Somerset Chantries*, S.R.S. Vol. 2
Jarman, S.G., *History of Bridgwater* (1889)
Leland, J., *Itinerary*, ed. Smith, L.T., 5 Vols. (1964) see Vol. 1
Martin, A.R., *Franciscan Architecture in England* (1937)
McLachlan, H., 'The Bridgwater Academies', *Unitarian Historical Society Transactions*, Vol. 8 No. 3
Murless, B., *Bridgwater Docks & the River Parrett* (1983)
Murphy, *Lieutenancy Papers, 1603-12* (1969)
Oldmixon, J., *History of England during the reigns of the Royal House of Stuart* (1730)
Peake, T.M., 'Somerset Clergy, 1625-42' unpublished thesis deposited at S.R.O.
Powell, J.R., *Robert Blake General at Sea* (1977)
Power, E. and Postan, M.M., 'Tables of Enrolled Customs – Bridgwater', Studies in the English trade in the 15th century (1933)
Rogers, J.P.W., 'John Oldmixon in Bridgwater, 1717-30', S.A.N.H.S. Vol. 113
Sedgemoor District Council, *Bridgwater, The Second Selection* (2001)
Slocombe, I.S., 'A Bridgwater Riot 1717', S.A.N.H.S. Vol. 113
Spencer, N., *The Compleat English Traveller* (1771)
Sprigge, J., *Anglia Rediviva* (1647)
Squibbs, P.J., *Squibbs' History of Bridgwater*, revised by J.F. Lawrence (1982)
Stieg, M., 'Laud's Laboratory', MS in S.R.O.
Toogood, J., *Reminiscences of a Medical Life* (1853)
Trenchard, C.T., *Siege of Bridgwater* (1929)
Underdown, D., *Somerset in the Civil War & Interregnum* (1973)
Williams, David, *Bridgwater Inns Past and Present* (1997)

Index

Abbot of Athelney, 8, 11
Albert Street, 36, 153, 163, 168, 175, 187
Aldermen, 26
almshouse, 61, 107, 120, **121**
Angel Crescent, 13, 167
Angel Place, 33, **181**, 182
apprenticeship, 89
archery, 75, 94
armour, armoury, 74, 95
Arts Centre, 166
Ashcott, 5
Assize, 115, 142, 151, 152; of Ale, 11, 24, 131; of Bread, 24, 27, 131
Assize hall, 125, 141, 142
Athelney Abbey, 7, 8
Axbridge, 9

Back, The, 32
Back Lane, 32, 148
Back Quay, 35, 136, **137**, **138**
Bampton, Robert of, 10
Baptist Chapel, 186, **187**
barbican, 19
Bascule bridge, 157
Bath, 98, 118
Bath Brick, 153, **153**, 169, **170**
Bath Road, 33, 142, 168, 172
Bawdrip, 6, 8
Beckington, Bishop, 40, 44

Beggars, 83
Binford Place, 35, **137**, **138**
Black Death, 13, 40, 42, 47
Blake: Bridge, 170; Gardens, 35, 81, **81**, 166
Blake, Humphrey, 83, 95, 104, 107
Blake, John, 41, 43
Blake, Margaret, 83
Blake, Robert, 83, 98, 107, **151**, 165, 166
Blind Lane, 36
Bloody Assize, 115
Board of Guardians, 146, 147, 156, 163
Bore, 2, 3
Bowen, John, 145, 147
Braose: Richard, 11; William, 11, 17
Brewer, William, 10, 23, 58
brick makers, 130, 149
brick, bricks, 80, 121, **121**, 123, 148-149, 153-154, 157, 171, **171**, 172, **173**
Brick & Tile Museum, 172
Bridge:
    Black, 158, 159, **159**; telescopic, 158, **159**, 176, 182
bridge repairs, 119-20

bridge, at Chilton, 181
bridge, medieval, 119
bridge, new, 1798, 137-9
Bridgewater, Massachusetts, 189-90
Bridgwater House, 20
Bridgwater Rural District Council, 177
Bridgwater Turnpike Trust, **144**
Bristol, 49, 57, 59, 83, 123, 131
Bristol Channel, 7, 176
Bristol Road, 142, 168, 172, 176
Bristol to Exeter Railway, 158
British Waterways, 175
broadcloth, 57, 59
Broadway, 30, 40, 168, 170, 185
Brunel, 156, 176
bull baiting, 94
burgage rents, 13
burgage tenure, 13, 23
Burgess Hall, 67, 68-70, 141
Burnham-on-Sea, 3, 172
Burrow Bridge, 99
butts, 20, 63, 76, 94

Canal, Bridgwater-Taunton, **4**, 5, 140, 157, **174**, 175, 182
Cannington, 5, 6, 40, 62, 97

193

Cantelupe, William de, 10, 43, 44
Carnival, 189
Cary, 3
Castle: 39; Ditch, 13, 105; Field, 3, 13, 21, 75, 113, 172; House, 34 152, **152**; Moat, 14, 29, 31, 34
Castle Street, 18, 34, 121, **126, 127**, 127, 129, 134, 142, 145, 166, 181
cattle market, 33
Chandos, Duke of, 125, 127, 142, 162
Chandos Street, 17, 127, 134
Chantries, 52
Chantry of All Saints, 52
Chantry of St Anne, 52, 54
Chantry of St Catherine's, 52, 54
Chantry of St Erasmus, 53
Chantry of St George, 50, 53
Chantry of the Blessed Virgin Mary, **23**, 50, 53, 54, 55
Chantry of the Holy Cross, 52, 53, 55
Chantry of the Holy Trinity, 50, 52, 53
Chapel Street, 120, 187
Chapman's Row, 33
Charles I, 26, 65, 97
Charles II, 28, 105, 110, 113, 114
Charnel House, 52, 53
Charter Hall, 153
Charters, 23, 24, 25, 26, 27
Chedzoy, 5, 6, 91, 99, 115, 118
Cheese market, 38, 110, 136
chevage, 21

Chew Magna, 62
Chilton Street, 6, 170
Chilton Trinity, 5, 31, 40, 41, 77, 163, 172
Chilton, 49, 109, 182
Chiselly Mount, 23
cholera, 163
Chubb, John, 18, 134, 135, **135, 136, 137**, **138**, 150, 151, 165
Church: ales, 62; bells, 49, 73, 185; House, 33, 63, 68; valuables, 55
Church of St Francis, 186
Church of the Good Shepherd, 185
Church Street, 181
Civil War, **102**, 97
Clare Street, 94, 148, 165
clay, 121
Cleeve Abbey, 44
Clock (church), 54
cloth trade, 103
Clubmen, 99
coal, 78, 95, **175**
Coalbrookdale, 138, 139
Coffee House Lane, 152
Coleridge, 5
Collector, 78, 85, 86, 127
Colley Lane, 6
Combwich, 5, 12, 59, 139, 172
Common Back, 32
Common Council, 26, 28, 64, 66, 72, 76, 109, 111, 122, 123, 138, 139, 141, 142
Common Hall, 14, 24, 67, 82, 94, 117
common oven, 14, 32
Commonality, The, 25, **25**
Confraternity, letters of, 44, 45
Congregational Church, 186
Conservatives, 161, 162, 167

Cornhill, 30, 31, 32, 49, 118, 132, 134, 148, **150**, 164, 166
Corpus Christi, 63
Council houses, 169
County Court, 152, **152**, 161
court rolls, 11
Court Street, 152
Crandon Bridge, 5, 6
Cromwell, Oliver, 100, 106
Cromwell, Thomas, 66
Crosses, 37-8, 181
Crouiles' Lane, 36
Crowcombe, 9, 62
Crowpill, 6, 30, 139, 156
Crowpill rhine, 30
Crowpill Road, 18
cucking stool, 24
Custom House, **157**
Customer, the, 25, 59
Customs Officer, 45

Dampiet Street, 35
Dead Woman's Ditch, 5
Delvys Tower, 19
Dissolution, 40, 42, 45, 55, 73
distillery, 127
Dodington, George, 129
Dodington, George Bubb, 129
Domesday Book, 9
Donyatt ware, 19
Downend, 5, 17, 23, 49
Drake, Sir Francis, 78
drawbridge, 19
dredger, **65**, 156,
dry dock, 73
Dunball, 2, 4, 142, 172
Dunwear, 6, 37, 49, 77, 99, 100, 109, 172
Durleigh, 3, 168, 170
Durleigh Brook, 7, 8, 11, 29, 30, 35, 36, 99, 122, 164

Index

Durleigh Valley, 7

East Bower, 5, 49, 77, 109
East Gate, 30, 31, 34, 40, 101, 103, 143
East quay, 119, 139, 158, 159, 173, **174**
east stile, 32
East Stower, 15, 26
Eastover, 34, 40, 101, 107, 133, 156, 181, 185, 187
Edington, 159
Edward I, 24
Edward IV, 22
Edward VI, 15, 71, 73
Edward VII, 166
Edward, Earl of March, 14
electoral corruption, 129, 160-3
Elizabeth I, 26, 71
Elizabeth II, 182
Enmore, 22
Entertainment, 63-4
Exeter, 123

Fairfax, Sir Thomas, 98, 100, 101, 103, 106
Fairs, 188
fee farm, 14
fish weir, 72
floating harbour, 156, **156**, 182
Fore Street, 19, 20, 34, 137, **139**, 182, 186
foreign trade, 120
Fountain Inn, 124
Frampton, Nicholas, 41, 42
Franciscans, 43
Frankpledge, View of, 42
Free Methodists, 187
Free School, 63, 94
Friarn Avenue, 45
Friarn Lawn, **180**, 182

Friarn Street, 35, 36, 43, 44, 101, 132, 135, 136, **179**, 181-2, 186
Friary, 36, 43-6, 56, 66
Frog Lane, 89
Frog Lane Bridge, 35
fulling mills, 59

gas works, 150
gatehouse, 18, 19, **19**, **20**
George III, 28
George Inn, 36, 124, 131
George Street, 36
George Williams Memorial Hall, **87**, 179
Gibbs doorway, **127**, 129, 166
gild merchant, 16, 23, 24, 25
Glass Cone, **125**, **126**, 127, 129
Glastonbury, 97
Globe Inn, 121
Goathurst, 94
Godwin's Lane, 33
Golden Ball, 162, **162**
goldsmiths, 90
Great Western Railway, 158
Guildhall, Gildhall, 11, 24, 30, 33, 67, 74, 89, 141, 142
gunpowder, 68, 75, 95, 101

Ham Hill, 17
Ham stone, 18, 19
Hamp, 3, 6, 7, 9, 37, 49, 77, 100, 109, 123, 148, 172, 185
Hamp Brook, 7, 8, 11
Haygrove, 3, 7, 11, 13, 15, 21, 37, 49, 61, 74, 77, 109
hayward, 12, 21
Henry III, 10

Henry VII, 64
Henry VIII, 40, 64, 76, 99
High Cross, 30, 32, 33, 34, 38, 70, 94, 134, **136**, 148
High Street, 26, 63, 94, 134, 142, 150, 151, 154, 162
Highbridge, 82, 172
Holford, 5
Holloway, Benjamin, 127-8, **128**, 129
Holy Trinity Church, 185
horse fair, 38
horse mill, 14, 81, **81**
Horse Pool, 35
Horsey, 5, 7, 9, 37, 49, 77, 109
Horsey chapel, 56
Hospital, 147, 148, **161**, 164
Hospital of St John, 27, 30, 58, 59, 66, 93, 103
Hospital, Union Workhouse, 154, **155**
Huntspill, 43, 79
Huntstile chapel, 40
Huntworth, 3, 97, 172
Hyatt, Richard, 71, 72
Hyatt's barn, 71, 72

Idstock, chapel, 40
Ilchester, 5, 9, 28, 39, 41, 110
Ilminster, 39, 101
inner bailey, 17
inns, 131-3
Inspeximus, 23
Isle, 3
Isle Brewers, 39

James I, 88, 93, 95
James II, 28, 99, 117, 182
James, Duke of Monmouth, 111, 112, 113, 114, 115, 117

Jan Swayne's Leaps, 118
Jefferys, Judge, 117, 118
Jocelin, Bishop, 39
John, 23, 39

Kelyng Cross, 30, 38
Kendale, John, 22, 26, 52
Kidsbury, 36
King Square, 18, **128**, 142, **143**, 169
Kings Sedgemoor Drain, 5, 7
Knowle Hill, 100

Labour, 167
Lady chapel, 52
Langport, 6, 9, 17, 78, 99
Langport Quay, 78, 136, **137**, **138**
Lansdown, 98
lastage, 57
Lent Fair, 26, 82, 111, 130
Leper hospital, 46, 47
Letters Patent, 10, 23, 29, 65, 74, 76
Liberals, 161, 162, 166
Lime bridge, 30
Lions, The, 63
Little Chandos Street, 127
London, 28
London & South Western Railway Companies, 159, 160
lower bailey, 17
Loxley Woods, 118
Lyme Regis, 98, 113
Lyng, 9
Lytell Mill, 7

mace, 14, 107, 108
machicolation, 19
Mansard roof, 179, **179**, 181
Mansion House Inn, 63, 140, **140**
Mansion House Lane, 33, 132, **140**, 165
Mariner's Chapel, 186
Market House, 30, 134, 135, 136, 150, **150**, 151, 187
Market Place, 19, 30, 32
Market Street, 36, **178**
Mary, 15, 26, 66, 71, 74
Marycourt, **116**
Mayor, 25, 26, 182
Merleswain, 8
Methodist Church, 187
Middle Stream, 7, 8
Middlezoy, 6
Midsummer Fair, 23, 82, 130
Milestone, **5**, 6
millstones, 80-4
Minehead, 31
moat, 14, 19, 20
Moat Lane, 132
Monmouth Street, 38, 143, 170, 187
Mortimer family, 11, 12, 20, 22
Mortimer, Margaret, 47
Mortimer, Maud, 11
Mortimer's Hall, 20
Mount Street, 29, 33, 99, 163, 168
murage, 29
Museum, 45, 56, **98**, 166
muster, 70, 75, 76

names, medieval local, 42, 59
Nether Stowey, 5, 23, 129, 145
New Town, 6, 169
Newtown Lock, **4**
North Bower (*see also* East Bower), 37
North Gate, 20, 29, 30, 31, **31**, 34, 36, 94, 104, 130, 137, 142, 168, 172, 177
North Gate House, 30

North Petherton, 19, 27, 40, 43, 65, 98, 103, 145
North Street, 30, 33, 91, 142, 163
Northfield, 181
Northover, 39

occupations, 1661, 109
occupations, 1727, 130
Old Oak Inn, 134, 135, 150
Old Oak Passage, 33, 135
Oldmixon, John, 114, 115, 127, 130
Orfair, 30
Orloue Street, 36
Otterhampton, 13

pantiles, 123, 171
Parks, the, 3, 13, 14
Parrett, 2, 3, 5, 7
Paynel, William, 10
Pedride, 7
Penel Orlieu, 30, 165, 170, **178**
Perry Green, 6
Pest House, 91
Pibsbury, 17, 59, 99, 119
Pig Cross, 33, 36, 37, 90, 100, 163
pig market, 124
pillory, 24, 32
piracy, 79
plague, 90, 91
Plymtree, 22, **22**
Polden Hills, 6, 17, 118
Polden Street, 37
Poor Law, 86
Poor Law, 1834, 146-7
Post Office, 150
Poulett, Honourable Anne, **183**, 184
pound, 94
powder house, 68, 95
preachers, 64-5, 105
Prickett's Lane, 36

Priory, **176**, 177, **177**
public health, 167-9
Public Library, 166
Punchbowl Inn, 137, **139**
Puritan, puritans, 65, 93, 99, 103, 104, 106, 110, 112
Puriton, 59
Puriton Hill, 142
Pynel Street, 36

Quantock Hills, 6, 59, 99, 168
Quantock Road, 170
quay, 17, 176
Queen Street, 19, 34, 152

rating system, 86
Receiver, 25, 70, 80, 83, 90, 92, 96, 101, 109, 110, 123, 132
Recorder, 26, 106
Reeves, 12; seal of, **12**
reservoir, 164, 168
Restoration, 109
Rhode Lane, 3, 169, 170, 185
Richard, Duke of York, 14, 22
Roman Catholic Church, 120
Roper's Lane, 36, 153
Royal Clarence Hotel, **141**, 142, 182

St Giles, hospital of, 46,
St John's Church, 107, **159**, 163, 185
St John's Street, 6, 158, 186
St Joseph's Roman Catholic Church, 187
St Mark's chapel, 21
St Mary Street, 30, 110, 135, 151, 164, 165, 179, 186
St Mary's Cross, 38

St Matthew's Fair, 88, 130, 188
St Matthew's Field, 3, 36, 59
St Saviour's chapel, 35, 56
salmon butts, 71, **71**, 139
Salmon Parade, 148, 164
salmon trap, 72, **72**
Saltlands, 3, 13, 14, 21, **159**, 172
Salvation Army Citadel, 186
Sandford, 5, 6
Saracen's Head, 64, 131
Saxon charters, 7
Saxons, 6
Searcher, the, 25
Sedgemoor District Council, 170, 177
Shambles, 32, 124
Shapwick, 97, 104
sheep market, 33
ship building, 73
Silver Street, 35, 44, 90, **90**
silver, silversmiths, 90, 107, 108
Sion Chapel, 186
Somerset & Dorset Railway, **160**
Somerset Bridge, 140, 156, 172
Somerset Levels, 3, 6
Somerton, 97, 113
South Bridge (Lime Bridge), 35
South Gate, 8, 31, 33, 120, 142
South Gate Oratory, 56
South Mill, 8
South Perrott, 3
Spaxton, 6
Spire, 49, 50
Stafford, Humphrey, Earl of Devon, 22, **47**
Stogursey, 5, 9, 23, 145
Stretcholt, 71, 72

stump, the, 32
Sully's wharf, 158, **175**
Swan Inn, 31, 118, 123, 124, 131
Swan Lake, 7
swimming baths, 168
Sydenham, 3, 5, 7, 41, 99, 186
Sydenham, John, 41

Tallage: 25; lists, 59
Taunton, 9, 28, 31, 70, 71, 75, 78, 99, 107, 110, 118, 153, 156, 164, 175, 184
Taunton Road, 30, 142, 150, 169, 176
tidal basin, 158, **175**
tide mill, 36, 72, 73
tile makers, 130
tiles, 69, 121, 123, 125, 148-9, 153-4, 157, 171, **171**, 172, **173**; medieval, 46, **46**, 47
tithe, 77
Toll house – Monmouth Street, **144**
Toll house – Taunton Road, 142, **144**
Toller Porcorum, 39
Tolsey, 33
Tone, 3
Tory, Tories, 123, 124
Town bridge, 72, 182; medieval, 57, **58**
town cellar, 20, 57
Town Council, 150, 151, 164, 170, 182
town crooks, 68
town ditch, 99
town gate, 40
Town Hall, 33, 108, 110, 119, 133, 135, 142, 152, 153, 154, **154**, 183
town mill, 7
Trades, medieval, 42

Trivet arms, **59**
Trivet, Sir John, 44, 58
tug, 157, **157**
tumbrel, 24

Union Workhouse, 146, 154-6
Unitarian Church, 186, **186**
United Reform Church, 186

Vicarage (former), **53**, 54
Virona, Hugh de, 10

Waleys, Nicholas, 49
Walford's Gibbet, 5
Walscin, 8
Walter of Douai, 8
Wards (medieval), 36
Watchet, 9, 31

water bailiff, 20, 56, 65, 70, 71, 78, 80, 120
water gate, 17, **18**
water mills, 14, 61
Weech's Wall, 7
weirs, 19, 20
Wells, 93
Wembdon, 5-8, 17, 30, 31, 39, 40, 164, 170
West Bower, 3
West Gate, 30, 33, 37, 44, 105, 119, 143
West Gate almshouse, 61
west quay, 20, 119
West Street, 3, 30, 33, 105, 132, 153, 163, 175, **178**, 179
Weston Zoyland, 6, 65, 113, 115, 118
Weston-super-Mare, 167
Westwayer, 12

Whig, Whigs, 28, 113, 123
willow industry, 6
Witches Walk, 7
withernam, 24
withies, 6
Woolavington, 100
workhouse, 89, 91, 92, 93, 122, 144-5, 154-6, 163
World wars, 169-70
wreck of the sea, 24
Wrotham, Richard of, 10
Wyndham, Sir Edward, 97, 99, 102, 103

Yeo, 3
York Buildings, 20
York Place, 19

Zouche, 11, 15, 27, 42, 43